TAIPAN SNAKE PIT

Michael D. Guard

CONTENTS

Preface

"It was the worst time, and the best time of my life." "An experience that I would not do again for a million dollars, nor would I give a million dollars for the experience." "It was a time of individual discovery and growth, if you lived through it." These comments heard thousands of times by returning American soldiers from a faraway place. A place far away in terms of distance to be sure, but even farther from our perceived realities, a place where time passed ever so slowly with no desire to catch up to the rest of the world. A place where peoples and their customs were so different from our own!

The Vietnam conflict was never a declared war—although those who served in combat would say it was indeed a war! History has recorded the conflict as the "Television war." In the early 1960s, I recall listening and watching the news stories from a foreign country where our U.S. servicemen were involved in battles. Images flashed across television screens all over the world of U.S. soldiers firing weapons at an unseen enemy in tall elephant grass or in the dense jungles. The enemy they called "VietCong," "VC," or simply "Charlie." We watched scenes of wounded American soldiers and Viet Cong corpses all bloodied and limp as they were carried away to awaiting helicopters. The television screen hurried through these pictures during the six o'clock local newscasts while the population had their evening meals.

Those images meant little to me as a young teenager, someone who had no political awareness. The morality of the waste and wanton destruction of peoples and their country was best left up to those who knew a lot more of the situation than I.

There were also the images of helicopters, dozens of them, landing into zones or "LZs"; there the troops would disembark from the hovering craft and stay crouched down until the helicopter lifted off again. These helicopter missions, called "sorties," were combat assaults. They were the insertion, extraction, and/or repositioning of ground troops into a landing zone. Other types of sorties included gunship air support, search and rescue, re-supplies of food and munitions, medical evacuation (medivac), and more. Likewise, the Vietnam conflict is also referred to as the "helicopter war." It is that helicopter war on which this experience is based.

More specifically, the Huey helicopter, originally dubbed "the Iroquois," it was manufactured by Bell Industries, then designated the "UH-1" by the military, it is a large utility aircraft with outstanding lift capability. The Huey was the backbone of the allied forces' mobility. Used primarily for troop transport, it soon became apparent that the helicopter was invaluable in most aspects of combat in adverse terrain. Early model Hueys were converted to gunships in 1967 to provide close air support to the Hueys that transported the ground troops into hostile territory. The gunship could provide gun cover for the troops on the ground whenever they made contact with the enemy.

The two popular versions of the time were the "Hogship," a helicopter fitted with two circular rocket pods containing a total of nineteen rockets in each pod. Then there was a "mini-gunship," with seven rockets each in two pods and two Mini-guns (a six- barreled, motor-driven Gatling gun), each capable of firing six thousand 5.56-millimeter (223-caliber) rounds per minute, although a two-thousand-round setting was normally used. All heavy weaponry was mounted on external attachment points on either side of the fuselage. A third version had a rapid-fire 40-millimeter grenade launcher mounted on the nose. Later, wire-guided missiles or "tank killers," were also adapted to the basic gunship.

My purpose for enlisting in the U.S. Army was to train as a helicopter repairman, Military Occupation Specialty (MOS), designation 67N20, commonly referred to as "Helicopter Crew Chief." Prior to arriving in Southeast Asia, I believed that to mean fixing or repairing of aircraft. A crew chief owns the aircraft, or more accurately is assigned an aircraft and is solely responsible for its care and maintenance. I felt that this would give me a good start in the aviation industry once my service had been completed.

But fate would redefine my MOS soon after arrival in country. Be assured I had no preconceived ideas about being in the Army or about being a soldier. I had recognized that there was a possibility that

I could end up in a country like Vietnam. But I truly, however naive, never believed that I would have to do anything other than actually be a helicopter mechanic.

Most of all the events pertaining to Vietnam have been explored and concluded, and although it may not be to the satisfaction of everyone's conclusion, there will always be opposing points of view. Between the covers and on the pages contained herein you will find no new insights about the cause and effect of the Vietnam conflict. However, you may find what it was like for an average hometown boy to be involved in war. Young American's who left the sanctity of their home in the United States for a vastly contrasting way of life in the Nam, giving up real freedom for the dictatorship of the military.

Make no mistake, a soldier is not free to do as he or she desires. The dictator is the "chain of command." Everything a soldier does is directed by orders trickling down the command chain until the orders are finally executed. This is how it must be for the military to function for the benefit of all.

This is not about any particular event or acts of heroism. This is about the bigger picture, the year-long adventure and a trial of endurance! It is my desire to take the reader back there, in country, so they can "feel" like they have been transported back to that time. To get a sense of what some of those young GIs caught up in the conflict might have endured. GIs ranked at the bottom of the command, namely, the front-line combatants, those whose lives were put on the line to serve the needs of the command.

The Huey pilots, those who answered the call to duty, who signed up knowing they were headed to Vietnam after flight school, deserve special recognition. The WOs, or "Warrant Officers," were neither enlisted men nor officers. Their rank was as unique as they were. Enlisted personnel did not address them as "Sir"; rather they were called "Mister." They did not conform to the institutional command structure, as did officers, although they could be promoted to officer candidate, from warrant officer to the rank of second lieutenant. Truly they were in between the enlisted man and the commissioned officer.

From my perspective they were not only brave beyond reproach, they were the ultimate professionals, each and every one. In Vietnam we depended on their cool nerves and flying skills as they depended on our maintenance of aircraft and weapons and our ability to shoot back even when shot at. Those few who might have made an error in flight did just that, and usually under very difficult and hazardous circumstances. Helicopters requires constant input from the pilot—add to that the mission responsibility, people shooting at you, etc… well, you get the idea. Piloting a Huey is ninety percent mental and ten percent skill. I did then, and would again, fly into hell with anyone of them.

The political atmosphere in the United States, and elsewhere, during the Vietnam conflict was, to say the least, ambiguous. American politicians were as divided on the effectiveness of the conflict as the civilian population was. I held no political beliefs until returning to civilian life. But I did learn to appreciate the American political system even if flawed, it is still the best on earth. Do not look for a political statement here although I have my opinions, they are mine alone. This book is not for any such purpose.

At the time these incidents took place, there may have been some natural animosity for having to undergo such a contrasting and conflicting way of life. I would have a hard time believing that any one person is ever completely satisfied with all the events of their lives. In truth I was willing to accept my fate. I harbor no bitterness towards any person or persons, institutions or situations described herein.

Having said that, many references to the soldiers to the Army of the Republic of Vietnam (ARVNs) are derogatory in nature. From the first day of my tour of duty, comments made by veteran GIs referring to our allied fighting man were mostly negative. There was so little interaction between these two forces that one had little to draw on to conclude an accurate summary. Our unit worked closely with the indigenous soldiers, providing air support and transportation. However, we never took the initiative to truly understand the individual, their beliefs or customs. Resentment for having to go to Vietnam because of the common belief that the ARVN could not defend themselves or their country may have played a part in the animosity. Today I have much respect for those who gave so much for so long, and guilt for not seizing the opportunity to better understand and to really know this courageous ally.

The incidents described in this book actually occurred. I have written of it in a "Narrative Non-fiction" style because writing it today seems as though it involved a third party, a surreal event that happened to another person much different from the person that I am today. As a young man, indeed a boy, my experiences seemed "normal" enough. After all, millions of young men shared the military obligation whether by enlistment or by having been drafted into service. We did what was asked, as did those before us, because our country had asked us to.

The names have been changed to preserve the rights of others. The events are real and the actions expressed were as described, although sometimes embellished to fill voids in recollection. The timing and sequence are vague and are put together as close as memory can recall.

A word of caution: conflict by nature is a gruesome and often brutal occurrence. I have held back nothing in describing the reality of war. To that regard I've also tried not to embellish on the offensively violent situations, but I felt it necessary to be honest about the events, and tell it as I experienced it!

Excerpt from President Nixon's Speech on "Vietnamization," November 3, 1969.

"Fifteen years ago, North Vietnam, with the logistical support of Communist China and the Soviet Union, launched a campaign to impose a Communist government on South Vietnam by instigating and supporting a revolution.

In response to the request of the Government of South Vietnam, President Eisenhower sent economic aid and military equipment to assist the people of South Vietnam in their efforts to prevent a Communist takeover. Seven years ago, President Kennedy sent 16,000 military personnel to Vietnam as combat advisers. Four years ago, President Johnson sent American combat forces to South Vietnam.

Now, many believe that President Johnson's decision to send American combat forces to South Vietnam was wrong. And many others I among them have been strongly critical of the way the war has been conducted.

But the question facing us today is, now that we are in the war, what is the best way to end it?

In January I could only conclude that the precipitate withdrawal of American forces from Vietnam would be a disaster not only for South Vietnam but also for the United States and for the cause of peace.

For the South Vietnamese, our precipitate withdrawal would inevitably allow the Communists to repeat the massacres, which followed their takeover in the North 15 years before.

-They then murdered more than 50,000 people and hundreds of thousands more died in slave labor camps.

-We saw a prelude of what would happen in South Vietnam when the Communists entered the city of Hue last year. During their brief rule there, there was a bloody reign of terror in which 3,000 civilians were clubbed, shot to death, and buried in mass graves.

-With the sudden collapse of our support, these atrocities of Hue would become the nightmare of the entire nation and particularly for the million and a half Catholic refugees who fled to South Vietnam when the Communists took over in the North."

UNIT HISTORY

of the

135th Assault Helicopter Company

The 135th A.H.C. was organized at Fort Hood, Texas on 01 February 1967. In October 1967 the unit deployed to Vung Tau in the Republic of Vietnam. At the time of deployment, the Australian Government dispatched a Navy Helicopter flight to Vietnam consisting of eleven officers and thirty-six enlisted men.

The Australian flight was assigned to the 135th, and the unit became known as an"Experimental Military Unit," or EMU for short.

The unit's first role in Vietnam was to support the Royal Australian Task Force and other free-world units working in South Vietnam's III and IV Corps.

To facilitate operations, the 135th moved to Blackhorse in December 1967 and then to Bearcat in November 1968.

Working as part of the 214th CAB and 222nd CAB, the EMUs wreaked devastation on the Viet Cong. Their missions took them from the southern edges of the U-Minh Forest, to the Bamboo of Bu-Dop, and east to the boundaries of II Corps.

On 8 September 1970 the EMUs moved again, this time to Dong Tam, supporting strictly Vietnamese Army units in the Delta.

As other Aviation units in the Delta deactivated, the only U.S./Australian helicopter unit in existence took up the slack. The 135th flew great distances daily from their base station in support of the war effort.

As the only completely integrated Multi-national Helicopter Company fighting in Vietnam, the EMUs developed pride and dedication in their motto,

"GET THE BLOODY JOB DONE."

The gunship platoon (TAIPANs) adopted their own motto,
    "GET THE JOB DONE BLOODY."

In 1971, The EMUs moved to Di An.
In June 1971, the Royal Australian Navy portion of the 135th deactivated and was replaced by additional U.S. personnel. The 135th continued to carry out their mission in the traditions established by the multi-force EMUs.

The EMUs flew their final mission, a combat assault, in support of the 25th ARVN Division at Tay Ninh, on 20 January 1972. Stand-down operations began the following day.

Vietnam Helicopter Language

50 CAL = 50-Caliber heavy machine gun, anti-aircraft gun

51CAL = 51-Caliber heavy machine gun, enemy's anti-aircraft gun

AA = Anti-aircraft fire

AC = Aircraft Commander, Pilot, Ranking Officer

AK-47 = Fully automatic rifle, Chinese Communist-manufactured 5.57-millimeter

AMMO = Ammunition

AO = Area of operation

Ao dai = Meaning "long dress" or "tunic" in Vietnamese.

AP = Armor piercing

ARTIE = Artillery, a firebase

ARVN = Army Republic of Vietnam, American allies (friendlies)

AWOL = Absent without leave, a court marshal offence

BIVOUAC = Camping without tents, to make camp without shelter

BODY BAG = A black plastic bag, zippered, with carrying handles, used to transport deceased persons

BODY COUNT = Number of KIAs

BUNKER = Inside dwelling safe area, a mud and log protective enclosure

C&C = Charlie-Charlie, command and control, flight commanders aircraft (flew at high altitude to observe the mission)

CA = Combat assault

CACHE = Hidden stockpile of weapons/explosives, usually buried

CHICKEN PLATE = Flack vest usually worn over chest and back, placed under seats by aircrew

CHIEF = Crew chief /gunner, responsible for aircraft, enlisted personnel

COM = IC, intercommunication radio frequency

COM-CORD = Communication cord attached to helmet

C-RATIONS = C-rats, individual boxed meals containing canned food and cigarettes

DEROS = Acronym for "Date Expected to Rotate Overseas"

DI = Daily Inspection, also Drill Instructor

DINK = (see GOOK) Derogatory depending on use

DOG TAG = Stamped metal plate with name, rank, serial number, and religion, used to identify bodies; issued in pairs as form of I.D. to be used in the event of death

E&E = Escape and evade (the enemy or the company duty officer)

ELIGIBLES = Eligible male, perceived or otherwise, a target (the enemy)

EM = Enlisted Men, e.g., "EM Club," (a bar for enlisted men)

EMUs = Two flight platoons containing twelve slick helicopters

ETA = Estimated time of arrival

FLESHETTE = Warhead on 2.75-inch rocket, filled with dart-shaped nails, a.k.a beehive round

FLIGHT = see EMUs

FNG = Fucking New Guy

FOX MIKE = FM broadcast radio frequency

FREEDOM BIRD = The airplane that takes you home

FROGSHIP = Huey gunship, like mini-gunship but with added 40-millimeter grenade launcher mounted in the nose

FULL SUPPRESSION = all guns/gunners firing at the same time

GOOK = A disparaging term for an Asian person, popularized in Vietnam during war

GUNNER = usually volunteer from Infantry, responsible for armament, enlisted personnel

GUNSHIP = Huey UH-1B or C model, earlier version, converted for heavy armament

HAMLET = Village or multiple villages

HE = High explosive

HEAVY FIRE TEAM = three gunships: lead, wing, and trail.

HO CHI MINH = North VN leader, Uncle Ho (enemy #1); died February 2, 1969

HOGSHIP = Huey gunship with thirty-six 2.75-inch rockets

HOOTCH (or **HOOCH**) = Dwelling (home) usually made of mud, straw, and bamboo

KIA = Killed in action

KLICK = Kilometer (1,000 meters) or 3,200 feet

KP = Kitchen police, duty in the mess hall, peeling potatoes, washing pots, etc.

LIGHT FIRE TEAM = two gunships: lead and wing ship

LRP = Long Range Patrol, Infantry personnel, also called "Leerps"

LZ = Landing zone

M.P. = Military Police

M.P.C. = Military payment currency, a.k.a. funny money

M-16 = Rifle, semi or fully automatic, sixteen-round clip of 223-caliber (5.56-millimeter) bullets

M-60 = fully automatic belt-fed, recoilless and gas-operated machine gun (7.62-millimeter bullet)

M-79 = Single-shot 40-millimeter grenade launcher

MI = Military Intelligence

MINI-GUNSHIP = Huey gunship with fourteen 2.75-inch rockets in two pods and two mini-guns

MO = Major overhaul

NEGATIVE SUPPRESSION = No one fires unless fired at

NVA = North Vietnam Army, regular Army, trained soldiers (the enemy)

O.D. = Olive Drab

PETER PILOT = Co-pilot, Subordinate Officer

PM = Periodic maintenance

POL = Petroleum, Oil, Lubricant, a designated area for refueling aircraft

PRC-25 = Field radio/telephone, a.k.a. prick-two-five

PREPPING = the act of shooting to create a response, i.e. to cause another to shoot back, or to purposely create an explosion

PSP = Pierced Steel Planking, used for quick assembly of semi-permanent runways

PUCKER FACTOR = various degrees of tightening of the anal sphincter muscle that occurs during period of high stress

PZ = Pick-up zone

R.A.N. = Royal Australian Navy, brothers–in-arms, allies, very friendly

R.O.K. = Royal Order of Korea, allied troops, a.k.a. Rocks or Roxie

RPG = Rocket-propelled grenade, shoulder-fired weapon

SAPPER = Slang for enemy whose weapon is a satchel charge explosive, thrown by hand

SECONDARY(s) = an explosion creating a second or multiple explosions

SLICK = Huey helicopter UH-1D or H, utility/troop transport

SLICK LOAD = Passengers, seven Americans with gear or nine Vietnamese with gear

SMOKE = A colored-smoke-producing grenade (red, yellow, green, or violet), on-explosive

SORTIE = A mission, e.g. medivac, resupply, air support, combat assault, etc.

SUPPRESSION = to inhibit fire with fire, shooting first

TAIPANs = One flight platoon containing five armed gunships (three onmission, two on standby)

TI = Tech Inspector, supervisor of all aircraft repair

TRACER = A bullet filled with red phosphorous, "a marking round," usually every fifth round on a belt of ammunition

TRAILING SMOKE = Holding in hand a smoke grenade at arm's length outside the helicopter door after igniting.

TROOP(S) DISMISSED = Released from duty, The End

UH-1 CREW = Four persons: Pilot, Co-pilot, Crew chief (right gunner), and Gunner (left gunner)

UHF = Ultra-high frequency

VC = Victor Charlie, Charlie, Chuck, sympathizer with North Vietnam (theenemy)

VHF = Very high frequency

WHITE MICE = South Vietnamese Military Police, wore white helmets

WILLIE PETE = White phosphorous, used as a marking round, or a weapon;burns, not extinguishable with oxygen present; used in grenade, rocket,and artillery form

South Vietnam Map
(circa 1969)

Foreword

January 1969, Fort Eustis, Virginia.

It is the final day of advanced training. The cold chill of the night air has made its way inside the unheated barracks as the soldiers prepare to depart tomorrow before sunrise. Mitchell Collins has been handed a set of orders that have come down from high command. Shivering from the cold, or maybe it was his nerves, his hands shook as he parted the envelope. Looking over the papers he discovers that he is on his way to Vietnam. Not really sure how to feel about it, he told himself, well this is what you've trained for. But there is doubt about his ability to deal with aggression on a scale never before experienced. Still there is a certain curiosity that drove him to accept his fate.

Mitchell has thirty days leave before reporting to the stateside Transition Company at Fort Dix, New Jersey. A civilian commercial aircraft under contract with MACV (Military Airlift Command Vietnam) will fly him to his final destination. Did I say "(final)," well perhaps, but let's not think about that right now.

Into the third week at home preparing for his eventual departure, Mitchell knows that his time is short. Convincing his girlfriend has been difficult at best, but there's not much time left.

"Honey, I am going off to war, I may not get back the same person that I am now, please, couldn't we do it just once before I die, please?" finally convincing her to concede to his cruel persuasion.

Having spent as much of the available time left to see friends, party hearty, and reflect on the future, the time has come to head out to the airport. There is a tearful goodbye with many of Mitchell's friends and relatives in attendance. It's true he was not going off to college, or the

Peace Corps, but still it seemed to Mitchell that everyone thought he was never coming back! Although they all said, "See ya next year," Mitchell wondered, *Well if I am going to be gone only a year, then what's all the fuss?* He was strong emotionally but seeing grown men cry has reduced Mitchell to tears also. Turning to board the plane, the realization that his life is about to change has impacted hard. Suddenly all the joking around about being a soldier has taken a very serious tone. Mitchell is heading off to a war zone, and all he knew about soldiering is the training he has had in the past year. He wondered if it would be enough to get him safely back home again.

Having been a soldier for so little time, Mitchell has learned much about himself and his ability to cope in a militarized environment. Physically, he is in the best condition of his life. Not only is he strong, but he was able to crawl at speeds most people run at, then get up and run a three-minute mile, climb, swim, leap, and hang by his fingertips.

He has acquired skills in hand-to-hand combat, hand-to- weapon, and can quickly break a man's neck. In weapons training he has shot rifles, stabbed with bayonets, fired machine guns, launched shoulder-fired rockets, and tossed hand grenades. Yet even with these "skills," there is a sense of vulnerability.

In the past months and having been exposed to so many people his own age but very different from himself, compatibility took on new meaning. They came from every culture on the planet, and from every neighborhood in America. "getting along" has taken on a new dimension. Yet now Mitchell will depend on them, as they will depend on him. Here they are just soldiers, and that's all!

At Dix, they've had a day being vaccinated with what seemed like every disease known to man. Then they lay around a couple of days waiting for any reactions to the concoctions put into their bodies. Medics give classes on the prevention of malaria, and venereal disease, there is much to learn, but so little time.

With the preparations complete, they march out onto the airfield to board the plane. Mitchell moved forward with curiosity, rather than courage. Everything that has happened in his brief military career has been a new and unique experience.

The soldiers on the airplane converse about their private thoughts of going to war. The spoken words produce images of battles with an elusive enemy, fighting what is termed "Guerilla Warfare," while they have just been trained in "Conventional Warfare" style. After all it is not really a war they said—"It's a police action." The conversations on the plane are as diverse as the public opinion toward the conflict.

It's been such a long flight, passing time zone after time zone. Time and dates do not mean much to a soldier; every day is just another day of service to your country. The Army has control over your time: you come and go at their discretion. Now they have a year-long adventure before them, and anything shorter than a year means something went terribly wrong.

There is a feeling that today is a day Mitchell will want to remember. It is the first day of what he hoped will pass quickly, and without incident to cause harm. So he repeatedly marked the day in his mind so as not to forget: March 17th, 1969…

The Snake Pit: Aircraft are parked in their respective "revetments", here the Taipan gunships, a/k/a/ "snakes", reside in the snake pit. In this case the revetment is constructed with empty shipping containers for the rotor blades, then filled with sand. Fifty-five gallon drums, sand bags, and PSP (perforated steel plates), are also commonly used.

Chapter One

A Bad START

It is pitch black in the strange void outside the Military Airlift Command 707-jet transport. Inside, a few of the overhead reading lights illuminate those who are reading, playing cards, or smoking cigarettes while quietly conversing. Mitchell Collins sat in silent anticipation with a plane full of soldiers. Most are fresh from state side training, but there were a few returning veterans. It was overheard that when asked, "What's it like where we are going?" they were told, "You'll see soon enough, Kid," by those who already had firsthand knowledge.

Looking at his watch he observed it is 3:30 a.m. nearly twenty-three hours have passed since he boarded the aircraft at Fort Dix, in New Jersey. The big, four-engine jet made one previous landing for fuel in Anchorage, Alaska. It was cold and blowing snow as they all ran into the terminal building to stretch their legs.

As they take off for the last leg of his journey, Mitchell's orders in the manila envelope that is stuffed in the seat next to him say he will arrive at Tan Son Nhut airbase in the Republic of Vietnam. Listening to some of the others, he learned that Tan Son Nhut is some place near Saigon, a name he has heard many times before on TV and the radio. But all he really knew for sure is that he was going to be somewhere on the other side of the world.

In the seat next to him is Mitchell's closest friend, big Richard. They are surfer buddies from Miami. Surfers are what they called themselves, but South Florida really didn't have waves suitable for surfing most days. Still the surfer lifestyle flourished, and hanging out at the beach is what they did most. Both were well tanned before entering service. Mitchell, the shorter of the two by an inch, was lean with a muscular upper body—

is reconditioned physique made possible by the extensive physical training in bootcamp.

Big Richard was, well, big—not fat, but big in stature. He is strong but without a lot of muscular definition. Blond-haired and blue-eyed, he looked older than his actual years. Already he sports a bearded shadow even though he shaved only eight hours ago.

Mitchell is glad to have Richard with him; not knowing what to expect on their arrival "in a war zone," at least he won't have to be alone. They joined the Army with two other friends from high school in what was called the "Buddy Plan," but only he and Richard were sent to Vietnam after completing Helicopter School in Ft. Eustis, Virginia. At Eustis they have been trained in helicopter repair, qualifying them for their new military occupation as Helicopter Repairman, or "Crew Chief."

They are volunteers in an Army comprised largely of draftees, those young men caught up in the draft through the lottery system, where the lower your number the greater the risk of being called to active duty. Mitchell had enlisted with his friends so that all of them could pick their assignment based on their initial aptitude tests. Helicopter mechanic is what each of them had qualified for. This would guarantee them that they would not have to beat the bush on foot in the steaming jungles with the infantry, or, as they were referred to by other soldiers, "grunts."

Likewise, flying over the jungle on maintenance flights sounded better than walking through it in combat. Mitchell had always been infatuated with airplanes from his earliest recollection. He found helicopters to be just about the most awesome machine ever to fly. Never having before flown in one prior to his training, Mitchell was hooked after his first flight. He wanted more, and this was going to be the chance of a lifetime for him to get some real flight time. Besides, they really had nothing better to do with their young lives.

Just moments prior to landing an announcement by the pilot gave them the first indication of what was to come.

"Tan Son Nhut Airfield is under a mortar attack so we will be circling for a few minutes before landing," the voice from the cockpit said calmly. Immediately the soldiers all strained to see out of the tiny windows to catch their first glimpse of war. Mitchell tried to remember what a mortar is, oh yea, a three-inch diameter tube, about four feet long, if you drop the projectile in at the top, when it hits bottom it fires and launches the projectile up toa mile away. So he concluded whoever fired them must be close to the base.

"Hey, Richard can you see anything?" Mitchell uttered somewhat above a whisper from the middle seat because couldn't see past Richard's large head that filled the small window. "Negative, just black shit." Richard has already learned to speak in the military vernacular.

Soon the stewardesses were preparing the plane for landing.
"Please place your seats in the full upright position, tray tables stored and locked, and extinguish all smoking material." The stewardess clicked off the microphone and waited. Then after a few seconds she passed it to another uniformed female who announced, "As you deplane…" She hesitated a moment to read from a small notepad before continuing, "…if you hear incoming mortar rounds exploding, hit the dirt, then get away from the aircraft as quickly as possible." She looked up to see the faces of the young boys staring back. "Then stay down until you hear the all clear," she said sternly. "Is she kidding, are they going to dump us in the middle of an attack?" Mitchell mumbled loudly enough that those around him would hear while nervously looking around for a confirmation.

Soon the doors to the plane opened and filled the cabin with a surge of super-heated air. At the same instant their young, sensitive noses detected an odd and acrid odor.

"Hey, Richard, what's that smell?" Mitchell inquired with an upturned nose.

They looked at each other wide-eyed, shrugged their shoulder sin unison, and continued down the center aisle towards the opened door. Dragging their duffel bags along by the shoulder strap, they expeditiously headed to the rear of the plane. At the door the stewardesses wish them luck and enthusiastically shake their hands as they disembark. Some of the ladies have tears in their eyes. One especially attractive lady says to each recruit who passes her, "See ya back here next year, OK, soldier?" spoken with moist eyes and a forced smile.

"Hey, Richard, why do you think they were crying?" Mitchell asked pointing a thumb over his shoulder, while they walked ontothe tarmac below and then to the waiting bus.

"I guess they know most of us won't make it back.""Shit yea, I guess so, but we will, right?"

Richard nodded his affirmative.
Mitchell and Richard promise to watch each other's back. Until now, dying here, in this place, had not been considered by either of them.

On the ground now they could not see any post effects of a mortar attack. Yet they all believed it had happened because the place is just so damn dark, and they still hadn't identified that smell hanging in the night air. Was it the smell of war? A plane-load of soldiers looking around, not fearful of incoming explosives, but rather in a curious manner trying to get a bearing of just where in the hell are they? Everything had seemed, well…so foreign.

They landed in the wee hours so there was little activity around the aircraft or on the base. A few sodium lights on wood telephone poles cast an eerie yellow glow over the darkness surrounding the base. On the tarmac there is a large assortment of aircraft parked, Mitchell recognized the F-4 phantom jets, Chinook helicopters,and C-130 cargo planes, but there are many that he does not recognize. There were no lights in the distance so someone in the group suggested it must be all jungle beyond the lighted area past the end of runway.

Drowsy from talking and playing cards for most of the twenty-four-hour flight, they walked fast in hopes of getting to a real bed soon.

Unruffled, they boarded a military bus, just like the yellow school bus that took them to school not so many years earlier,except it is painted in olive green camouflage and has metal bars on the windows.

"Hey, driver," came a voice from behind the person in the driver's seat, "what are the bars for?" Not waiting for his answer he continued, "You wanna make sure we don't bail out on ya, eh?"

The driver not giving it much thought, rebutted, "Naw, it's to keep the VC from tossing in an explosive." He continued, "During this past TET offensive, the Vietnamese New Year, a whole bus of GIs was blown up when a VC Sapper Commando ran up to the bus and threw a satchel charge into an open window!" The driver peered up into a mirror that allowed him to see rearward and the faces of the soldiers.

Is he kidding? Mitchell thought. Then came the sound of a few half-opened windows slam shut as a few nervous laughs ensued, followed by complete silence.

They kept their eyes peeled outside the dust-covered windows for anything that looked like a VC. As the bus rolled on, the headlights revealed the roughly paved streets and drainage ditches that parallel both sides of the roadway. The route is now completely deserted, with all the buildings boarded up tight. There is an abundance of coiled concertina wire, with its sharp warning not to trespass. Sand bags are stacked high in between and around the buildings. *It's beginning to look like a war zone*, Mitchell thought, even resembling the prisoner of war camps he had seen on the TV.

Heading for a transition company somewhere on the base, most were too tired to care where they are, or where they go. At the Transition Company tomorrow, the group will receive further orders and an assignment to a unit that is to be their new home for the next year. At this point only the U.S. Army had control of their future. They knew nothing of where they would live and work. Mitchell felt he could take whatever came his way as long as he and big Richard stayed together.

Exhaustion settles in when they arrive at a temporary barracks. Inside, rows of double bunks have the three-inch thin mattresses folded in an S-roll at the head of the bed, exposing the flat springs underneath. Some GIs slowly unpack a few items to prepare for sleep, and some headed for the showers. Mitchell lay back on the bare, flat springs put his head on the mattress roll, and pulled the baseball cap over his eyes. And that was the last thing Mitchell remembered, as he slipped into a deep, coma-like sleep.

He woke up in the next morning to the sound of low flying helicopter overhead. The heavy whopping rhythm of the rotor blades beating the air like huge jungle drum. In the distance Mitchell heard the phantom jets; thunders roar while taking off from Tan Son Nhut. Then there was the passing sound of jeeps and trucks hustling their cargo about the base. Mitchell wanted to rise up to see what all the activity was about. But he felt like he had been on a week-long drinking binge and was still groggy and disorientated. He checked himself over, still in his new uniform fatigues, combat boots on and laced, and lying on bare springs. Straining his brain trying to remember the recent past, all he could recall is having arrived last night.

Suddenly he was aware of that smell as it fills his nostrils again. He wondered, *what is that smell?* Mitchell lifted the brim of his cap and got himself up onto his elbows and looked around at the empty barracks that, just hours ago, had a busload of soldiers in it. He has become accustomed to the almost primitive construction of a military barracks. This one, like the barracks he had in basic training at Ft. Gordon, Georgia, and then at Eustis, is all wood;the shiny linoleum floors are buffed to a high shine. The brown steel double bunk beds are aligned perfectly down the length of both sides of the barracks. The only noticeable difference was the lack of wall lockers and foot lockers that weren't needed for transients.

Unable to get up yet, despite the hunger in his gut, Mitchell lay still, waiting for someone to return. Assuming everyone else had gone to the mess hall for morning chow, Mitchell decided his need for sleep was greater than his hunger. He sensed it was light outside the barracks, and he heard voices in the distance. Although it was hard to hear them, he knew it is not English they are speaking. With his eyes closed he strained to hear more. A couple of hours have elapsed, and Mitchell wondered, *wherein the hell is everyone?* He lay there waiting for anybody to rejoin him but no one has returned. In his daze he remembers this is the Army. One, sleeping in past reveille is not allowed and, two, getting separated from your troops in a combat zone could get you killed. Mitchell reached for his duffel bag. Okay, it was time to get going!

Outside the sun is very bright, and it's hot and humid. As Mitchell breathed, the thick, moist air filled his lungs with each short gulp. Squinting up into the brightness of the day, Mitchell is hazily aware of people busily moving about the company area. However, one sight caught his immediate attention: a small figure squatting down in black, silky pants and a white, long sleeve shirt and a straw hat that is round and cone-shaped. It appears to be too large for the head wearing it. He can't see her face, but the long, black hair protruding from under the straw hat and the petite figure indicated to Mitchell that it must be a female. Her arms work in between her knees as she squats flat-footed at the edge of the small water-filled ditch, washing clothes. Next to her a small pile of saturated black and white silks await a scrub with tiny hands. Beyond her is a large animal, blackish gray in color. Although this is the first time Mitchell ever saw one in real life, he thought that a water buffalo is a menacing looking creature. It is pulling an antiquated wooden plow; even the blade of the plow is made of wood. A skinny man, with the same round straw hat and no shirt, stands on the plow as it carves out a line in the thick mud. He trails behind the creature with a stick and string attached to the end as if a whip. An ugly beast, its back is covered in dried mud. The horns are thick and sharp, like some kind of primitive helmet. The pair labors onwards seemingly in slow motion.

Looking around and out a far distance across open fields,he sees there are parallel rows of palm trees and not much else. Mitchell felt that he has stepped into a time machine, going farback in time to a place preceding his life span by many times. Certainly, there is not much resemblance to the modern world he just left behind.

Now Mitchell knew the source of that smell; he could tell it's the whole damn place. He knew it was in the ground, and in the air, everywhere. A smell like a burnt forest mixed with thick, fertilized muck and laid out to bake for a thousand centuries. He wondered if the whole country smells like this. He sure hoped he didn't have to smell this shit for a whole year.

The first mission was to find Richard.
"Where have you been, you missed roll call this morning," the staff sergeant snaps.

"Gee, sorry, Sarge, just woke up, I didn't hear reveille and everyone's gone. I am looking for PFC Richard Stockmen."

They stepped into the small office of the company commander.The sergeant lifted page after page of typed names from the thick binder until he found the alphabetized names that began with the letter "S."

"PFC Stockmen has been assigned to the 174th Transport Company in Da Nang."

"Where's that?" Mitchell asked. "North in eye corps."
"Oh, well how do I get there?" he replied.
"You don't." The sergeant smiled. "You've got orders for the 135th Assault Helicopter Company, sez here you're going to Bearcat, that's in three corps!"

A chopper from the 135th on a maintenance flight to pick up spare helicopter parts at Ton Son Nhut was notified to receive Mitchell and return with him to Bearcat.

"Be ready to hop aboard your helicopter in 30 minutes, troop."

Why, Mitchell wondered, *didn't Richard tell me he was leaving? Did he even plan to return and let me know? And what if I leave here, this base right now, I may never see Richard again.* Suddenly Mitchell felt very alone, and vulnerable and maybe even a little scared.

The flight aboard the Huey UH-1D to Bearcat yielded his first opportunity to see this country. It is flat, not so unlike Mitchell's home state of Florida. He once flew over the Everglades and thought Vietnam looked the same. Leaving the congested area of the base, Mitchell could see the city of Saigon in the near distance even though he could not see anything in detail; from up there it looked like any other metropolitan area. They flew east over an area the pilot called Cholon. At an altitude of two hundred feet, Mitchell saw they were over a very despairing part of the city—cardboard shacks all merged together, some made of discarded plywood, some with corrugated sheet metal on the roofs. Clothing that was presumably just washed hangs from everywhere the sun reaches and seems to add to the dense congestion. The passageways are so narrow, two people walking side by side have to turn slightly to pass each other, and there are no paved streets. It seems very dirty, and smoke rises ever so slowly from the many small fires used for cooking. Chickens and pigs are free to roam, and the foul odor rises from below.

They climbed to a cruising altitude of fifteen hundred feet. Mitchell glanced over the instrument panel to assure himself that the gauges were of the same kind he remembered from helicopter school. Altimeter, airspeed, HSI, check, N1 tachometer, temperature and pressure gauges all in the green. Mitchell felt more at ease remembering these things. Everything else seemed so different, he just needed to know that he had remembered his training to perform his duties correctly. That is if he was going continue to fly maintenance missions.

As they approached Bearcat, the base reminded him of a small western town from the days of cowboys and Indians. Except there is a raised perimeter, a mound of dirt six-foot high, that surrounds the base camp. And beyond the perimeter are rows and rows of concertina wire.

The narrow roadways are unpaved reddened dirt, again with a drainage ditch on each side. All the buildings are wood and pretty much all looked alike. A forest surrounds the base and is thick with trees, but the camp itself is all but void of any green plant life. Near the airstrip are large, canvas-covered Quonset huts used as aircraft hangers.

Mitchell saw military personnel on the ground, but also some Vietnamese wearing that funny-looking, straw conical hat. He pondered how he would be able to distinguish the Vietnamese from the Viet Cong. What kind of hat did the VC wear? It seemed strange to him that the Army would allow the Vietnamese civilians onto a military base in such large numbers.

The helicopter crossed over the perimeter and landed near the base tower. A jeep was sent to take Mitchell to his new home. During the short ride past the airfield he noticed all the aircraft parking areas, called "revetments," were empty.

"Where are all the helicopters", Mitchell asked the driver. "Out flying missions, they are usually back by five or so"," Suddenly Mitchell couldn't wait for them to return. "Do they all come back at the same time?" he inquired. "Nope, those that do come back, come back in flight groups."

The driver continued, "We have several units on the base, some go north, and some south, depends which unit you belong to"
"The one thirty-fifth, where do they go?" Mitchell wanted to know his destination.
"They usually fly their missions down south in the Mekong Delta."

Mitchell Collins reported for duty at the company commander's office. As he entered the single-level building where the office is, a large sign hanging overhead has the unit's crest, and unit name, along with the motto, "Get the Bloody Job Done." He looked at the sign and wondered whose blood the sign is referring to, the enemies, or his?

Inside he found another enlisted man typing at his desk.
"You'll be assigned to a duty after receiving your in-country training," the desk clerk told him. He was told that he would go to Bien Hoa the next day, just twenty miles northeast of Saigon, for one week, to learn about Viet Cong booby traps and mines. *More training*, Mitchell thought, *hell I've been in the Army for six months now training to come to Vietnam, and now that I am here, I get more training. He wondered, when do I get to do some cool stuff?*

The company area is comprised of three two-story buildings, or barracks, and two single-level barracks for the enlisted personnel. An underground bunker is placed between each building. A short walk to the mess hall, and enlisted man's club or bar, and of course the company commander's office. Also, there is an arms room across the hall from the commander. A small, detached hut painted red, white, and blue is the company mailroom.

Imagine being assigned to an assault helicopter company, and Mitchell found himself on his way to Bien Hoa in a "Deuce and a half," a large, heavy dump truck. Mitchell bounced with every bump in the road as he sat on long, hardwood bench seat. With his new jungle fatigues and steel helmet rattling around on his head and his M-16 rifle, he felt more like an infantry man than he did an aviator. He wondered if he'd see Richard at Bien Hoa; he sorely hoped so. Mitchell was still pissed off that Richarddid not tell him that he was leaving that morning at the Transition Company. Perhaps it wasn't Richard's fault, he thought, trying to justify the absence; maybe they wouldn't let him go back to the barracks where Mitchell lay sleeping. He really wanted to see his friend again.

The truck rumbled through the village of Long Thanh, with a few of the other new soldiers riding with Mitchell back in the bed of the truck.

"I hear the gooks throw their babies in front of Army trucks to collect twenty-five dollars from the Government," a fellow passenger says.

"But they get five hundred if we kill their water buffalo," says another.

"They can't spare their buff's, but they don't need more mouths to feed, so they toss 'em," said the expert new guy.

They drive past rickshaws, cyclists, and women walking laden down with heavy loads dangling from bamboo sticks they carry across their shoulders and behind their necks. An assortment of small cars, the kind of which Mitchell has never seen before, go zipping by. *It must be true what they said, this place is just so weird*, he thought.

On arrival at the training facility, they check in their M-16 rifles at the arms room there; actually it was just a steel shipping container with a lock. Mitchell figured Saigon must be a secure area. They are told to get some food at the mess hall, then get some rest, and that class will begin tomorrow.

Suddenly Mitchell spotted a familiar face. "Hey Brian, you made it here!"

It was not the face of his best friend, but a welcome sight nonetheless.

"It seems like a long time since basic training, eh?" Mitchell said. Brian agrees.

"So where did you get assigned?" Mitchell sort of hoped he would say Bearcat.

"Saigon," Brian says with a bright smile.

Mitchell, along with Brian and his buddies from Miami, drank beer till it came out of their ears upon graduation from basic training. He decided Brian is a good acquaintance to have here.

"Wanna go into town for a beer?" Mitchell asked. "Sure."

Mitchell sensed his friend feels the same about being here alone. They walk off the base towards Saigon, a place that Brian has had a few days to get to know. Walking and talking they decided to hitch a ride on an Army truck, and then hopped a pedicab for the remainder of the twelve-mile distance. Mimicking the lingo of the other soldiers that have been here awhile, Brian spoke.

"Papa-san, we go to number one club, OK?" he told the old Vietnamese driver.

Saigon is a bustling city of people, bicycles and mopeds, and a small number of automobiles. Very few signs over the doors of local business are in English. Children going to school are in uniforms and carry books like those of their counter parts back in the States.

The military vehicles look more out of place here, as they are too large for the narrow streets. As they came to a traffic jam they decide to disembark from their human-powered cab and walk the remaining few blocks. When the two neared the intersection where all the traffic has come to a halt, they saw the source of the delay, a two-and-a-half-ton military truck has run over an operator of a moped scooter. The deceased was transporting a watermelon strapped to the fender behind him; when the truck ran over him, it popped his melon and his head in one gruesome roll of the large tires. The corpse lying in the street was complete except for the head, which had its gray matter coming led in the street with the red matter of the melon. No one bothered to cover up the body. Mitchell was somewhat puzzled at the lack of attention the scene created other than the disruption of the traffic. No large crowd gathered to gawk, besides those few who were actually involved in the incident, everyone else went about their business as usual. Mitchell and Brian took a long, hard look and moved on.

The Bar on Tu-Do Street is simple in decor with twelve or so round tables with four chairs at each. The rusty old ceiling fans turn unusually slow, and some are making a slight squeaking sound. A long, mirrored bar has but one bartender and no barstools. Indigenous music is playing over the boom box radio that sits on the shelf above the rows of glasses behind the bar. Mitchell found the music irritating, it sounded sort of like a twangy, three-string guitar, and the female voice is too high-pitched as she blurts out the Vietnamese love song in her native tongue. The club has only a few soldiers inside, but there are a dozen or so women, or more accurately girls. Youthful stares and smiles are directed at the two of them as they enter. Mitchell and Brian look for the perfect table to see everything.

Once seated they order two beers, and the bar girls begin to strut their stuff in front of them. The girls say nothing; they are looking for a response from the pair of newbies. Then Mitchell spotted an angelic face and made eye contact. They smiled at each other as she walked towards their table. He could feel his heart pounding as she drew near. He noticed that she is not wearing a typical *Ao-dai* dress. Her clothing is more western, with her short skirt on the verge of being a mini. It reveals a sleek, smooth thigh above perfectly proportioned calf and thin shin bone. The hips sway seductively, and she flips the long, jet-black hair to one side;he thought her absolutely gorgeous. Mitchell motioned for her to sit with him. His heart is beating fast and he feels nervous, but he does not want to appear like the inexperienced admirer that he really is. Brian and Mitchell made some small talk, but mostly they stared at her, in awe of her skin that is flawless witha perfectly shaped face with high cheekbones and green eyes thatare more round than the others yet still look Oriental. Her smile produces perfectly straight, blindingly white teeth. She told them she is half-Vietnamese and half-French. She acts coy, and there is innocence in her voice, Mitchell could easily have fallen in love with her. He asked her if she has a boyfriend.

"Oh I have many GI boyfriends. I make beaucoup boom- boom." Brian, who had little experience in the Saigon life style, interpreted what she has just told them to mean she is a prostitute. Not ready to send her away just yet, he asked her if she would like something to drink.

"Yes, Saigon tea, pweez," she said, her eyes diverted downward.
Mitchell ordered the drink, and she placed a hand on his thigh and squeezes lightly. Mitchell smiled.

The two of them asked the girl a thousand questions about Vietnam, about the language, history, all the sort of things the Army did not teach them.

Hours go by as Mitchell and Brian slam beers down with reckless abandon. Another bar girl has joined them, as Brian needed some love too! Mitchell has successfully persuaded his beautiful slut onto his lap. Soon the beer started talking sex, but to his dismay she did not refuse his advances, but rather she stated that it is very late and he must get back to the base before curfew.

"Shit I forgot all about that," Brian said. But both were so wasted and it was already dark outside.

"Where did the time go?"

"Man, we could be in big trouble", Mitchell replied nervously.

"I saw this little hotel and no one saw us leave the base so let's stay in town, and tomorrow we can head back to the base", Brian offered.

"Good idea", they finished their drinks, kissed their new love interests good-bye, and headed to the hotel. Any other time the two would have been fearful of walking these streets after curfew, but tonight they are beer brave.

"Maybe we could go back there tomorrow", Mitchell asked,

"Yea" Brian says, as they stumbled on.

At the hotel, they paid a small fee for two overnight rooms. What a dump, even in a drunken stupor they could see this is a flea bag hole in the wall. Upon entering the room Mitchell reached for a light switch, and saw a small room about ten feet by eight feet, a brass bed with a high head board fills the room along with a toilet and sink in the corner, no doors or partitions. A ceiling fan suspended by a six foot pipe turns slowly overhead, as he looked up, the height of the ceiling seems odd, sixteen feet high at least, making the room feel like he was at the bottom of a large square can. There is a small round stain glass window near the top of the wall at the side of the bed, no good for viewing or escape. Well no sense in watching more paint peeling from the walls Mitchell thought, as he unlaced his boots and retired.

The pounding on the door down the hall was loud, as Mitchell is startled from a deep sleep. He realized someone is knocking on doors and yelling for everyone to step into the hall. The voice has a distinct accent,

Vietnamese, could be VC. He decided to stay quiet. Soon the stranger was knocking on his door, yelling in broken English and Vietnamese.

"Come out, come out now".

Mitchell hurried out of the bed and put his ear to the door. The footsteps sounded like two maybe three people. Mitchell thought of his options and decided to bluff.

"Look I am an American, I have a weapon with me, If you try to enter I will shoot you", he yelled through the door after first checking to be sure it was locked. Man I wish I had that M-16, he thought. There is a moment of silence, and then he heard the footsteps go down the hall to another door and yell some more. Whew, it worked and so the chatter goes on a little more and then quickly fades away. Mitchell's heart was still pounding, when he realized how hot it was and he was sweating profusely. After going to the sink to wash his face with some cool water he lay back down trying to comprehend what that was all about.

The light of a new day peers through the little stain-glass window and awakens Mitchell. Hung over he felt for his boots and tried to recall the events of yesterday. Then he remembered the training is today, gotta hurry. Down the hall he knocked on Brian's door, it took him a long time to answer.

"What the fuck was that shit last night" Brian asks yawning as he spoke. Mitchell told him of his bluff, and Brian told him he just ignored the whole thing.

"Gee I wish I had thought of that", Mitchell said.

"Hey Brian what time you got, he inquired".

"1040 hrs." Brian replied.

"Shit man, we missed the start of training", Mitchell felt panic.

"Well let's get some grub, I am hungry and then we can figure out what to do". Stuffing themselves with military cuisine back at the base, they had to wait until noon to slip in to the mess hall without being noticed.

Brian has a plan, "maybe we should go back into town, OK", Mitchell thinks Brian is going to be a bad influence on him.

Well they couldn't just walk in the training session late, what if the instructors asked "where have they been?" they decided to wait until tomorrow to try again.

Back in Saigon, they found their favorite club. As they enter Mitchell's eyes search for the whore that he hasn't been able to stop thinking about since he met her. Disappointment struck him hard when he saw her siting on the lap of an infantry soldier wearing a well-worn boonies hat. Judging from his equally worn fatigues, he had the experience to score the best of the clubs whore's.

Mitchell decided to drink to his loss. It wasn't long before Brian and he are drunk again. They have switched to drinking CC & 7 that by now they drink like water. All the women are looking beautiful to them, and both have a new attitude towards the hookers. Mitchell told his new girl to dance for him. She then stepped up unto the table and began to gyrate to the music. Suddenly a strange feeling swell's inside of Mitchell, he decides this girl wants him badly. He started at her knees and slid his hand up past her thigh and felt for her panties while she danced. Mitchell took her smile as a sign of approval as he pulled the panties down exposing her pubic area. He didn't know why he did it, he just felt the urge to put his face into her soft mound and taste her, and so he did.

Fortunately Brian got them back to the base before curfew, they are almost out of MPC (military payment currency), what they called funny money, and might have had to spend the night in the streets. Mitchell tried thinking about that new hooker. Funny he thought she had no teeth, oh what did I do. Then he thought of all those G.I.'s she must have been with and the black syphilis they were warned about in those training films about Vietnam. He wondered if his lips would blister or would his tongue fall off?

They never made it to any of the classes that week. With the money all but spent, they went on walking sightseeing tours trying to learn as much as possible about their new environment. But mostly they laid around trying to avoid getting caught. Their first week in Vietnam and they have been A-W-O-L. This is an offense that in a combat zone, they could be shot by a firing squad for, quite literally! On the last day of training, Brian and Mitchell hung out outside the classroom until the end of class, which ended early. All the trainees filed out and headed for the arms room, where all of the weapons have been stored. Mitchell and Brian secretively fell in line near the end. As they entered the arms room, a training sergeant looks at them and says,

"Where have you two been"?

"In-country training Sergeant", they respond in unison.

"I don't remember seeing the two of you", he said with a suspicious eye.

"We went to the other class", that lie just sort of spilled out.

"Well grab your weapons and find your truck back to your unit". Mitchell really did not think he believed them, but there really was another class. Besides it was all over, or just maybe the Sergeant did not want to be responsible for their executions.

"Oh God, our weapons are missing", Brian uttered almost in a whisper.

"Aw shit, fuck, now what are we going to do", Brian looked worried.

"I have already been warned that losing a weapon in a combat zone is a capital offense". Again they could get the firing squad. The Sergeant took pity on them as they explain their dire situation.

"Someone probably just grabbed the wrong M-16's, if there are any weapons leftover there yours", the Sergeant said shaking his head.

"But sarge, the serial numbers won't match", they cried.

"Just have them change them in the log book, back at your unit, they'll know how".

It was a relief to know the Army would make it so simple to save their ass. Absolute exhilaration comes as the last trainees grab all but two beautiful M-16's.

"I hope the idiot that grabbed our weapons gets court-martialed", Mitchell told Brian. Still they felt good that they have cheated death twice already.

Mitchell and Brian promise to stay in contact. They wish each other luck and Mitchell boarded the half-ton truck, for his return to Bearcat. He was glad to be returning to his new home, Mitchell has had enough fun for a while. Although he did have some fond memories he was exhausted. With his first Vietnam experience behind him, he thought about the hookers, getting drunk, and flying.

Bouncing along in the back of the truck he remembered the staff sergeant in the States, back in basic training. It was late at night and he had just finished KP duty, (kitchen police, and a.k.a. dish washer/potato peeler). He went into the shower to wash off the more than 12 hours of food stench. Mitchell did not notice it at first because his drill sergeant was facing the shower wall. As he entered he could see only his naked side profile. As Mitchell stepped under one of the shower heads, a few down the wall from the drill sergeant. When the DI turned to rinse his backside, Mitchell had caught a glimpse of the scars. They were an inch wide, maybe wider, and stretched across the entire width of his buttocks and up to his waist level, three, zigzag reddish purple marks that were raised well above the level of the surface of his skin. As he rinsed he completed a turn and Mitchell saw the same gross scars on the DI's lower abdomen. There was only a small section above both his hips that were not heavily scared. He looked as though he could have been cut in half and sewn back together.

"Bad accident, eh sarge", Mitchell had to know how it happened.

"Something like that, more like bad luck", the DI stated.

After some small talk and prodding he began to relate the experience that caused his wounds.

"I was in the Nam, serving in the infantry, we were out on patrol, beating the bush one day", the DI stopped a moment to rinse his face.

"The point man halted the platoon to check something out ahead of us", he continued.

"He was going to be awhile so I went to sit down to eat my C-rations, and sat my fucking ass right down on a fucking land mine".

Mitchell heard that a land mine can kill a multitude of persons and sensed an amazing story of survival. He then asked how the sergeant could have lived through it.

"At first I was just totally stunned and I remember lying on my back, I struggled to sit up, ya know, kinda up on one elbow then the other", he said demonstrating as he talked.

"Then I was up, I looked down to see my stomach and all my intestines blown out", he looked down at his scars.

"My insides jus-sort-a laying in my lap, and all over my legs and in the dirt", the DI reached for his towel.

"I must have been delirious cause I just sort of started scooping them up and shoving them back into the hole in my stomach", he said as he made a motion using both hands and his towel to indicate the displaced organs. Mitchell stared at his naked torso trying to visualize the fresh wound.

The sight of his grotesque scars left no doubt that his statements were honest and accurate. Mitchell was beginning to feel a little woozy as the Sarge continued.

"Our medic came and wrapped his poncho around me, shot me up with morphine and then I passed out. Later I was medivac out to Japan".

"God, It looks like it was real painful, Sarge", Mitchell said.

"Naa…Didn't feel much at all, everything was kinda numb, and the morphine did the rest".

Suddenly Mitchell wished he had gone to all those classes about the booby traps and mines. Jeezus what a bad start, things can't possibly get any worse. Oh what the hell, I'll be flying in the helicopters, Mitchell thought. I am sure I won't need to know about the land mines and shit like that. Hey, at the very least…he was going to be optimistic about his survival chances, after all he's come this far unscathed!

A Taipan Snake, one of the top ten deadliest snakes in the world, is endemic to Australia. A suitable mascot for the gunship platoon.

Chapter Two

F-N-G's

Mitchell's unit, the 135th Assault Helicopter Company is an Experimental Military Unit, "E.M.U.". It is the first ever in the history of U.S. armed forces to live, work, and fight alongside foreign allies. In this case the Royal Australian Navy or "RAN", helicopter detachment. A fighting contingency made up of Army and Navy personnel, someone surely had a sense of humor.

Two platoons of six helicopters each had the call sign EMU, which ironically enough is also an Australian bird that does not fly. The choppers are Huey's, model UH-1D's and H, but everyone referred to them as slicks. Although few of the Aussie's were pilots and crew, most are assigned to non-combat roles such as maintenance, armament, motor pool, etc. Occasionally some Aussie's would volunteer to fill in for absent crewmen on combat assaults. Doing so affirmed to the American combatants that they were as capable as their counterparts. They too enjoyed a good fight but were sometimes held back for their countries political stance on the conflict.

The remaining flight platoon carried the call sign, "Taipan", they fly the gunships, UH-1C models. C-models are smaller, older aircraft, capable of lifting a four-man crew, armament, and not much else. Most everyone seemed to avoid the members of the gun platoon. The Taipan's, aptly named after an extremely deadly snake from Australia, are reputed to be a rough bunch and very confrontational.

The first week back at Bearcat, Mitchell was miserable. He had been given all the worst duties exclusively available to FNG's. Filling sandbags, digging ditches, dumping trash, KP, and the dreaded shit burning detail. There he supervised the total burn down of human waste that had been collected in the latrine's underside containers made from the bottom third of fifty-five gallon drums. The two boys who made up the detail were Vietnamese, eleven and thirteen years of age. They came to the base each morning, except Sundays, with the hundreds of hooch maids that were trucked in from the local village and had security clearance to work on the base.

"Shit one", the older boy, and "shit two", the only names Mitchell ever heard anyone call them. They seemed to enjoy their work, as they poured in the diesel fuel into the smelly urine and feces mix. Then ignited the potent concoction with their own matches, the same one's used for lighting up their hand rolled cigarettes. They had stirred with metal rods until all the liquid dissipated in the thick black smoke, whenever the wind changed direction they played hide and seek with the dark gaseous plumage.

It is not at all what Mitchell had expected of Army life in the Nam. He prayed for a change of regular duty. He felt that he really didn't want to go on carrying out the non-combat roles for much longer. If he had to be here, away from home, might as well make it count for something. That following morning at roll call, the duty officer commanded Mitchell to the arms room to clean the weapons stored there. He was to report to the black hippie sergeant at oh ten hundred hours. Great Mitchell thought, more shit stuff to do.

As he walked towards the HQ building, where the arms room was to the right and the Company Commander's office to the left, he noticed the shaded area in front of the small complex. Deciding to stay in the shade he went the most direct route to avoid the intense sun's rays. Stepping up unto the covered walkway that ran the length of the complex, he turned right, towards the arms room. As he approached the breezeway that separated the two rooms, he heard what sounded like a gunshot. Mitchell stopped and listened for a confirmation of the shooting but he didn't think anyone else had heard it. Thinking for a moment, maybe the arms room sergeant accidentally discharged a weapon his suspicion was immediately confirmed. Just then another black soldier came out through the door of the arms room. Mitchell did not recognize him as someone he knew. Out he came rotating on one stiff leg, spinning around several times while crossing the walkway. Shouting as he goes down, "I've been shot, I've been shot", then the black soldier hit the dirt grabbing at his crotch. As Mitchell was only ten feet from the door now, and he could see the blood on the wounded man's pants.

Damn, someone's gone crazy and is going to shoot me too Mitchell thought. His heart was racing as he backed up to the front of the building. He then began to inch his way towards the open door. Mitchell was opposite of the wounded soul brother who is writhing in pain on the ground still screaming. He couldn't tell if the wounded man was alone and shot himself or, if someone else did it. Mitchell looked around for anyone who might help, or at least have a weapon with them, just in case. He was alone and it seemed that no one heard the shot or the man still screaming in pain. Now but a few feet away from the door to the arms room he first saw the pistol appear, then a black hand, an arm, too far away to go for the gun and to close to run, Mitchell froze. Sure as shit when he sees me he's going to shoot me too! Better get him before he gets me, Mitchell then lunged for the man but the wood walkways were made of uneven planks and he tripped stumbling forward. As he toppled, the shooter ran out so fast that Mitchell missed the attempted tackle with him. Startled, the hippie sergeant then turned to look at Mitchell and dropped a 38-caliber pistol on the ground.

"I am sorry man, I didn't mean to do it" he said to Mitchell, obviously mistaking him for some higher authority.

To Mitchell's great relief they went together to the aid of wounded soldier. The wounded man has now begun removing his pants while still flat on his back, trying to determine the extent of his own injury.

"You shot me in my dick, muthafucka", his hands shaking as he reaches down to feel for the wound. The hippie shooter ran to the infirmary to summon a medic. Three other GI's have appeared and give assistance. Mitchell tried to hold the wounded man's hands from feeling what he feared is going to be exactly what the man has said.

Help arrives quickly and a medic is cutting away the pants to observe the wound. A 38-caliber punctures through the middle of his black dick, from side to side, exposing a perfect pink hole. Mitchell's first thought was that he could put a pencil right through it. After passing through his penis, the projectile entered the inside of his leg without an exit.

A stretcher arrived moments later and the wounded is taken away. The MP's have arrested the hippie shooter, and Mitchell has been excused from weapons duty.

Later that day Mitchell heard the arms room sergeant was spinning the chamber of the revolver, in simulated Russian roulette fashion. When his friend came in to talk, he soon realized that the Sergeant playing with the pistol was a bad idea. He asked his soul brother buddy to put the gun down. The hippie Sergeant did not realize that there was a live round left in the chamber when the trigger was squeezed to indicate there was no need to worry. The shooting was ruled accidental and the shooter was reprimanded, then sent back to his duties.

New guys in country do not ask a lot of questions, so when Mitchell was told to take ammunition to the dump just outside the base camp and burn it he complied without hesitation. Another low ranking FNG and Mitchell loaded up corroded, bent, or otherwise damaged bullets and dented 2.75 inch rockets without explosive warheads, unto the back of the flight line jeep and drove off base to the dump. A continuous fire was burning in the eight-foot deep and twelve-foot wide ditch that was half as long as a football field. This was a popular place for Vietnamese locals to hang out and scavenge whatever didn't blow up or burn.

Never having before the opportunity to see inside a rocket, Mitchell unscrewed both ends of the round casing only to find another tube inside made of solid rocket propellant. The propellant had a hollow core and Mitchell surmised that the thin wire inside the core was the igniter that carried the electric current to fire the rocket. He threw the first core into the burning ditch and soon he thought it was going to rocket right out of the ditch. In seconds flames shot out of both open ends of the tubular core. Amazed, he watched scorching flames blasting out and extending ten feet or more. A loud pulsing roar with a high pitched whistling sound. In seconds there was nothing left but a metal tube.

"Hey, got another that was cool", Mitchell said while the other FNG dumped the bullets.

The noise of the rocket propellant burning caused quite a stir among the fifty or so local Vietnamese. They grouped together standing several feet away mumbling in their native talk. Mitchell decided to ignite the other one with his cigarette then tossed it into the ditch. He observed that the other core had burned from both ends toward the center. So holding the solid propellant at the center, he touched the tip of the cigarette to one end and fired her up. Again, in seconds there were flames, bright yellow thrusting out both ends, the noise almost deafening, as it burned down the heat transferred near his hand. When it got too hot to handle he flipped it into the ditch where the other FNG had thrown the bullets.

Mitchell backed up when he heard the bullets popping off, because he knew that they shot off in indiscriminate directions when not guided by a gun barrel. But no one ever told the Vietnamese that hung around the dump that. An elderly papa-san hobbled up to Mitchell pointing a shaking finger and loudly accusing said,

"You shoot", "you shoot", indicating that Mitchell had shot him in the leg.

"What? Where?" Mitchell asked.

"I haven't touched my gun you asshole".

Mitchell wondered how much trouble this is going to get him in. "Look, I take you to GI medic", he said trying to avoid a confrontation with everyone looking on. Mitchell thought fast, he did not want the MP's that stood guard at the dump to be alerted. They loaded the papa-san into the Jeep and drove off to the base infirmary. Enroute the old man showed Mitchell the open wound centered in his right thigh. Mitchell had to admit to the FNG driving the Jeep that it indeed looked like a bullet hole.

"But I didn't shoot him", Mitchell reiterated.

They pulled up and dropped old papa-san in front of the all-white painted building, with the doublewide screen doors and a big Red Cross over the door.

"Go", Mitchell said pointing to the doors, and then they quickly drove off.

Changing out of uniform and into the only civilian set of clothes Mitchell had, the one's he wore to Fort Dix before coming to Nam. They feel good on him and allow him to feel like a person from the real world. That evening Mitchell headed for the enlisted man's club for a cold beer and to listen to a band of Vietnamese musicians that played popular Rock and Roll from base to base entertaining the troops. Inside the EM club other members of the 135th are lined up across the bar, a few sit at tables. At one table a large crowd has gathered. Mitchell asked one of the Australians observing the game being played as to the nature of the ruckus, "Well mate, they're playing Crown-n-Anchor".

Mitchell peered over the shoulder of one of the young Australian's still in his uniform who seemed the most excited as he scoops up a hand full of the multicolored paper cash.

The crowd thickens around the game, some are ecstatic, and others are cursing. Mitchell asked out of curiosity how the game is played.

"Well mate, you have six symbols on the board, four are like your poker cards", he says in the modified Queens English.

"A black spade and a club, a red heart and a diamond, plus the red crown and black anchor, six dice are rolled, all have the same symbols on its six sides",

"If you have a buck down on a crown for example, and 4 sides of the six dice show the crown, you are paid four times the amount laid down in that square, quite simple really".

Mitchell watched a little longer, it did seem easy enough and he couldn't see any way to be cheated. He reached into his pocket for a few crumpled MPC notes. Putting his funny money down on the board he came up a winner, and doubled his investment. Hey this is a good game Mitchell thought.

It did not take long before he was almost down a month's pay, the money saved to send home, now gone. It was hard to leave the game when he could get it all back with one lucky roll of the dice, so he just kept going until there was none to spare.

Music began to play loudly outside on the little stage built for such occasions. Discouraged at his performance inside, Mitchell went outside to watch another. The band is playing a popular rock song, some of the GI's are singing along. Bummed out, Mitchell guzzled the beers down and stared at the Vietnamese lead singer in the red sequined mini skirt. She sings like a musician but looks like a hooker he thought. Towards the end of the night, the band sings another popular hit by Eric Burden and the Animals,

"We gotta get outta this place- if it's the last thing we ever do", drunk now, Mitchell joined the band in a modified rendition.

"We gotta get outta this place- girl there's a better life back- in-the- states".

Morning roll call brings good news. Finally, a chance to fly, it's a supply mission to Bien Hoa for aircraft parts. A short hop over familiar territory, still he'll enjoy the flight. This is his first in-country flight as a crewmember. In newly issued Nomax flight suit and gloves, Mitchell has traded in the canvas and leather combat boots for the all leather combat boot of aviators. With his own flight helmet with a drop down tinted visor and boom microphone, his uniform is complete.

A pilot, co-pilot and Mitchell make up the crew, as they board the Huey UH-1D, troop transport. Mitchell was anxious to show he could be a professional crewmember so that he might get more opportunities to fly. When the pilot called, "coming up", to hover the aircraft, Mitchell cleared the aircraft around the tail boom to be sure there were no obstructions. He kept a sharp eye on the instruments, and mentally reviewed his crew-chief duties. He soon found that he needed more practice with his communication skills with the pilots. Mitchell had to remember that he needed to depress the microphone switch when he talked and then released the switch when he finished. For several minutes he forgot to release the mike button and the open mike hissed in the pilot's ears. The noise prevented the pilots from hearing important communications from the air traffic controller in the tower. He felt really embarrassed for that error. Mitchell tried to imagine what being in combat must feel like from his seat in the helicopter. It sure had to be exciting and beat all the hell out of the rear echelon bullshit duties he has had. Mitchell decided this is what he really came here to do.

While Mitchell, the units newest FNG, struggled through his monotonous days, the missions of the 135th continue. The company has commenced an operation down in the southernmost region of Viet Nam. In an area called the "Delta", the three platoons of the EMU's and the

Taipan platoon begin their day... In a remote farming area outside of the city of Cai Lay the first flight takes off and sets a course for the landing zone. The 9th ARVN division has the duty to secure the area and rid the outlying villages of Viet Cong. It was a large area to cover and every available man of the ninth was in the field.

The only way to cover the distance required was to insert a small group of troops into a landing zone where the enemy had been openly active. Three slicks would load up with twenty-one ARVN troops and insert them into the first LZ. Then the ground troops would commence a search and destroy mission, if nothing was found they would call the choppers back, hop aboard, and fly a short distance to the next LZ. Following the first insertion, another three ships with a group of ARVN's would land in the distance between the first insertion and the second. In all, twelve helicopters were used, three flights of three ships. They continued the procedure until contact is made with the enemy. Filling in the gaps as they went along, this was referred to as "leap frog insertions". The missions had been going well and the ground troops had found evidence of the enemy's presence, but no bad guy's yet.

Four , Taipan gunship's, split up into two light fire teams to provide air support for the insertions, fire team's "Alpha", and "Bravo".

Alpha's lead ship has the call sign, "Taipan Three-One", and in trail is "Three-Six. The two Taipan helicopters of fire team Alpha had been covering the mission for most of the morning. The command and control ship has just discharged them from the Area of Operation to refuel. Bravo, the second light fire team, had been called in to cover the insertions while Alpha was at the base refueling. Fire team Alpha would remain at the base at Dong Tam until the two gunships in the AO ran low on fuel, or ammo, whichever occurred first.

The entire helicopter operations are under the watchful eye of the Command and Control ship, orbiting above at high altitude to observe the entire playing field. C&C is the mission leader and ranking superior officer. He commands the EMU's and the Taipan's. With him is an ARVN Colonel. He is responsible for the troops once they are on the ground. For the most part they got along well, the two of them commanding their respective Army's for the benefit of the mission task. But there was always those times when things did not go so well.

Meanwhile the Taipan gunner's decided to grab some extra ammo, while the pilots got out stretching their legs and the crew-chief's fueled the ships. The peter-pilot of the lead gunship had continued to monitor the mission frequency when he heard a call from one of the EMU slicks. The EMU's reported being shot at as they inserted the troops into the LZ. Taipan team Bravo had fired on the enemy expending most of their ammunition. The EMU's were now bringing in more troops to assist the small group now under heavy enemy fire.

The peter-pilot frantically waved for his pilot to come and listen to the frequency.

"What's up"

"EMU Two-Niner, has been hit and our guys are running low on ammo" he reported.

"Call C&C, find out if he wants us up"

"Roger"

The peter adjusted his microphone nearer to his lips and depressed the PTT switch on the cyclic.

"Ahhh Charlie-Charlie, Taipan, ah Alpha lead"

"Go lead"

"Ahhh roger, do you require the first team at this time, over"

"Lead, I am a little busy right now, stand-by"

The peter pilot relayed the message but the pilot predicted that they would soon be up, and called his fire team to their ships to "crank-em up".

They sat for a few minutes after bringing the ships to idle. Then C&C called.

"Taipan lead, what is your ETA to LZ, Yankee-four"

"Roger, one-seven minutes".

Lead was able to respond accurately because the co-pilot had previously plotted their navigation.

"Make it ten"

The Taipan's wasted no time twisting the throttle to get the engine tach r.p.m.'s into the green and lifted off. They flew at very low altitude to avoid having to climb to a safe altitude, and then having to descend. At twenty-five feet the ground passed by quickly. They were cruising at 92 knots, about all they had when fully loaded on a hot and humid day. Sometimes they had to pull pitch just to clear a tree line.

In the rice paddies, women worked in ankle deep muddy water with their pant legs rolled up and wearing those round straw hats. Bending over at the waist while planting the small sprigs that would eventually rise to become a stalk of rice. They were never deterred from their duty even when the thunderous helicopters buzzed at low level over their heads. The second fire team departed the AO and headed for Dong Tam to refuel and rearm. Taipan lead and his wingman were two minutes away.

Arriving on station they found a fierce firefight had commenced between the ARVN's and the VC. Bullets were flying everywhere. And somehow the ARVN's had commingled with the VC and both were firing at each other, and at the aircraft above. ARVN troops had taking up shooting at their helicopter support in a frenzy of anger for having to be dropped off in a hot LZ. As outrageous as it sounded for these allies to shoot at another it was certainly not the first time, nor did anyone expect it to be the last.

Another lift of ARVN's had been initiated but C&C held them off until he felt it was relatively safe for the choppers to get out of the LZ without being shot by the "friendlies". There were no American's on the ground to act as advisor to the foreign troops, so C&C had to deal with his cohort. He had argued with the ARVN Officer to radio his troops and have them refrain from firing at his EMU's.

"Colonel, if your troops do not cease their firing on my helicopter's, I am going to have the gunship's blow them all to hell, you understand me".

The Colonel had made a scornful face, then C&C added.

"And then I am going to throw you outta my ship", he threatened with a finger first pointed at the Vietnamese Colonel and then out the door. To drive his point home, C&C instructed his crew-chief to relieve the Colonel of his pistol and keep the weapon aimed at him. The repressed Vietnamese Officer began screaming at the ground troops through his radio.

C&C brought the next load of ARVN soldiers in and ordered the Alpha team gunship's to hold their fire until they were in the LZ and then only provide cover for the departing slicks. It was out of the ordinary for C&C to be vague about the rules of engagement but the ARVN Colonel was already nervous and C&C didn't want any more problems in the command ship. The gunship door gunner's heard the orders but they are trained to protect their aircraft. If they got a visual on someone firing at them, it was their duty to return fire, no questions asked and no explanations needed. That was their "rules of engagement".

As the three slicks approached the landing, the gunships flew on either side of them. Just as the slicks came to a hover, barely a foot off the ground, the gunship on the left made contact with the VC. The enemy just popped up out of nowhere and began shooting, frantically waving their AK-47's, and spraying bullets everywhere.

"Taipan Three-One, receiving fire", the pilot called out calmly over the radio.

"I got three Victor Charlie, breaking left to engage", he continued.

Three-One banked hard, the door gunner's opened fire on the enemy while the co-pilot attacked with mini-guns. The enemy had been dispatched within seconds.

The wing gunship that had been on the right of the flight had repositioned himself to cover Taipan Three-One. But by this time Three-One had already completed their first assault run. They remained at low altitude to draw more fire. Circling right, the lead ship's crew-chief spotted several more VC. At that same moment one of the enemy soldiers looked up, and again fired on the gunship.

"Taipan Three-One, taking heavy fire, Three-Six, take evasive action we'll get them on the next pass". It was apparent there was many more enemy below.

Now Three-One and Three-Six, were a fire team again. They decided to attack from another angle. After climbing to strike altitude they banked right thirty degrees to set up the run. Three-One in the lead ship, Three-Six has the trailing wing position. The separation between the two gunship's will allow the lead ship to clear out of the way for the wing man to begin firing once lead has finished at the bottom of his run.

Three-One noses over his aircraft downward to begin firing rockets when he sees five of the enemy, who take up running to the right of his position. They are in the open for the moment but are heading towards a tree line that they hope will shelter them. The lead gunship had to bank right again to align the ship and get the enemy in his sights.

Both the door-gunner and the crew-chief were firing out the side doors, but when the helicopter went straight on the enemy they lost their angle and could not see the VC.

They fired to the side of tree line where they thought the VC was heading just in case the bad guys are hiding in the trees already.

The co-pilot again fired a short burst of mini-gun but the helicopter bucked and bounced as the pilot tried to hold the craft steady in spite of winds, thermal drafts, and of course the enemy bullets. Four of the enemy had made it into the tree line and continued to fire upon Taipan Three-One. The co-pilot had a visual on the muzzle flashes of those weapons trained on them, so he fired another burst into the trees. Only the pilot saw the single enemy that had stopped short of the tree line and turned to face the charging helicopter.

Covered in crusty mud the disheveled soldier raised his automatic weapon and fired furiously at his airborne adversary. The small fragments of the plexi-glass windshield stung the pilot in the face, he turned his head away for a fraction of a second. As he again looked ahead the windshield had been obscured with the crimson colored fluid.

They were so low now, they looked upon each other eyeball to eyeball. The back seat gunners never stopped firing into the tree line as they had become target fixated on the muzzle flashes coming from the trees. The pilot could feel the impact of the projectiles into his body, and although he hadn't felt any pain, the blurring of his vision and the inability to speak had validated that he had been mortally wounded. He wanted desperately to tell the co-pilot to take over the command of the aircraft, but could not. His only thought now was to kill the man who had killed him, before he could kill the crew. He dove straight in on the shocked enemy soldier ready to fire a rocket. The co-pilot had glanced over to the pilot when he felt they had gone below a safe height to recover from the dive. He instinctively grabbed the cyclic control to pull the aircraft up. But the dead pilot had a death grip of the control as the ship ran out of altitude.

The nose of the aircraft slammed into the enemy soldier, crushing him like a bug under foot. The helicopter impacted solidly into the earth, no bounce, no skid. Implanted into the ground at a forty-five degree angle the crumpled mass was still.

The fuel bladder had broken through the rear bulkhead and tore a gaping hole on the sharp twisted metal. The fuel leaked into the cargo compartment and ran down onto floors surface, then under and around the dead crew-chief and gunner. The volatile liquid oozed forward towards the electronics bay and the battery that had been in the nose compartment.

Taipan Three-Six witnessed the collision, they had watched as the gunners fired all the way into the ground. The dismayed crew in the wing ship descended upon the wreckage. Just as they leveled off at fifty feet the downed aircraft erupted into a huge fireball sending flaming fragments into the air. Three-Six watched hopelessly as the helicopter burned.

"Charlie-Charlie, we have a ship down, Three-One is down"

"Ok, Three-Six, stay calm, are there any survivors"

"Negative, negative, the ship just exploded, oh God da…"

"The LZ is still hot, I say again, L-Z is hot"

"Ok Three-Six, I'm sending in a medivac, and fire team Bravo is inbound", then he added,

"Three-Six, back off and wait for Bravo". But Three-Six didn't back off,

"Ok guy's, shoot any fucking thing that moves down there", the pilot ordered his back seats.

On their second orbit the crew-chief noticed something moving in the burning debris. The pilot slowed the ship, and they saw a figure of a person stand up in the ruin of boiling flames. Watching in horror as the co-pilot stood up while totally engulfed in flames, he stood erect and walked out of the ashes. He was only recognizable by his gangly build and shuffled walk. There was nothing to impede his movement in any direction, at his feet was just ashes. Nothing above him or to the sides, and nothing to climb over, it was all gone, he simply walked away from the crash while himself burning.

Three-Six had to do something, ignoring protocol to inform C&C of his intentions he lowered the collective and instructed the crew,

"We're going in".

Quickly and without hesitation the pilot circled and set up an approach to land as close as he dared to recover the victim that had now fallen on the ground. Although the flames had been extinguished, the form of the man lying there was still smoldering.

Three-Six came to a sliding halt just in front of the victim. They could still hear the report of small arms fire coming from the tree line as the crew-chief unbuckled and went to aid of his comrade. The gunner had opened up with his machine-gun from the left side of the aircraft to lay down suppressive fire. The crew-chief didn't know how to grab the victim and feared hurting him. Then he shouted asking the victim if he could hear him. The co-pilot nodded his head and moved again to rise. As they walked towards the waiting helicopter the two pilots watching through the windscreen couldn't believe the image before them. The downed co-pilot's flight suit had entirely burned away except for where the leather of his pistol belt encircled his waist. His body was blackened except for a couple of patches of bright red, his lips and nose was burned off. Wisps of smoke emitted from his feet as the bootlaces melted away and shards of his pant legs gathered around the boot tops.

As the crew-chief laid him down on the cargo floor he tried to remove the crispy helmet still strapped on. As he lifted the shell of the helmet off, the crew-chief could see that the Styrofoam liner had melted onto his hairless and blackened skull. It had seemed the co-pilot felt no pain, or perhaps it was shock. He remained conscious and his burned eyelids could only partially hide the eye's that darted back and forth trying to say something, but he never uttered a word.

The ammunition in the still burning aircraft began to "cook off", the slight popping noise alerted Three-Six to get going. He pulled in pitch and edged the chopper forward but the helicopter did not respond as it should have. They were over-weight, but they'll try again, still unable to get off the ground the pilot hopped-up the aircraft away from the tree line. Each time Three-Six pulled in pitch the low RPM warning buzzer would scream in their ears while the enemy continued to fire on them, and the gunners would shoot back. The noise of the co-pilot firing the mini-guns at ground level was deafening. When it became apparent that they were not going to be able to get airborne again, Three-Six thought to instruct the back seats to dump all the guns and ammo to lighten the ship, but he hesitated when the radio hissed.

C&C broke in over the radios and told Three-Six the medivac ship was a minute out and that Bravo team was with them. More enemy fire came from the tree line and Three-Six had taken more hits. The pilot pulled in pitch to hop up about three feet and fired four rockets towards the trees while his co-pilot fired the mini-guns. All on board continued to fire until the r.p.m.'s bled off and the chopper came to rest again on the ground.

The pilot of the medivac ship was now on the same frequency as the remaining half of Alpha team. They asked them to cease firing from the right of the aircraft while he landed next to the gunship. Both back seat crew of the medivac ship came to carry away the crash victim.

As the medivac lifted off, Three-Six were able lift also and provided cover fire for the departing ships. Clearly the courage of the medivac ship had saved them all, not just the victim, Three-Six would never have left one of "theirs" alive on the ground, it was all, or none!

Both gunship and medivac headed to Dong Tam. The medivac landed at the field hospital while Three-Six hovered to the refuel and re-arm point. Three-Six returned to the hot LZ and expended all their ammo on the enemy, and returned to rearm again.

C&C demanded Three-Six to shut down his aircraft, but Bravo team were out there now and by God so would they be. Three-Six rearmed three times before the Military Police at Dong Tam ceased their act of revenge.

The burned co-pilot lying on the stainless steel gurney succumbed to his injuries shortly after his wingman shut down his bullet-riddled aircraft.

Bearcat, one-week later.

Encountering long days of mundane duties, more K.P., Guard Duty, and sand bags that always needed filling, Mitchell waited for another chance to fly.

Finally one afternoon he was called to the company commander's office.

"The Major wants to talk to you," the clerk says.

This is the first time Mitchell has been one on one with the Major.

"Specialist Four Collins, reporting as directed Sir", he said while snapping up a salute. After returning his salute the Major spoke,

"At ease soldier, have a seat".

The major is seated behind his desk looking down at an official looking folder with papers inside. Mitchell feared the report contains information about his going AWOL during the in-country training, or losing his weapon there. Or perhaps it was the accidental shooting of the little papa-san at the dump.

Nervously, Mitchell waited for him speak.

"Collins, you've only been in country a little more than two weeks",

Oh, oh, here it comes, Mitchell thought as a bead of sweat ran down from his temple.

"Technically I can't put you in a helicopter on flight status until you have been in country for three months, that's your acclamation period".

Hey, maybe this is good news, Mitchell thought. The Major continued,

"But we have had some losses lately, and I am short of crewmen".

Is this good news or bad, he couldn't tell?

"But if you want to volunteer, I can put you on flight status immediately".

Mitchell heart began pounding, the veins in his neck are pulsating, and his mind racing as he thought to make the right decision.

"You can give me your decision tomorrow Collins, if you want".

Suddenly he remembered all that shit duty he has pulled lately.

"No sir, I'll do it",

"Fine, report to the gun platoon tomorrow, a.m.", the Major commanded.

The gun platoon, did he say the gun platoon?

The following morning Mitchell gathered all his belongings by hastily stuffing them into a duffel bag.

"Where you going Collins" a bunkmate inquired.

With a big grin, Mitchell told him that he had been reassigned to the Taipan gun platoon.

"Oh yea, I heard some of their guys had been killed".

"What, I didn't hear anything about that", Mitchell said.

"FNG's don't need to know anything", the bunkmate seemed delighted in telling him that. Then unexpectedly, Mitchell remembered the Major's words, "I've had some losses lately", funny how he didn't think to ask what the Major meant by that.

The Taipan platoon is housed in the northern most two story barracks, on the second floor, the furthest point from the company commander's office. Down the stairs and to the left is the latrine. And to the left of that are the showers, a simple rectangular building with one row of twenty shower heads on one side and three wood benches on the other, and an appropriate number of sinks and mirrors. The water source is a large black rubber bladder that sits up on a tower above the height of the building. The bladder had to be replenished daily by a water tanker truck.

Upon entering the new living quarters, a fellow Taipan directed Mitchell to a bunk and locker that was previously used by the recently deceased member of the Taipan gun platoon. He introduced himself as JJ, and seemed quite unlike the reputed Taipan. While making up his new bunk and hanging clothes, Mitchell briefly thought about the man who previously occupied this space. What he might have looked like, and did Mitchell ever see him? Maybe he had stood next to him at morning roll call. After all there were more than a two hundred enlisted personnel assigned to the unit but Mitchell actually knew very few of them. Mitchell wondered if he had been a good crew-chief. His morbid curiosity tried to imagine how it was that he got himself killed. Mitchell felt he should learn how it happened so that he would not make the same mistake. Suddenly death became a reality to be avoided at all costs.

Mitchell never did ask of what happened to his predecessor, nor did anyone else ever speak of the departed Taipan to him.

When the Taipan's returned to base that evening they seemed exuberant. The screen door to the entrance of the barracks swung open and slammed back against the wall, three crewmen burst in excitedly.

"We blasted the shit outta them fucking gooks today", one of Mitchell's new bunkmate's says to JJ.

"We lose any choppers", JJ replied.

"All present and accounted for".

The others enter, looking tired and dirty. Each have what looks like a dark unshaven five o'clock shadow? Even the fair skinned blonde hair guy had a black beard. They carry over their shoulders, their helmets, an M-16 and bandoleers of ammo. Mitchell looked at the combat aviators and envied them because they have successfully flown their missions today and returned home to talk about it. How great the feeling must be to return from a day of combat missions. Like winning the biggest game of your life, only you get do it every day. And the day you lose it doesn't matter cause you ain't gonna be around to care, the game is over and that's all there is. Just then Mitchell realized no one has acknowledged his presence.

"Nobody just goes straight to the gun platoon", the man who occupies the bunk across from him says.

"You gotta do your time with the slicks first", he continued.

"If you can't hack it as a slickie, you sure as shit ain't gonna make it as a gunny", he concluded.

Of course, there was no way for the new platoon mate to know it, but there isn't anything, or anybody that could have discouraged Mitchell.

"Maybe none of those chicken shit slickies wanted the job", Mitchell said, trying to offer some excuse. In reality Mitchell really did not understand why he was chosen by the Major to complement the platoon.

"So, I volunteered, besides I didn't want to be a slickie", that should break the ice, Mitchell thought.

Then JJ spoke up, "You fucking volunteered, you pecker head, sure as shit you're gonna get your ass dead".

"Come on newbie lets go get a drink".

Hey, this JJ, he's not such a bad guy Mitchell surmised. The two headed out of the barracks for the EM club.

Sitting at one of the tables in the smoke filled club, JJ tells Mitchell that he is a door gunner in the platoon. He has flown previously with the second slick platoon for three months and had transferred to the gun platoon because he was bored with flying slicks. JJ has only sixty days left on his tour of duty. Originally he was a Grunt, he had asked for a reassignment into a helicopter company because the squad he was in was ambushed one night. It was only the third time he had been out on patrol when they were attacked. All the others had been killed, JJ was the sole survivor. He had been rendered unconscious when a booby trap exploded killing the man in front of him. The explosion sent the man's body flying into JJ, knocking him out and the corpse fell on top of him. The blood running down both of them probably saved JJ life since the Viet Cong thought they were both dead and quickly left.

Mitchell asked JJ if he and the guy's in the gun platoon got along ok. JJ had said not at first, but warmed up a bit afterwards when they found out he had been a grunt and was combat savvy.

"Don't expect too much from the guy's", he said.

"They don't like newbie's, FNG's get people killed".

Mitchell's new drinking buddy is just so full of encouragement.

"The guys probably won't like you for a while, but if you make it through a couple of months, well maybe….".

JJ hesitated a moment then added, "Hey don't worry about it, your life expectancy now as a helicopter crewman in the Nam is only three months, ninety days is what they say you got to live".

JJ lit a cigarette and took a long sip from his drink.

"Ain't nobody's gonna get close to you anyhow", "If you get too close with someone they just go and get themselves killed and it just makes you feel bad", JJ took another big swig from the amber liquid.

"You ain't gonna find no friends here, only acquaintances, and they just need you to watch their backs and they will watch yours, that's all there is man, that's all". JJ looked seriously at his drink before lifting it again to his lips. Mitchell felt that JJ knew well of the crewman who had been killed and in his own way was telling Mitchell that he missed him.

JJ's words of encouragement go down harder than the CC & 7, so Mitchell too just keep drinking.

"Just exactly what does the gun platoon do on the mission", obviously Mitchell couldn't be expected to know that.

"Well", JJ began, "We provide gun cover for the slicks when they are in the LZ".

The ice in JJ's plastic cup clinked softly as he shook the cup then held it up at eye level to observe the quantity of alcohol remaining.

"You'll be flying just above the trees tops, circling the flight when they're on the ground" he explained as he used his cup to simulate the helicopter. JJ stopped for a moment and drank again, then held the drink over his head.

"A heavy fire team, three ships, lead, and two wing ships", JJ brought the drink down in a circling motion while Mitchell tried to see what JJ did.

"Then when the slicks depart the LZ we provide the close air support for the troops that the slicks just dumped on the ground", he says. JJ is looking at Mitchell as if to see if he really understood him. Mitchell had to admit that the military vernacular is sometimes difficult to translate, but he was beginning to get used to it.

"We stay in the LZ while the slicks go back to the pick-up zone for another load of gooks". His mentor sips again from his drink.

"Usually three or four loads will do it, then we standby until C&C calls us back to extract the troops or pull some other sortie, got it"?

Mitchell nodded affirmatively although he still could not visualize it all, it did not seem so difficult.

JJ finished his whisky on the rocks, got up from the table and walked over to the bar and ordered another round for the two of them. Sitting back down JJ spoke again.

"Our main job is to draw fire from Charlie, so we know where he is, and then you get to blast the motherfuckers to hell". He said grinning.

"Shit happens fast out there in the field, so be alert or you'll be fucking KIA".

At eighteen years of age Mitchell felt he should be able to handle this, hell he has made it this far. Certainly his new job sounds more exciting than burning shit.

"Anything else I should know", Mitchell inquired, as the door was open so why not ask.

"Yea, don't shoot up the good guys or our helicopters".

JJ looked at Mitchell sternly and said, "You won't be worth shit if you do". All the other questions Mitchell had even sounded stupid to him so he kept them to himself. So with his classroom training over, Mitchell and JJ resumed their drinking.

The rest of the night Mitchell tried to imagine himself in the gunship, flying the combat missions, and what it must be like. Mitchell hoped he doesn't do anything stupid tomorrow. His ambition now is to fly in the most professional manner possible. He swore to himself that he would do right by the platoon and not screw up. Besides this was his ticket away from the base and all that fucked up duty.

Back in the barracks most were asleep already, some are writing letters home, and a couple play cards on one of the bunks. The card players speak softly as not to disturb the sleeping crewmen. Mitchell lay back on the bunk, his head in the pillow, he put his hands behind his head and stared at the ceiling while contemplating his conversations with JJ. He wondered how he could ever sleep thinking about tomorrow. His eyes blinked slowly twice before he dosed off. Mitchell rested easy that night.

The EMU's mascot, a flightless bird native to Australia.

Chapter Three

A New Gunner

That first morning came early, the wake-up call was at 0400 hrs. just enough time to shit, shower, and shave. Roll call is at 0430 hrs. Breakfast in the mess hall at 0445, then on to the flight line by 0530, then at 0600 hrs. for the scheduled take off. This was going to be Mitchell's new agenda and his first mission. He knew that it would take some time to get accustomed to, but that it did not matter as long as he could continue to fly.

It was still dark outside during roll call, a small group of gunners and crew-chiefs walked on to the mess hall. As he followed the team, a minor but important detail popped into Mitchell's brain.

"Where do we eat lunch at", he asked.

"On your ship, grab a box of C-rations on your way out of the mess hall", a fellow crew-chief say's.

"Yea man, better eat good now cause if the gooks don't kill ya, them C-rats will", another says with a chuckle.

Breakfast was the best meal of the day, your choice of eggs, anyway you liked them. Bacon, or sausage, potatoes, grits, pancakes and SOS, a/k/a-shit on a shingle, (chipped beef on toast to civilians), local green bananas, apples and toast.

Although this morning Mitchell couldn't eat much, he managed to down three cups of coffee. He felt he needed to be really alert today. On the way out he went over to where the C-ration boxes were piled three high on a table, he stood there a moment searching over the boxes trying to read the contents for a tasty meal.

"Grab one and move on", a higher-ranking cook says sternly.

Man, Mitchell thought do I really have to take this shit from a cook this early in the morning?

"Wad-ya get" a fellow Taipan asks.

"Let's see", "Pork Slices", Mitchell said, reading the top of the little cardboard box.

"Swap you my Ham and Lima beans", "It's really good, but I just can't eat those beans" the Taipan grimaces while holding his stomach.

"Sure, OK", I don't mind Lima beans, I've had them before", Mitchell said hoping to make a friend and remembering those buttered beans his Mom would cook up.

The sky is just beginning to lighten up a bit as they walk to their assigned helicopters.

"Where's three five niner", Mitchell asked referring to the last three digits of the aircraft's serial number. Another Taipan crew-chief points to a chopper parked in a revetment.

"It's that's piece of shit on the end".

The revetment, an L-shaped barrier is about four feet high, used to protect the helicopters from incoming mortar or rocket attacks. The barrier was made from sandbags and large steel tubular canisters. The canisters were used to ship pairs of replacement rotor blades for the helicopters in from the States. Apparently they used an awful lot of blades.

Helicopter 359, is a bird badly in need of a bath. An old looking aircraft, her exterior dull olive drab paint is blackened along the length of the top of the tail boom from the turbine's exhaust. The landing skids are a combination of black peeling paint on exposed green primer and bright exposed bare metal where people have stood getting on and off the chopper. The sides of the tail boom are lettered with a faded flat black, "United States Army". There are doors for the pilots, but the large sliding rear cargo doors have been removed. There are two seats for the crew made of three-quarter inch aluminum tubing and a faded green canvas seat. Mitchell climbed inside to view the interior and hopped up onto the seat. He leaned back against the rear bulkhead of the cargo bay area and noticed the interior had no silver quilted sound deadening blankets. Unlike the shiny aircraft they learned on at helicopter school, these aircraft were stripped of everything but the bare essentials. In fact there is not much paint left either. It really looked more like it belonged in a junkyard. Mitchell also noticed small square metal patches, eight in all, some on top of the roof and some on the bottom of the cargo door opening that are spray painted only with fresh Zinc Chromate, a yellow green primer.

The ships configuration is a "hog" ship, referring to the armament, she is carrying thirty-six, 2.75 inch rockets, in two round rocket pods of nineteen each, mounted on either side of the aircraft. Accessories on board included, are two M-60 machine-guns, two M-16 semi-automatic rifles with a bandoleer of ammo for each, just in case they are shot down. And both pilots have, 38 caliber revolvers in waist holsters, presumably to shoot themselves in case of pending capture. An assortment of colored smoke grenades for marking targets hangs on a wire mounted on the rear bulkhead separating the rear seat crew from the engine and transmission compartment. The crew-chief and the gunner can reach the "smokes" quickly in the event they take fire. A smoke is dropped to mark the location of the bad guys. There was also a case of fragmentation grenades, for destroying the targets. Or sometimes they would include white phosphorous grenades, a/k/a "Willie Pete", for burning down enemy hooches. The seasoned gunner explained all of this to Mitchell while they "readied the ship".

Some of the other gunships replaced the large rocket pods with, two smaller rocket pods of, seven 2.75 in., and two "mini-guns", a five barreled gun that spun like a Gattling gun but is motor driven, and fire two thousand rounds of 7.62 mm ammunition per minute each. They also carried the same sort of accessories.

A large stainless steel water cooler sat behind the center console between the pilots. Mitchell checked the ships logbook to determine her airworthiness, all maintenance completed, no red X's entered that would ground the aircraft. Then a pre-flight of the bird, checking all the fluid levels, and inspecting her from the tail stinger to the chin bubble, from the "Jesus nut" that held the whole rotor system together, (If that nut ever comes off, better pray to Jesus), down to the landing skids. Happily he determined that although she is rough in appearance, to Mitchell it is the most beautiful machine he has ever seen. So it looks like they fly today.

As the pilots arrive from their mission briefings, two of them exit the jeep opposite Mitchell's aircraft. Their helmets are in O.D.green cloth bags and they carry maps under one arm. They look more like cowboys than pilots with their 38 caliber's, on their hips and in leather holsters.

"Morning Sir", Mitchell says crispy, while saluting. That action just brought giggles from them both.

"Hey FNG, you don't have to salute us on the flight line, we are all equal out here, got it", one of the pilots remark.

"Yes Sir", feeling like he fucked up already.

"And don't call us Sir".

"Where's the gunner", a pilot asks.

"Picking up our sixty's <u>sir</u>", shit did it again, this time he just looks at Mitchell with a raised brow.

The pilots open their respective doors, pilot in command in the right seat, and co-pilot in the left. In the gunships the pilots reversed their seating as the instrument panel on the right allowed for better visibility through the chin bubble. Mitchell was not sure where he was supposed to sit in the back but he did noticed that the logbook was under the right seat. Mitchell surmised that only crew-chiefs write into the log, so he took up behind the pilot. The pilot climbs up into his seat, while the co-pilot did another pre-flight, but it was not as thorough as Mitchell's was, he finished quickly and joined the pilot in the cockpit.

They begin the start-up sequence, circuit breakers in, twist open the fuel throttle full open then back to the idle stop… The co-pilot is reading from his briefing notes, as he dials in today's radio frequencies, to contact ground control, our control and command ship, artillery, etc., and writes them in grease pencil on the windshield along with the code word today and just underneath each letter, he writes a number.

B L A C K H O R S E

0 1 2 3 4 5 6 7 8 9

The code is used to prevent the enemy from listening to radio transmissions and learning what channel we are communicating on, by giving a letter that corresponds to a number. Everyday a new primary and alternate code word is circulated to the pilots.

Mitchell slipped his helmet on and plug into the overhead communications box jack, then adjusted the boom microphone to his lip. As he did he could hear the pilots talking about hovering over to the POL point to refuel.

"COMING HOT", came a yell from the pilot in the cockpit, as the co-pilot depresses the starter trigger. A verbal warning that the turbine is cranking and soon the rotor blades will turn. Mitchell looked up to be sure the rotors were clear of obstructions.

What is taking the gunner so long, Mitchell hoped that he would not have to chase him down. He was sure the pilots would be upset if we had to wait on him to return. Mitchell listened to the slow whine of the starter motor begin to turn the turbine engine to life. Next came the soft ticking sound of the ignitors, sparking the air/fuel mixture into an explosion of contained gasses, to be used by the turbine to turn the transmission and eventually to turn the main and tail rotors.

The gunner shows up on the right side of the aircraft and hands Mitchell a clean, like new M-60 machine-gun. He took it from him and examined it like he was going to buy it. With a nod of approval the gunner and his sixty, makes a dash for his seat on the left by briskly walking around the front of the aircraft, smiling and flashing a peace sign with his fingers at the pilots as he does so.

Overhead, the rotor blades r.p.m.'s are slowly building. The high pitched whine increases, and the Warbird begins to waddle side to side, back and forth, almost in unison, then it smoothes out as the rotor speeds increase. Soon the helicopter is at full idle. The chatter over the intercom is hard to sort out for new guys, but Mitchell managed to pick out the flight is prepared for lift off. Well lets go, Mitchell couldn't wait to do something cool like shoot his new machine-gun with real bullets.

Twelve slicks and three gunships make up the flight, looking around Mitchell could see all the rotors of the flight turning, and he knew something was going to happen soon. When the throttle is twisted, to full green rotor rpm, the bird is ready to fly.

Over the radio he listened to the communications between the pilot's and the base tower.

"Bearcat Tower, Taipan lead"

"Go Taipan"

"Ahh roger, Taipan heavy, request hover from the snake pit to P-O-L"

"Taipan, report hover check, winds east at eight, D-A two niner niner two"

"Lead, roger"

It was all really said too fast for him to comprehend, then he heard,

"Coming up", the pilot announced over the intercom.

"Clear right <u>sir</u>", shit Mitchell said it again, but this time the pilot just shook his head. Mitchell stretched his neck out the cargo door opening to be absolutely positive that nothing will impede their hover sideways, out of the revetment.

"Clear left", came the voice from the gunner in a matter of fact tone. The pilot pulls up on the collective, the control arm that is located to the left of the pilots seats, adjacent to their left knee, it is used in an up or and down motion, to add or subtract pitch to the blades. It is the control that "lifts" the bird off the ground.

Slowly the old bird rises, looking down, the skids move inward slightly as the weight of the aircraft is reduced to zero. In the next half second they are at a hover, fifteen inches from the ground.

Floating on a cushion of air, this heavy machine loaded with enough armament to wipe out Mitchell's whole neighborhood back home is defying gravity. Then another contact with the tower,

"Bearcat tower, Taipan lead, hover check complete"

"Taipan lead, cleared to taxi, follow EMU trail, report clear the active"

They hover out of the revetment and fall in line behind the gunship ahead of them, who is following the gunship ahead of him, who in turn is following the twelve slicks in front of him. What an awesome sight for Mitchell's eye's to behold before the rise of the sun. Fifteen helicopters, all with red rotating anti-collision lights flashing their warning not to get to close. Red and green navigation lights to indicate direction of travel. The turbines produce a constant scream and the sound of all the rotor blades whopping in rhythm, literally creating a dust storm. And then there is the strong odor of the burning JP-4 aviation fuel as it sears the nasal passages. There is tremendous excitement in the air, or maybe it was just the way Mitchell felt. Anyway, he hoped that maybe they will have an opportunity to engage in combat today. Mitchell felt great to be a part of the mission, finally a sense of purpose for being so far from home.

Mitchell was mentally prepared for combat, when the pilot announces he is coming right to the P-O-L.

"Clear right", damn, Mitchell thought, I can't believe I forgot about refueling the aircraft.

The helicopter sat back down on a corrugated metal pad, opposite a large black rubber bladder, the last in a long line of bladders, a permanent refueling point along the far side of the runway. Mitchell unfastened his seat-belt, laid down the M-60, and leaped to the ground to grab the hose and nozzle that will deliver the refined kerosene Jet Propellant grade four (JP-4), to his bird. Mitchell ducked under the tail boom close to the fuselage to be sure his head stayed out of the tail rotors, the smaller, vertical blades at the end of the tail that compensate for the torque of the main rotors. Those blades had a nasty habit of slicing through human skulls that got in the way.

Dragging the hose to the right side of the aircraft to the fuel inlet, Mitchell remembered to ground the nozzle to the inlet to prevent static build-up that could cause a spark and blow them all up.

OK, feeling like he has got it all together now, Mitchell filled the tank then brought the hose back to the bladder and laid it on the pad.

The gunner has stepped down from his seat and then walked a few feet from the aircraft unzipped his pants and began to urinate on the runway. A steady stream of yellow fluid christens the tarmac. Mitchell thought he felt the helicopter move slightly. He glanced inside and noticed both of the pilots are watching the gunner pee. The pilot has increased the pitch of the blades to create the air turbulence that caused the pee from the gunner to produce a misty spray all around him. He seems unaffected by the silly prank, although the pilots are having a good time with him.

The odors from the exhaust of the turbine, and the JP-4 fuel that Mitchell is pumping, did not mix well with his breakfast. He began to feel somewhat nauseous when he climbed back into his seat.

"Coming up"

"Clear right"

"Clear left"

A bright orange sun is beginning to peak over the horizon, as they hover to the centerline of the runway. Holding at their fifteen-inch hover, the pilot noses the aircraft over,

"Taipan Three five, on the go".

"…Cleared for November departure, climb to two hundred, left turn heading one seven zero, contact artie.." came the chatter through his headset but he still couldn't understand it all and felt it was making him feel more dizzy.

The aircraft nosed over to attain airspeed. Oh shit! The takeoff weight is too high, Mitchell thought. A bolt of fear surged through him, were gonna crash! From his rear seat he could see the end of the runway through the green tinted window over the pilots head, as the helicopter stands on its nose. Mitchell braced his hands to the ceiling and his right leg to the door center-post for the crash that never came. Observing the rest of the crew, they did not seem affected by their imminent demise. As the aircraft struggled to gain airspeed, to attain transitional lift, the point where they would go from a hover to a full-fledged flying machine. It took a light bounce on the ground to the forward portion of the skids before they were off. Mitchell's stomach's really was not feeling to well.

All the other helicopters he has flown had sufficient power to lift off with only a slight nose down attitude, but a loaded gunship fully armed, needed full power and a delicate balance on the nose, and long take off roll to get airborne.

The cooler rush of the morning air is helping Mitchell feel better, as they climb to their cruising altitude of twelve hundred feet, a distance from the ground to avoid being shot down by random small arms fire. As they clear the north perimeter of Bearcat, they turn west then south. For the back seat crew, this is the time to prepare before a mission, going to and from the A.O.

The gunner fired up a cigarette with much difficulty, as the winds inside the helicopter without doors are fierce. Mitchell wasn't sure if smoking was permitted but no one has said anything to the gunner. Mitchell reached into his flight suit for his pack of Salem's, withdrew one and the gunner handed him a Zippo lighter. Mitchell switched the communication box to "intercom" to speak privately to the gunner.

"Hey, you know where we are going", he asked.

Their first stop is at My Tho, for refueling to begin their first mission of the day.

In route Mitchell can see the slicks at two thousand feet and ahead of them by an estimated three miles. Looking out of the door to the west, he could see Saigon in the distance. As they flew by Mitchell thought of his buddy, Brian and what would he think if he could see him now. They fly further south and the terrain begins to change. Dried up rice paddies, rivers, tree lines and thousands of round swimming holes, no can't be? Maybe bathing pools for the water buffalo's, no wait, there bomb craters! Yea, that had to be it, rows and rows of bomb craters, dotting the countryside like acne on a pot faced kid. Why would they drop so many bombs on the rice paddies? There must have been an awful lot of Viet Cong here once, he ascertained.

In less than an hour they arrived at My Tho, a large village, with several paved roads leading to and from its center, with an adjacent air base used by a variety of military services, and aircraft. After refueling, the flight of slicks, move over to the opposite side of the airstrip where there are twelve individual groups of nine ARVN solders lined up. These are forces of the Seventh Army Division, Republic of Vietnam. Young Vietnamese men who will climb on board the slicks, and then are air lifted into the LZ. Once there, it is their job to make contact with Charlie, and kill him or be killed!

Whoa, Mitchell just had a thought about shooting at people. He wondered if he could even shoot at another person. Or worse yet, what if they shoot at him? Mitchell could only hope for the best when that time came, so he tried not to think about it.

The first loaded flight to the LZ takes off, and climbs to altitude. The Taipan's in trail, follow the flight just above tree top level. Somewhere high above the slicks and them is a "Command and Control Ship", a/k/a "Charlie-Charlie". Onboard is a high ranking American officer, usually a Colonel, and a Vietnamese officer, likely a Major or higher rank. They are in radio contact with intelligence, artillery, etc. Between the two of them, they decide where and when the flight moves, who lives, and who dies.

The pilot alerts Mitchell and the gunner that they are nearing the LZ. Then he reminded them there will be negative suppression in the LZ, in other words, it is a cold LZ, shoot only with permission, or when shot at.

"Hey there Chief, aim that gun outside, I don't feel like getting shot in the back today", the pilot said to Mitchell.

"Not to worry Sir, I'd probably miss anyhow", he said, trying to be amusing. Besides the pilots sit in armored plated seats, so what's he got to worry about Mitchell thought.

The LZ is an open area of rice paddies, divided by narrow dikes that separate each paddy and allow people to walk along the twenty inch or so wide top, to move from paddy to paddy in the wet season, when they are full of water. Although dry this time of year it looks muddy. To the south and east are two tree lines, with thick underbrush. Mitchell kept his eyes peeled out for anyone in the LZ. The flight is "in bound" descending down from their high altitude. The Taipan's have arrived ahead of them because they did not have to climb and descend. Mitchell's ship is positioned behind and above the other two gunships. As "wing two" their job is to provide gun cover to the other two who are flying at tree tops, circling the LZ, trying to draw fire. Should they receive fire from the ground the two will "break out" and bank either left or right. Then wing two will dive onto their position firing their rockets as they go.

"If you have to shoot, chief, do not shoot until Lead and Wing are clear, you copy?"

Stepping on the microphone floor button, "Yes _sir_", Mitchell said quickly realizing he had used the word "sir" again. Now the gunner was laughing too!

The flight arrives moments later all twelve slicks flying a formation in a single line, one behind the other, as they headed for the LZ. They come in high and fast and when the lead slick flares out to land, they all begin the flare in unison. From Mitchell's vantage the slicks seemed to fly too close to each other for comfort. The slicks touch-n-go and the troops dive out and hit the ground. Some of the Vietnamese soldiers lay flat in the prone position, others kneel down to see over the rice dykes. The flight of the now empty slicks departs and disappears in seconds. Well that seemed easy enough thought Mitchell. The troops get up and spread out, and start walking very slowly towards the tree line. The Taipan's continue their flight pattern, circling the LZ at tree top level. Mitchell observes carefully the troops on the ground to see where they go, if he has to fire his machine-gun he does not want to hit the friendlies on the ground.

The pattern continues until the slicks return with the second group of ARVN's, who will join their counterparts on the ground.

When the second flight returned, the first group was just a few yards from the tree line and stopped. Then came a voice transmission over the intercom from the Command and control ship.

"The ground troops report they have possible contact in the tree line to the south".

Then command ordered the Taipan's, "Three One, check it out".

Mitchell's excitement builds at the prospect of seeing his first VC. The lead gunship has over flown the tree line where the contact was. All eyes are glued to the tree line.

"Negative enemy contact", says Taipan Three One,

"Taipan Three Eight, ready smoke, go in slow, Three Five's got you covered", said Three One.

"Roger",

As the first wing ship slowed above the tree line, the radios burst into excited voices.

"Two eligible males running to the south", someone reported.

"Three Eight, you got-em"?

"Negative"!

"Three Five, rolling in".

"Three Eight breaking right".

"Roger Three Eight, Three Five's clear to fire".

"Fire back there", said Mitchell's pilot, as they were still to the north of the tree line and maintaining their original altitude. Mitchell caught a glimpse of two people, skinny males, unarmed and wearing nothing but black shorts, together they ran full stride into the open rice paddy away from the tree line and the advancing ARVN's. Running across the southern rice paddies towards another tree line, they are behind Taipan Three eight who has just flown over the top of them. They did not look like bad guys, just two typical peasant farmers running scared. At first Mitchell thought they must have been referring to some other "eligible males".

Mitchell looked around excitedly to see if it was him who the pilot wanted to fire the machine-gun. The gunner in the left seat was not able to get a shot at the enemy on the run because the eligible males were to the right of the aircraft. Mitchell had the only clear shot although he thought they were up too high. The gunner with a sense of urgency in his eyes yelled, SHOOT!

Nervously Mitchell turned, took aim and squeezed the trigger, and the heavy gun bucked in his arm. He held tight and watched the red tracer's head for the two as they ran. Mud and dirt was springing up from the ground below. Like intermittent little fountains of dirt all around the two, following them as they ran, sometimes to the side, then in front of them, then behind, but not hitting them. Mitchell dared not take his finger off the trigger as they were now directly above them. He was shooting straight down at their heads from about four hundred feet. Mitchell's foot is searching for the microphone floor button while he is still firing.

"Go down, down, down we got to get lower", he yelled excitedly, even surprising himself for yelling at the pilot.

As inexperienced as he was, Mitchell could tell it was not his aiming but rather their distance from the targets that made the grouping of bullets so wide apart.

"Wait, I'll come around", the pilot said.

Not waiting, Mitchell was still firing to the rear almost under the tail boom. He could see the two Viet Cong nearly at the other tree line. His pulse is pounding, adrenaline soaring through his veins. Mitchell knew he had to keep firing if there was any chance to stop the enemy from getting away.

"Cease fire back there, cease fire", the pilot yelled, "GODDAMIT CEASE FIRE, CHIEF".

Mitchell let up on the trigger of the smoking, red-hot machine gun, then turned forward in his seat and sucked in a deep breath.

"Leads rolling in on the target, hold your fire", the pilot commanded.

Mitchell watched as they banked to the right, and lead, Taipan Three One, who was behind them now, had his gunners open up on the enemy. Mitchell looked to the rear and could see that they are at low altitude, possibly seventy-five feet or less. They can't miss from there he thought.

But they did miss, the two made it to the tree line and disappeared. C&C called for a cease-fire and were sending the ground troops over that way to capture or kill the bad guy's.

"Get back and cover the flight", came their orders.

Mitchell then glanced over to the gunner who pointed to the communications box, reaching for the dial he switched to "INT", to speak privately again with Mitchell.

"No way to have got those two from that high up", he says. Nodding in disappointment, Mitchell had to agree, well next time…

The rest of that morning went pretty smooth, all the troops were now in the LZ, and the Taipan's are headed back to My Tho for lunch. Time now 01130 Hrs. The adrenaline is fading fast and Mitchell is feeling very tired. Reminiscing of the excitement of having shot at his first bad guys he realized that he was not shooting to kill them he just wanted to stop the eligible males from getting away. He really hadn't thought of what would have happened if he had not missed, and how he might have felt. Everything just happened so fast. Mitchell's confidence had been given a serious boost knowing he could do what needed to be done.

As the helicopters wind down and the blades come to their ever so slow stop, crews strip themselves of their helmets and shirts. Some go to the fuel tank drain, (used for checking water in the fuel), and draw a sample into the small round cans from yesterday's C-rations, and ignite the fuel for cooking their rations today. Others like Mitchell eat them cold. "Whatcha got," asked Mitchell's gunner,

"Ham and Lima beans",

"Oh, ham-n-muthafuckers", he says while snickering.

"Well I had pork slices, but traded them this morning", he said trying to redeem himself.

"Never had ham-N-muthafuckers before, eh", "You got ripped off"

Mitchell searched the contents of the box for the P-38 folding can opener issued in every box. It took a little time to open the can, but Mitchell finally had the now can of mysterious sustenance opened. Carefully, he tasted the hard packed concoction only to find it inedible.

"Damn this shit tastes bad, that asshole knew what he was trading me for", Mitchell said as he looked around for a place to spit, another lesson learned. Upon reading the box in detail, Mitchell found the C-rations had been packed fifteen years earlier. Some later, if you were lucky enough to get the better tasting food. The C-rats sat warehoused in cardboard boxes, thousands of them, maybe millions, until they finally had another war to distribute them. Who could have ever planned for this so long ago?

"Come up, Lima, Alpha, Oscar, Decimal, Echo", the C&C ship radioed to Mitchell's pilot, giving him the radio frequency from the code word of the day. The pilot transcribed the frequency from the numbers below the "BLACKHORSE" code word. "L" is 1, "A" is 2, "O" is 6, "Decimal" is a point, and "E" is 9, hence 126.9 is the frequency to contact the American advisor to a company of ARVN's who have made contact with the enemy, and has asked for an immediate Dust-off of his wounded. C&C decided one gunship would escort the medivac ship, just in case. Wing two is called up for the sortie. In route to the area where the American has called for help Mitchell and the gunner straighten up the ship and stuff their garbage into small compartments in the airframe.

The LZ was cold and the medivac ship got in and out quickly without incident. So Taipan Three Five returns to My Tho, and shuts down again to await further orders. With his extra time Mitchell decides to look over the helicopter. During an inspection of the aircraft, just to be sure they didn't have any extra bullet holes, the gunner looks at one of the primer painted patches and stated he was flying the day this bird was shot up. The gunner began to relay his story of the day he had been flying, "and all hell broke loose"…Mitchell listened intently to his stories.

Hours go by, and the Taipan's and EMU's are called up to extract the troops that they had inserted into the LZ earlier. When they arrived at the LZ, they could see the ARVN solders awaiting the return of the slicks for the ride home. Mitchell heard that the two males who ran earlier were never found. He wondered where they could have hid, because the land is all open area except for the tree line. He knew right then, the ARVN's might not have looked very hard for the bad guys. Those were two very lucky Viet Cong!

Back at the base, Mitchell stepped into the shower room and laid his shaving kit down on the little wood shelve above the sink. When he looked up into the mirror, he noticed a dark five o'clock shadow, on his cheeks and chin. Since Mitchell barely shaved at all, he stood back and briefly admired his new manly look. Then he washed off the gun grease, mixed with the black gunpowder from the machine-gun. With his helmet visor down while shooting, the hot black residue has stuck to the exposed areas of his lower face and neck.

Mitchell was feeling good after returning from his first day of combat missions and having survived, without any major mishaps. Today he became a Taipan gunner! Mitchell hurriedly dressed, I think I'll celebrate this evening at the EM Club, he thought, yea I'll have a drink, or two!

The bar was to the left of the entrance door, and eight round wood tables on the right, each with six metal folding chairs. Looking around the place for a familiar face, there was none in the full house. Mitchell bellied up to the bar and ordered a brew. Turning to observe the crowd, he noticed a table where a couple of Taipan's sat, seemingly in a heated conversation. They were openly conspicuous by their black scarves and blue unit patch on the right breast pocket. He did not approach them nor did they invite him to join them. Feeling a little like an outcast, Mitchell realized he was not fitting in here. Not quite accepted as a Taipan by his peers, nor was he accepted by the EMU platoon because he was a Taipan. As a Taipan, the rear echelon personnel avoided him also, because they were reputed to be "crazed killers". An image probably brought on by the platoons need for release after rough missions. His fellow Taipan's were not quite ready to accept the "fucking new guy", who never flew a mission prior to today. But all that was ok with him, he did not need friends here. He would keep to myself, try to get along and do a good crew-job.

So it was decided, and for those reasons he stood alone chugging down his ice-cold beer, then ordered another brew.

Indigenous Personnel: This photo depicts a crew chief, and baby-san who would visit the remote airfield to beg for the cold apples this chief would bring for her.

Chapter Four

Deadly Cargo

Over the past few days, the missions had been fairly routine, The Taipan's shot up a lot of tree lines, killed some rice paddies, burned down a VC hooch, and sunk an unoccupied sampan sitting on the bank of a river.

Although yesterday, while the rest of the flight ate their lunch Taipan three-three took a couple of hits from small arms fire when it was up on a defoliation-mission. C&C called up three-three to provide cover for another Huey especially outfitted for spraying the herbicide dioxin, "Agent Orange".

Flying down alongside a riverbank the spray ship reported "receiving fire", three-three rolled in on the tree line, firing the rockets as they went. Both door gunners prepped the area trying to draw more fire from below and had used up a whole ammo can, two thousand rounds each, but saw no enemy in the dense vegetation. The mission was aborted when it was discovered the defoliation ship had taken some hits from an AK47 down in the thick underbrush below and was losing hydraulic pressure.

Just as Mitchell was getting used to flying in his own ship, the total flying hours since the last P.M. was done, indicated that another Periodic Maintenance Overhaul was due on the helicopter. So Mitchell has been temporarily assigned for a few days to another ship until his own helicopter had completed its inspections and repairs. The pilot whose call sign is "Taipan three-seven", flies a clean, recently reconditioned helicopter. Quite obviously the better ships are crewed by the more experienced crew-chiefs, while FNG's get the old tattered one's.

Mitchell had asked the gunner on this ship, a tall kid with red hair and freckles, to bring an extra box of grenades today. Mitchell needed some practice of throwing them from the flying platform. It took a lot of lead on the intended target to hit the mark. When the grenade would leave his hand it was traveling at the same speed as the helicopter, so he would throw early, ahead of the target, but only enough as the grenade slowed its forward momentum as it fell to earth. It was also necessary to compensate for the various altitudes.

"They ain't got no frag's, but I found these incendiaries" the red headed gunner said smiling.

"You ever use one of these", Mitchell asked.

"Yea, their great, they'll burn through anything, even the engine block in your car back home, sit it on the carburetor, and in fifteen seconds it'll drop out on the ground through the oil pan, guaranteed" he said happily while looking for Mitchell's approval.

Sounded like bullshit to Mitchell but what the hell.

"Well we only got a few frag's, OK, let's try-em, load them in", he said.

Funny thing, Mitchell flew with this guy for the past two days and he just noticed his name was Gardner, never did ask his first name. He was short anyway, which meant that he was soon to rotate out of country and go home!

"Twelve days left, I am too short to fly" Gardner had said.

"Then you should've been an EMU, because they can't fly", Mitchell waved his arms up and down mimicking the flightless bird.

"You're still on flight status so get your ass in gear Gardner".

After loading the small wood crate filled with its hot cargo, the gunner inspected the ammo cans. Coiled to the top of the Fifty Caliber ammo can is the continuous belt of two thousand rounds of 7.62 mm bullets. The ammo belt is all linked together with dull black metal links, snapped tightly against the bright color of the brass casing. The ammo can sits in-between the legs of the gunners and feeds into the breach of the machine-gun. When firing the M-60, the long belt was fed over the left arm and into the breach of the machine-gunweapon. While the left hand grasped the carrying handle just above the barrel, with one hand on top it was easier to turn the gun upside down to shoot out the rear without jamming the belt into the breach. The right hand always stayed on the trigger.

Every fifth round on the ammo-belt was a tracer, it looked like the other bullets, except for the orange painted tip. But when fired, its hollow core was filled with a phosphorus material that burned red, so that the shooter could see where the other rounds were going as the tracer round made its way to the target. From the air, "walking the tracers to the target" is a popular form of aiming.

As the flight takes off for the A.O., Mitchell had gotten used to the overweight, helicopter nosing over sharply to gain flying speed, so much so that he no longer felt the need to brace himself from falling forward. With full fuel and full armament, and the four-man crew, the total weight created an "Over Gross" situation. On hot muggy mornings the gunship helicopter required a lot of runway to get airborne. This restored bird has been equipped with the two mini-guns and fourteen rockets but feels lighter than Mitchell's ship. Or maybe it was just the newer engine, anyway it did not have to bounce on the skids to takeoff.

The assigned crew-chief of this war-bird did not "free hand" his M-60, he has opted to use a short bungee cord that is attached to hang point overhead in the door opening, and hangs down with a hook that is used to fasten to the carrying handle of the machine-gun. Mitchell had never used the bungee, but decided to give it a try today.

As they fly south to today's A.O., near Ben Tre, the pilot decides to test fire a rocket into one of the tributaries that led in towards Saigon from the Mekong River Delta. A new rocket pod had been installed to replace the one hit by ground fire the day before. To verify the operation of the new pod, a test fire was appropriate prior to a combat assault. So Mitchell has asked for and received permission to test fire the M-60sixty at the same time with the intention to feel the handling characteristics with the bungee cord.

"Hold your fire until we are over the river"

The ship picks up speed as the pilot noses the craft towards the river.

"Open up back there, Chief" the pilot authorized his crew.

With his seat belt loosened to allow him to sit at the outer edge of the seat, the upper half of Mitchell's body was able to be outside of the aircraft. He rested his right foot on top of the rocket pod, and his left foot braced to the doorpost, next to the floor microphone button. Mitchell leaned forward to fire straight ahead at the muddy brown water. The pilot fired a rocket from the left pod. Mitchell did not like the feel of the rubberized resistance to his aim, although there was no perceptible weight to the gun, which was a good thing, still, when he tried firing to the rear he got tangled up in the cord. That's it, Mitchell thought as he unhooked the cord from the gun, then reached forward to hook the loose end out of the way to a point forward of where it hung. Free handing the machine-gun just worked better for him.

With the river dead, they flew to My Tho, to refuel, before going on to Ben Tre, to commence the day's missions.

The morning insertion into the LZ goes smoothly. The first flight in had "full suppression" into the LZ, Charlie was somewhere in the area. They shot up everything in sight as they landed. And the Taipan's fired a few rockets into the tree lines, mostly to make lots of noise, in hopes of keeping "Charlie's" head down. A couple of hooch's in the LZ started smoking and soon erupted in flames. After all three insertions were completed they headed back towards My Tho, to re-fuel and re-arm.

"Don't get to comfortable", the pilot told them before shutting down the turbine engine.

"We may be up soon, were waiting on C&C to decide another mission for us" the pilot announces.

Mitchell and Gardner decide to eat their C-rations, while the pilots walked off to discuss the possible mission with the other Taipan pilots.

Pilots always knew what was going on. If they did not hear it while at the mornings briefing, then they got the information on the UHF radio.

While, in the back seats they listened to the Armed Forces Viet Nam Network (AFVN). It is the only rock-n-roll music station in country and broadcasts out of Saigon. They spent a lot of time listening to the music that brought them home mentally every day.

"I am not scared of dying- and I- don't really care- if its peace you find in dying- well then- let the time be near", came the song from the Fifth Dimension rock group. Words to live by Mitchell had thought, the music was as deep as their jobs here. They switched to the working channels during the mission, but as soon as they could, they would switch back to AFVN, to escape the reality of their surroundings.

"Ya know I heard they use salt peter in the C-rations, to keep GI's from getting too horny", Mitchell said to Gardner.

"I think it's true, I've had problems getting it up at the massage parlor lately, I plan to stop eating them before I go home" Gardner said.

"I wrote in a letter to my girlfriend that if she wanted to be the first when I get home, don't let your mom answer the door", Gardner laughed.

"Imagine jumping your future mother in-law, anyhow if I am not horny when I get home, she's gonna think I've been mess'n around over here", Gardner say's in a serious tone.

One of these days I'll think I'll try that massage parlor, Mitchell promised himself.

"The pilots are coming, let's get ready", Gardner says as he leaps down from the helicopter to grab his cans of C-rations off the ground to prevent them from flying up into the blades. They always policed up after themselves because the VC could use the ration cans or anything else left behind, to make booby-traps and such.

"What's up, Mr. Dickerson", Mitchell asked the pilot.

"We're going to do a defoliation mission, where three-three was shot up yesterday", he looked down to read some notes he had made.

"Were flying a heavy fire team, Three-four is taking the lead, we are the wing, and Three-two is taking the rear in trail", Dickerson continued,

"I don't need to tell you boy's to keep a sharp look out, but the area is hot, I want you guys to call out anything that don't look right, OK"

"Got it"

"Right"

It was a bit unusual for all three Taipan's to be up for a sortie, so they knew someone expected gunplay, which only made the Taipan's more intent and mission ready. In route to the AO, Mitchell and Gardner prepared the ship.

"Open the box of grenades, just in case we need-em fast" Mitchell told Gardner.

Mitchell unhooked the tie-down of the aircraft's main rotor blades, assisted the pilot with his seat belt, and then slid his armor plate forward to shield his head and upper torso. The plate was an extension of his armored chair. Then he closed the pilot's doors. A quick glance over the aircraft, and he climbed in. Feeling down under his seat

Mitchell checked the position of his "chicken plate", a heavy bullet proof vest, that helicopter air crews rarely ever wore as designed, but left it under the seat to protect the scrotum. Whenever they were shot at from the ground, the bullets came tearing up through the floor.

Since their jump seats were made only of thin aluminum tubing and canvas cloth it made more sense to protect the bottom portion of the anatomy, especially the family jewels.

The Taipan's listened to the UHF as the two defoliation ships contacted them and reported their position. The Taipan's departure has been coordinated as to meet the spray ships in the AO at the same time. They inform the gunships of their intended flight path along side of the river, flying from the southeast to the northwest.

"We got to be right on top of the trees for this stuff to work", the pilot of the lead spray ship radioed.

"If we receive enemy fire we will roll out towards the open rice paddy on the north side of the river, yesterday our boys thought the fire was coming from the south, across the river, over" he explained.

"Roger, good copy", says Taipan three-four.

"We appreciate your assistance on this aaah, alright let's get busy", the spray ship responded somewhat nervously.

The gunner on Taipan three-four sees the sprayers flying into the AO at his eleven o'clock position and in turn tells his pilot, who in turn informs the rest of the flight.

"OK Taipan flight, lets stagger our altitude now", says three-four. The trailing gunship, climbs to five hundred feet, while they climb to two hundred and the lead ship will fly just above and behind the second spray ship, which in turn follows the lead spray ship

As all the helicopters enter the AO, one behind the other, but at different altitudes except the spray ships, which fly in formation at the same altitude and are offset to the sides. The sprayers are H model

Huey's with a large white plastic container in the cargo area and two long poles that protrude from either side of the ship that expelled the deadly chemical onto the foliage below. In a couple of days there won't be anything green around here for a very long time.

The sprayers start with the tree line on the north side of the river, there is another tree line on the south bank also. Both are thick with green vegetation that nearly covers-up the seventy five-foot wide river. To the north is an open paddy area about a mile wide then another tree line, to the south is dense jungle. The sprayers are just above the trees now. Mitchell's helicopter was high above, and to the rear of the two spray ships. He watched the chemical spray being expelled from the two ships. A toxic misty cloud trailing behind the two sprayers falls ever so slowly into the green mass below.

Taipan three-four is slightly ahead and below them. Looking out to the rear and just above them is Taipan three-two.

How would anyone expect us to see anything down there, Mitchell thought, I can't even see the ground under the…just then the radios burst into excited screaming.

"RECEIVING FIRE", "BREAKING RIGHT", "GET IN THERE I AM STILL TAKING FIRE".

Immediately followed by, "there right under us", the sprayer's voice was calm but crackled.

"AW GEEZ, WERE TAKING HITS, WERE HIT, WERE HIT",

It all came so fast, the call for help from the lead spray ship.

"OK, Taipan's, stay calm, wait for them to clear, I am going in, I'll pop smoke on the way out" three-four commanded his heavy fire team. Three-four was too close and had to slow up to let the sprayers get clear of the incoming rounds of the mini-gun burst. Three-four's co-pilot fires a three second burst of mini-gun into the tree line, four thousand rounds with eight hundred red tracers raining down that disappear without a revealing their destination. His gunner has popped a smoke grenade and is holding the red smoke at arm's length outside the aircraft until he is over the target. When he finally drops it, the smoke makes a red trail through the air, as if pointing to a target hidden deep into the underbrush.

When three-four slowed down to let the sprayers get out of the way, Mitchell's ship had to slow also, nearly coming to a hover above the tree line which made them extremely vulnerable to the ground fire.

"Three-seven, put some rocket fire on that smoke", lead requested of Mitchell's pilot. Their ship noses over, Mitchell leaned out to fire and cover three-four, who has already banked out to the right. Gardner and Mitchell shoot through the red smoke, the rockets leave the pods with a bright flash and fierce whooshing sound, a faint trail of sparks and smoke mark its path. Firing two at a time, the pilot launched six deadly missiles towards a shrouded enemy in the bush.

"Three-four is still receiving fire, watch it three-seven"

Then just as they are approaching the red target smoke, Mitchell heard the report of small arms fire from below. A faint rapid popping of sounds against all their ambient noise, yet it was still very audible. Mitchell was out to the limit of his seat belt, and then some. He knew that the only way to stop them from shooting is to shoot at them first. Mitchell hasn't let up on the trigger since they started into the diving airstrike. Breaking out before over flying the red smoke he fired to the rear and noticed Taipan three-two beginning his airstrike from five hundred feet. Mitchell's ship has barely cleared the trees when three-two starts walking his rockets up to the smoke. Mitchell could feel the concussion of the rockets exploding on impact, as they continued to initiate a climbing right turn.

Mitchell heard the enemy still firing at the helicopters, but could not tell if it was at them, or Taipan three-two.

"Were receiving fire" Mitchell told the pilot, better safe than sorry.

They continue their hard banking turn around to the right while at the same time climbing for more altitude. Taipan lead, is now where three-two started his airstrike, and is preparing to begin his strike as soon as three-two is out of the way.

Three-two is clear when three-four rolled in, mini-guns blazing, rockets streaming to their target. Just as they pass over the target area the flight heard the radios squelch,

"Taking hits, Three-four, taking hits",

"God Almighty, we're getting shot up pretty good here", "cover me, cover me", his voice was calm but deliberate.

"Three-four get outta there, we got ya covered" Mitchell's pilot says, as he jerks the helicopter harder right, they approach the tree line at a forty five degree angle and open fire with everything they've got.

What about the back seat crew, Mitchell wondered if anyone had been shot!

"Ah shit" the pilot says, then transmits,

"Three-seven's hit, three-seven's hit".

Hey that's us, Mitchell thought, damn it, but he kept shooting into the trees attempting to restrain the ground fire. Although he did not know where they were hit, or how serious it was, he did know they are still flying and the guns are still working. Only one thing left to do, Mitchell continues to suppress the fire, with fire.

Man, whoever is down there, sure is pissed off at those sprayers, Mitchell thought to himself. After the third pass he was out of machine-gun ammo, so Mitchell grabbed his M-16 and began shooting with that. He noticed that the experienced Gardner had conserved his ammo appropriately.

"Three-fours low on ammo, how you guys doing, over"

"Three-two, just about gone"

"Three-seven, same over"

"OK, there's a fire base about ten klicks from here, I gave them a Sitrep, (situation report), they will re-arm us, then C&C wants us back here ASAP, over-out", Three-four heads for the fire base, and the two Taipan ships follow in trail formation. An EMU had been dispatched by C&C to supply the firebase with rockets and ammo for the gunships.

On arrival at the firebase, someone on the ground has popped a yellow smoke to indicate wind direction and where the gunships should land outside the perimeter of the small artillery base.

The artillery unit at the firebase has received a fire order into the AO that the Taipan's just departed from. The big cannons will pound the area until the Taipan's return. After landing, the pilots bring the hot turbines to idle, as the crews re-arm along with the help of the co-pilots and others at the base.

"Got into some shit, Eh" the big burly infantryman, who came to help, says.

"Yea, were getting shot up pretty good today" Mitchell said as a matter of fact, while trying to mask his anxiety.

The pilot is looking over the aircraft to determine the extent of their damage, which appears to be not so bad. There is a couple of holes in the tail boom, and one in the windshield just above the pilot's head.

"That one came in while we were diving in on the target" the pilot told Mitchell. "It must have gone over my head", he said.

Hey, I sit behind him, if it went over his head it must have gone over mine too, Mitchell thought. Then he checked around and found an exit hole through the roof of the helicopter just behind the pilot's head and two feet in front of his. The small diameter of the hole in the metal did not appear menacing, but the thought of being shot in the flesh did!

The big bangs of the 105 howitzer artillery pieces firing into the same tree line from miles away have Mitchell wondering what will be left when they get back. The howitzers continue their pounding while three-four checks his damage. While the helicopters are at still at idle, a few of the crewmen walk over to three-four's ship to inspect the hits that he reported back in the AO.

"We took seven hits, near as I can tell" says three-four, "All the systems look good to go, let's get back into the air boy's"

Going back was not easy. For the first time their vulnerability has been exposed to Mitchell. Up until now Mitchell didn't think the gooks could even hit them. Now he has to look at the hole in the top of the cabin two feet ahead of him caused by one of the two bullets that came in through the windshield. They had determined that because the hole was oblong the bullet hole was the wrong shape. On further inspection they discovered another exit hole over the left shoulder of the pilot. It appeared that two bullets came through the same hole, but from separate angles. The bullets would have had to criss-cross in front of the pilot's face. Whether or not it was at the same time, or not, was hard to imagine. The armored chairs don't do much for the pilot when getting shot at from straight on where only Plexiglas separates them from the bullet.

Whoever was shooting at Mitchell's ship while they were shooting straight at him had to be very brave, or a very stupid person. He tried to imagine the gunship diving out of the sky with blazing guns and punching off rockets straight at the enemy. Mitchell thought he'd try to find a mighty deep hole to crawl into, yet this individual raised his single rifle and fired directly into the windshield. Mitchell wondered if he could have survived the attack.

Back at the AO, a cease-fire at the artillery base were they had just departed from, is in effect. The huge holes in the rice paddy adjacent to the enemy's tree line, indicates most of the heavy rounds exploded away from the trees, creating more water pools. Three-four, decides to make a high speed run over the top of the tree line to draw fire.

No such luck,

"Receiving fire", "popping red smoke", "three-seven, their all yours"

"Roger, three-seven rolling in."

"Crew-chief reports the target is twenty yards to the south of smoke"

"Roger that"

It was not as active as before, maybe some of the enemy were eliminated by the Howitzers. When they were directly above the smoke Mitchell did not hear the faint popping sounds of ground fire. Deliberately he eased up to conserve ammunition, but put a few bursts behind them just in case. On the second pass they came in low, and slow.

It sounded like one AK-47, a short burst fired straight up as they rolled out. One bullet had found its target coming up from under the helicopter. It came tearing through the floor directly under Gardner's chair. It impacted hard against his "chicken plate". It hit with such force that it drove the plate up and into Gardner's buttocks so hard that he thought he had been shot.

"I am hit, I am hit" screamed Gardner.

In a moment of panic he had unfastened his seat belt, spun around towards Mitchell, and dove to the floor.

"I am fucking shot, man, I got shot", his fists were pounding on the floor while his legs flailed. Then he looked up at Mitchell with the most pathetic look in his eyes. Mitchell had only taken a quick glance but believed Gardner had been wounded. But he was alive and talking so Mitchell kept on shooting back towards the tree line.

Once they were well clear of the tree line Mitchell put the M-60 down on the floor in front of him, unhooked his seat belt and went to Gardner's aid.

"Where are you hit, man", Mitchell asked with deep concern.

"In my fucking ass, man, oh fuck it hurts", said Gardner in tears.

Mitchell did not really know what to do for him. But at least he knew what bullet holes looked like, remembering the papa-san at the garbage dump and the Black soldier shot through his penis. So he began to look over the backside of Gardner's pants. Lifting his shirttail, Mitchell's eye's rapidly searching for that telltale pink hole or trickle of blood. Gardner is still on his stomach and Mitchell looked over the back of the Nomax flight suit, on his butt, the back of his legs, lower back, nothing.

"I don't see anything, there's no blood man, are you sure your hit"

"Fucking A, I think it went all the way through me", Gardner said a bit calmer now.

"I really don't see anything", Mitchell said.

The helicopter jerked side to side and bounced up and down as the pilots repositioned for another run. Mitch was anxious to get back in his seat.

The pilots have been so busy that they had no idea what was going on behind them. Mitchell waited to tell them of the gunner being hit until he knew what to report. After Gardner calmed down a bit he rolled over on his back. Meanwhile Mitchell got back into his seat, convinced that the gunner was ok.

Then Gardner began unfastening his pants and pulled them down, he got himself up to his knees and pulled down his underwear and flashed his bare ass towards Mitchell.

"Can you see anything", Gardner yelled.

He had to yell because he did not have his helmet plugged in. The pilot heard the yelling and turned around. Mitchell also turned to look at Gardner, on his knees with his exposed backside to him, hiking up his shirt, and still wearing his helmet.

"What's going on", the pilots voice pierced the intercom.

"Gardner thinks he's been hit", Mitchell responded.

"Well has he"

"I don't see anything".

"Then tell him to put his pants on and get back in his seat, we are going back around".

Mitchell was almost in tears himself, with laughter.

Gardner is on his hands and knees looking for the bullet hole in the floor. He found the hole and the indentation in the chicken plate. He knows now he's ok! But he sure was pissed off, short timers do not like getting shot at.

The ground fire has subsided, as they make another pass above the tree line. Mitchell has decided to toss a couple of grenades. Gardner was back on the machine-gun, cussing and shooting like a banshee. The pilot has the controls and fires the rockets, the co-pilot has the mini-gun sight and trigger, it seemed that they could use a few grenades.

The incendiaries wouldn't be of much good in the dense vegetation, so Mitchell opted for the fragmentation grenade. These were smooth round and slightly oblong and just a bit smaller than a baseball. There are four main parts to the frag, the pin, the spoon, detonator, and the "Composition B" explosive body that is wrapped within a smooth casing. The spoon is really more like a spring-loaded lever that was attached at the top, to the detonator, and curves down the length of the frag. Once the pin is pulled, it unlocks the spring-loaded spoon. After the spoon is ejected, the detonator is a time delay fuse that will explode the frag in exactly <u>seven</u> seconds. Holding the spoon to the frag after the pin is pulled will delay the detonator until released. To throw the frag, it is laid in the hand with the spoon towards the fingers, so that only the fingers are restricting the spring load, and then simply open the fingers until the spoon is away and throw. In training you are taught to mentally count those seven seconds each time you throw a hand grenade.

Reaching over, between Gardner and him, the frag hung on a wire tied on the bulkhead, between the two. Mitchell grabbed one of the three remaining frag's with his left hand, while holding the M-60 down in his lap with the right. Mitchell pulled the pin out by the ring attached to its closed end, and kept the fingers of his left hand tightly wrapped around the frag to secure the spoon. Then Mitchell peered out to see where he was going to toss his handy little explosive.

Approaching the intended target area, Mitchell squinted into the rush of the oncoming air looking down on the tree line. As they zoomed above he thought he caught a glimpse of a person on the ground moving about in the brush. Mitchell's right hand still held his sixty securely in his lap, his left hand held the little explosive ball. There's no time to use the gun, *quick*, throw the grenade.

His fingers opened and the spoon landed on the floor in front of him. Mitchell kept his eye on the target now passing below them. No time to count Mitchell thought only of getting that grenade to the target. With a great sense of urgency his left arm arched to throw the grenade as far behind them as possible. Mitchell was looking back as he brought his arm around in a rapid movement when something went horribly wrong.

Mitchell's left-handed speedball was halted when he felt the sharp jerk of his lethal hand. The frag is pulled from his grip and spun backward out of control, and fell onto the floor. It had been caught up on the bungee cord that he had hooked up out of the way. The detonator snagged the rubber loop, stretched, and pulled it out of Mitchell's hand, then flung the frag backwards inside. And it lays now, armed and extremely dangerous on the floor of the cargo compartment.

Mitchell panicked as he instinctively reached for the device but was stopped short by the seat belt. Twice he made an attempt to kick the frag across the floor with the toe of his boot. Mitchell has scooted down against the seatbelt, with the machine-gun still in his lap, his boot barely able to make contact. Oh God please let me get that out of here, Mitchell felt real panic now, how many seconds left?

Mitchell looked up to Gardner, he has his back to him fiercely firing his M-60, the pilot, maybe he can reach it, Oh God, no time!

The machine-gun slid down off his lap when he went forward to grab at the fallen explosive. How much time do I have, Mitchell begged, Oh God please.

Stretched to the limit, so tight he has made the seatbelt, his right hand has released the catch, but the pressure exerted by the strain to save their lives, continues to resist the merciful opening.

The heart is beating so fast, breathing is labored, triggering the adrenaline, and the thinking is accelerated. As though he had all the time in the world, he thought of the impending disaster. Wondering what the fireball will look like when the exploding red-hot shrapnel reached the fuel bladder, and the flame ignites the jet fuel. And the crew, they will never know what happened to them? Oh God, Mitchell stretched ever more, please dear God.

A finger barely touched it when it rolled a half turn towards him. He laid three fingertips of his left hand on the top of the frag, pressed down and slid the unwanted deadly cargo across the floor and out the door. His eyes followed the source of his profound anxiety, as it falls down and behind the tail boom. Mitchell snapped forward in his seat, in an attempt to hide from the explosion.

The detonation came almost immediately, and the concussion rocked the helicopter, Mitchell sat petrified.

"What the hell's going on back there", the pilot's said sternly through the earpiece inside Mitchell's helmet that moments ago, could hear only a pounding heartbeat. The pilot was turning in his seat to look into the cargo deck,

"Must have had a short fuse on that last grenade", Mitchell said, still in an extreme state of anxiety, hell, he just couldn't tell him the truth.

"Well, take it easy back there", his words wasted, as Mitchell has already sworn never to touch a frag again.

After the shaking subsided and he calmed down a bit, Mitchell thanked God, then looked over to Gardner, then to the pilot wondering if they had any idea how close they came to becoming a fireball in the sky. His mind raced as he recounted the horrifying incident. The scene playing over and over in his head, each fraction of the event and mentally counting, he was sure, absolutely positive, more than seven seconds had elapsed before detonation. But of course that would have been impossible, right? The hand grenade always detonated in seven seconds.

The incident terrified Mitchell and he chose never to tell anyone about it. Gardner never knew how close he came to being killed twice that day. Fortunately he never had to fly another combat mission, and went home with an unceremonious departure.

Although Mitchell had to stay, the time would come again when he had to use his deadly cargo of hand grenades. But in the future he would be a lot more careful handling them!

Inbound to the Pick-up Zone (P.Z.): Here, troops will board the aircraft for a lift into the Landing Zone (L.Z.).

Chapter Five

Dauntless Obligation

1967, Ft. Eustis, Virginia, United States Army Transportation school;

On his first flight ever in the Huey the instructor pilot flew the students out to fire the M-60 machine gun from the open door. The whole class was on the airfield, where they were split up into small groups that would board the choppers two at a time to take the twenty minute flight, and take their position as left and right door gunners. When Mitchell's chance came he took up in the left seat. The gun was in the stowed position, barrel pointing straight down and locked in the clip that held the barrel in place.

The big D-model helicopter picked up into a hover about three feet high, Mitchell leaned out to clear the aircraft for takeoff. Mitchell could hardly resist the experience of defying gravity, like floating on a cushion of air. As they hovered he was so impressed with the machine's ability that he knew right then and there that flying was for him. They lifted straight up to about three feet, then hovered to the active runway and headed out over the James River near Newport News. Unlike the airplane the helicopter flies with the nose pointed slightly down, so the view from the back seat is exceedingly panoramic.

Once over water, the gunners were allowed to arm the M-60 machine gun with the belt of 7.62mm "blank" bullets. Every crew-chief trainee had a belt of 100 rounds to fire at the imaginary enemy to get a sense of what it was like in combat. The blank bullets had no projectiles and fewer grains of gunpowder that caused frequent jams of the gun. How fast they could clear the jam and continue firing graded the gunner students. It never occurred to Mitchell that this training was ever to be useful in the future.

Over the rivers water now they fly over a pair of fisherman in their small open boat. The aircraft commander makes the comment that the boat is actually a Vietnamese Sam-Pan, and the local fisherman crew is in fact a Viet Cong enemy soldier with AK-47's to shoot us. They drop down for the kill. Mitchell aimed and squeezed the trigger towards the fisherman who, to his surprise ignored them as though were not there. The loud report of the two guns firing in unison should have created some concern for the two, but obviously the fishing was more important. Mitchell was having a great time when the gun stopped on its own and he discovered the jammed brass casing stuck in the injection port. With one hand he lifted the breach lock and with the other he slipped the malfunctioning round clear, repositioned the belt and began firing again until he was out of ammo.

The right gunner had a malfunction at about the same time as Mitchell but was not able to clear it. The pilot cursed him and demanded he get the gun firing again. He was unable to do so, mostly because he was nervous from the pilot yelling at him that if he didn't shoot "right now" they all would be killed by the enemy. Once the pilot landed the helicopter back at the airfield he made the gunner drop to the ground and do fifty push-ups. Mitchell was really thankful for not having so much difficulty in clearing his weapon.

Somewhere west of Ben Tre in the Mekong Delta, the slicks were landing in the LZ to pick up the waiting troops to return them back to the PZ after a day on "search and destroy" patrol. It was a tight LZ with limited space for the entire flight to be in at one time. Tall palm trees surround the mud filled rice paddies on all sides. The approach was steep and the whole flight of twelve helicopters had to get in and out together.

When EMU Two-Two got in they had to hover sideways, to the left, in order to avoid collision with the ship in front of them. They touched down heavily, very close to the waiting troops that were grouped together waiting to load up for their ride back. The left landing skid of Two-Two sunk into a deep hole obscured by a clump of tall grass.

As the weight of the helicopter came down on the skids the chopper tilted hard to the left. The rotor blades struck the muddy rice paddy sending huge globs of earth flying in all directions. The impact of the spinning blades on the counter rotation downward was sufficient enough to send the fuselage leaping back over to the right, and slamming down on the harder ground to the right side of the aircraft. It came to rest on its side, the blades disintegrated and the tail boom snapped off. It all happened so quickly, two, maybe three seconds. The left pilot door opened as both pilots began climbing out of the wreckage. The gunner was the first one out and was assisting the pilots to the ground while white smoke bellowed out from under the engine cowling.

On their low-level pass around to where the now vertical rooftop of the helicopter could be seen, it became apparent that Two-Two's crew-chief was in serious trouble. Mitchell could see him face down in the mud, arms outstretched and motionless. The top edge of the cargo door opening has him pinned down across the middle of his back.

The rest of the flight departed, seemingly as though nothing happened, but of course they knew they could not risk their choppers and crew to stop and assist in an unsecured LZ. That work would be left up to another crew to affect a rescue mission. EMU Two-Two's crewmembers that were now secure on the ground came around the nose of the wreckage and over to the ill-fated crew-chief. The aircraft commander bent down over the crew-chief and shook his head in a negative fashion. The other two moved in closer for a look at the crash victim, then turned and walked off to set up a protective perimeter around the downed craft. The victim did not move and the others did not touch him, he was surely dead. Mitch wondered who it could have been. From behind and with the helmet on his head, there was no way for him to know the identity of the crewman. And of course the helicopters were all the same with no unusual markings. After all that really did not matter, the crewman was one of them, an American soldier, and an EMU. He gave his life in an effort to help them all get the out of the

Nam. Now he will head home before any of them, stuffed into a grim body bag.

One of the ARVN soldiers who was to go aboard Two-Two, and had nearly escaped death himself when the debris from the shattered rotor blades had knocked him down, went over to examine the body of the EMU's fallen colleague. As they continued to circle low over the wreckage Mitchell spotted the ARVN soldier squatting over the still crew-chief. He watched intently not really trusting the ARVN's motives. Was he going to try and remove any of the personal effects of the deceased? Mitchell was really getting pissed off that they couldn't get in there and do something. That fucking gook is acting very suspicious down there, Mitchell was getting angry. With his machine-gun at the ready he has not fired on the ARVN because he seemed to be just curious. Instead he decided to allow the gook time to leave. He knew he can't shoot to kill the ARVN, after all they are allies. But he could shoot close to him signaling a warning that he was not to molest one of them.

The ARVN went down on bended knees, removed his helmet and laid it next to the crew-chief who is still face down on the ground. Then he reached into a canvas satchel that was looped over his head and shoulders. He withdrew an object from the bag that Mitchell could not see from the air. Then leaned over and touched the dead crew-chief around the midsection of his upper torso. Mitchell reached for his M-16 rifle and selected semi auto. If he had to fire he did not want C&C, flying high overhead, to hear the report of the heavy gun or see the telltale muzzle flash. Mitch then raised the rifle to fire into the ground, but as they flew around he lost sight of what the gook was doing. He waited for the next circling pass. When they came around again he took aim with the weapon and anticipated firing a couple of rounds as close as he could to the ARVN's feet. But then Mitchell saw he was using his bare hands to dig out the muddy ground from around the crew-chief. Why would he do that, he decided to hold his fire.

C&C radioed Two-Two to inform them a medivac ship was in route to the crash site. Then commanded Two-Two to escort the next flight in then back to the PZ for another sortie. They left the downed aircraft feeling the pain of losing one of their own, and maybe even a little angry for the senseless death. Nevertheless the missions go on and they are the professionals who have the dauntless obligation to provide the service.

The sortie brings them close to an area that was a known VC village at night and a peasant-farming village by day. All the villagers have been forcefully evacuated due to heavy enemy activity in the area. Anyhow they were all suspected VC, women and children included. The powers to be thought it better to disperse the villagers, rather than kill them all.

Having arrived ahead of the inbound slicks, the Taipan's discover the village has been recently lived in. Smoldering fires and a few chickens scurrying nervously and flapping flightless wings under the roar of the war-birds overhead indicated occupancy. Chicken, fish and rice are the staple of the Vietnamese diet, they never would have left any of those from behind.

The Taipan's widen the circling flight path around the village to the surrounding rice paddy. Far across the paddy to the north is a narrow river, and as they approach from the east turning northward, the pilot spotted the sampan with a lone male rowing his hand carved wooden craft. Long and thin, it almost appears too small for its human powered occupant. Tall Nipa Palms line both sides of the narrow river that shade the man in the boat. The Taipan's close in on the suspected enemy, lurking overhead just above the trees but are still a safe distance from the possible VC. Meanwhile the co-pilot has changed frequency on the radio and calls to C&C for clearance on the eligible male.

"C&C wants to know what he's doing" the co-pilot asked the pilot.

"Tell him rowing northwest away from the village, but the sampan has cargo that is covered with a cloth, we can't make out its contents"

"Roger that"

The co-pilot informs C&C, and his response is to, "wait one for clearance".

As they wait for C&C to decide what to do with the man in the craft, they continue to circle above him. Watching, and waiting for the eligible male to make a bigger mistake, other than being in the wrong place at the wrong time. They assume he is not alone but the ARVN's that will be inserted just outside the village in a few moments will have to search for the others. In the meantime this target belongs to the Taipan's.

The three fully armed helicopters get closer and closer as they attempt to intimidate their suspect into reaching under the cover for his weapon, or try to hide. Either action would have created a quicker response from the gunners. They know they can fire, if fired upon, but if he tried to hide, the delay for clearance could allow the enemy to escape.

As Mitchell watched his every move he couldn't help to feel a little sorry for this individual, he looked quite young and appears to be alone. He is wearing only black pajama pant bottoms, typical of the Viet Cong and the NVA hiding out in the south. Unlike most Vietnamese, he does not have a straw hat on his head. The pilots discuss the hat issue.

"It's midday and the fucking Dinks always have that hat on", one said.

"Yep, jus could be he has one of them NVA pith helmets hidden under that cover", the other pilot responds.

"If he had the Dink that he should have been wearing it, if he has a helmet, I think he would have hidden it as not to expose himself as the enemy".

A reasonable deduction Mitchell thought.

"Charlie" continues to paddle unhurriedly downstream in the dugout. He looks only straight-ahead and his moves are deliberately slow. He is overwhelmed by an unimaginable firepower and probably knows it.

A call back from C&C has ordered that the eligible male is a Viet Cong.

"That village is not supposed to have anyone there", C&C said.

"Taipan's are cleared to fire".

The pilot responded to the order speaking slow and precise.

"Roger, Charlie Charlie, understand Taipan's cleared to fire".

"You are cleared to fire", the order is repeated.

Alone and vulnerable the VC in the boat continues to look directly ahead. Now he has stopped rowing, he is adrift in the middle of the muddy river. His luck has run out as he sits motionless in the sampan on bended knees and sitting back on his heels. Perhaps he understood his future as a mortal is over, and now prays to Buddha to prepare for his afterlife.

They are the lead ship, the pilot has the controls and as they bank around to the right, the helicopter slows and flies head to head with the sampan. The pilots voice presents a soft command into Mitchell's helmet.

"OK, chief he's yours"

Mitchell raised the M-60 they are so close now he could not miss, even if he had wanted to, the others would know that he couldn't do it. Mitchell would be derelict in his duties and would not be allowed to fly any longer, maybe even a court-maritial. Mitchell drew in a deep breath; this is for the dead crew-chief lying back in the LZ and for all the other American soldiers that will live with your passing. Your country's aggression has brought this upon you. Mitchell squeezed the trigger.

The short burst of machine-gun fire found its target. His body did not react to the bullets penetrating his torso as Mitchell thought it might. Instead of being knocked out of the boat, his head slumped forward and he fell back and slid down into the floor of the boat. His blood flowed through large, perfectly round holes in his body.

The first wing ship came around and opened fired into the boat with a long burst that partially sunk the sampan. The water turned a deep red and the enemy was pronounced KIA, (killed in action). Taipan Wing Two then made a pass around and was to shoot up the cloth cover, to create a secondary explosion in case there were explosives under the cloth. When no explosion occurred, that gunner continued to shoot into the body until the head was severed from its trunk. Bits and pieces of the wood boat and the head of the corpse floated about in the muddy water and blood filled hull. The Taipan's broke from their circling pattern and formed back up into the Vee formation while climbing for altitude.

Although Mitchell was credited with his first confirmed kill, somehow it did not feel like an honor. He would have made any excuse not to have the credit for such an unpleasant act. Was this the reality of the price that he had to pay for his silly desire to want to fly? Mitchell wondered now if any of this was worth it. The image of that young person, before and after, repeatedly flashed in his brain and Mitchell didn't like it one bit.

Heading back to base that afternoon, he retreated to the AFVN radio station, hoping for some soothing music to take him someplace else. Mitchell stared out over the passing landscape, feeling kind of numb. If he had been alone in the helicopter he knew that he might have cried. Not for himself, and not for the dead crew-chief, and not even for the VC, but just for his whole fucking stinking situation.

Back at the snake pit, Mitchell took his time performing the daily maintenance on his chopper. He had the fire extinguisher filled with water and the engine cowling off ready to clean the turbine engine. The co-pilot stayed behind to do the run-up on the engine. Meanwhile Mitchell hand pumped the water from the extinguisher directly into the intake of the turbine engine to flush out any dirt or other contaminates through the engine and out the exhaust. The combustion stage of the engine produced such extreme temperatures that everything melted into oblivion, even water simply turned into exhaust gases.

Mitchell was completing the entries into the ship logbook when the crew-chief from Taipan Three-Eight walked over to the revetment and asked him,

"Hey did ya hear about Larry"?

Mitchell assumed he was referring to the chief of the downed helicopter earlier today, his name must have been Larry.

"Yea, I almost shot that gook that was fucking around with him"

"Good thing you didn't huh, hey by the way, nice shooting today man, you're not a virgin anymore", he seemed to be congratulating Mitchell.

Mitchell let the comment go over his head as the crew-chief waved bye and headed for the barracks, dragging his helmet and rifle over his shoulder. Then it struck Mitchell, why did he say it was a good thing that I did not shoot the gook fucking with Larry? It was too late to ask as he had already disappeared in the direction of the barracks area.

Mitchell was in bad need of a shower, even though he was not any dirtier than any other day of flying and shooting, it was just that he felt really dirty. A truly hot shower was needed to bring him back to feeling righteous. Unfortunately, the intense sun's rays on the black rubber water bladder high up on the tower generated the only warmth brought to the shower water. As the warm cleansing water flowed over Mitchell's head and down his body, he could feel all of the day's events melting away down into the drain. Soon he would be so drunk that any resemblance of that boy, who today, was ordered to perform a loathsome task, will be missing in action, until the next day's missions begin all over again. Yes sir, he'll head over to the EM club for some liquid soul saver. Tonight, Mitchell promised himself, I will drink myself into a long uninterrupted sleep.

Mitchell grabbed a towel and wrapped it around him, then slipped on a pair of rubber flip-flops. Stepped out of shower building ready to transform into another person, the one who could accomplish the impossible, the one who could destroy as well as create, the one who could…what the? Approaching Mitchell appeared a familiar face, he recognized him as one of the slick crew-chiefs, but he has been hurt, and has been bandaged around his skull and forehead.

"What the hell happened to you", Mitchell asked somewhat puzzled?

It was Larry, no one had told Mitchell it was he that had been injured. Mitchell even though he saw him this morning on the flight line, suited up and flying with the slicks today.

"How did you get like that", Mitchell asked not believing his eyes.

"We went down in the LZ today", Larry was actually smiling.

"When? I flew today and I didn't see you go down", Mitchell said still trying to put the pieces together.

"When we landed, the chopper flipped on its side and I got trapped under it"

Larry then lifted his O.D. green tee shirt to revel another bandage wrapped around his rib cage. The whites of his eyes are blood red, but other than that he looked pretty good.

"That was you under the slick that crashed in on the first sortie", Mitchell questioned.

"Yea, did you see me", Larry seemed proud to relay this to Mitchell.

"Yea, but I thought you were dead", Mitchell caught himself, "I mean, I thought the crew-chief on the ground was dead".

Mitchell does still not believe this is the same Larry as the one he had thought died on the field of battle today.

"I thought so too", Larry started, "but some fucking gook saved my ass". Larry was much more serious now.

"My pilots thought I was dead too", Larry went on.

He proceeded to tell Mitchell that when the helicopter fell to the left, Larry felt the blades strike the ground, he unfastened his seat belt and jumped to the ground, on the right side, but slipped and fell on his stomach. When the fuselage flipped over to the right, the roof section above the cargo door landed in the middle of his back, pinning him to the ground. He had been knocked unconscious and a broken rib had punctured his lung, and filled his lung with blood. Unable to breathe he was only seconds from certain death.

The gook was an ARVN medic, who went over to help Larry.

"When I came to, I couldn't move or talk but I could see this gook squatting over and staring at me" Larry continued, "I wanted him to help me but I couldn't tell him with that fucking chopper crushing me", Larry took a long breath.

"He scared me shitless when he pulled a knife out of his bag, felt between my ribs and then stuck the knife all the way into my lungs to drain the blood out", Larry grimaces as he recalled the pain.

"I thought he was trying to kill me".

Once Larry was able to breathe again, he was pulled out from under the chopper and airlifted to a hospital, treated and released.

Mitchell's opened mouth was catching flies as he was still in a state of shock at Larry's account of the situation. If he had seen that medic with the knife, he might have killed the ARVN Medic and unknowingly killed Larry too!

Mitchell still could not believe this was the same Larry, the one that he knew, as the same one who was under the crashed helicopter. How could it have been that he did not recognize him, sure he had his face down in the mud with his flight helmet strapped on and covered in loose dirt, and a helicopter crushing him. Still, he felt he should have known, someone should have said who was down there. Then Mitchell realized it was of no consequence there was nothing more or less that would have been done.

He was very glad to know that Larry survived, it made Mitchell feel a little less vulnerable too. However, now he wished he had not felt the anger that he did when shooting at that eligible male in the LZ earlier today. Professional service should come without emotion. It's just my job he told himself as he headed to the barracks to get dressed, and then for that big drink.

So far, his time in Vietnam seemed to have passed quickly, and he felt like he has done fairly well for a young man. Mitchell has already experienced more than he could have ever imagined, and done things he felt he could never do. Somehow it seems impossible that he could ever make it out of Vietnam. If I continue at this pace, I just don't know how I will avoid disaster, Mitchell thought. So much happens so fast, one moment of hesitation or visual alertness diverted for just one fraction of a second could spell disaster for himself or the crew.

Mitchell wondered too about the Viet Cong, and just exactly how many of them are there anyhow? Could he possibly make any difference, just how many will he have to kill to survive? Is that how it works, kill or be killed? Just kill until one of us is all gone? No, that can't be the way it is Mitchell concluded. I'll just provide the professional service that we have been trained for. Fly right, shoot straight and everything will be ok. The cocktails were helping convince Mitchell he had this war figured out.

In the following days, Mitchell Collins and still just eighteen years of age earned his first Air medal for twenty-five aerial missions over hostile territory, and was credited with several more confirmed kills. He has earned his Taipan black silk scarf with unit patch, worn in recognition of his performance of duty, namely to kill.

It has been one month and one week since his date of arrival in country.

This crew chief readies his M-60 weapon to prepare for engagement with the enemy.

Chapter Six

Going Down

The hooch maids are Vietnamese women who seek employment working for the American soldiers. They were brought to Bearcat each day except on Sunday's, by eight a.m. sharp, and by four p.m. their workday was done. They were loaded into the big two and half-ton trucks at Bien Hoa, twenty miles away. Some maids traveled a far distance from their villages to Bien Hoa for the opportunity to work on a military base. They had all been previously screened thoroughly and given a security clearance and picture I.D. badges. No badge, no work.

It took several trucks to get them all to the base. Crammed into the aft bed of the truck, there were not enough seats, so most of the thirty or so women squatted down between the two rows of bench seats for the journey to Bearcat. They all carried with them a woven straw shoulder bag that contained several small aluminum containers that is their lunch and some personal items. Every bag was checked by the Military Police prior to entering and leaving the base. Although, when need be, the maids could be very resourceful in getting past the MP's with unauthorized items. Sometimes, although rare, the bag leaving the base was heavier going home due to the theft of a soldier's belongings.

There is one maid for every two G.I.'s and they are paid fourteen dollars a week in Military Payment Currency, those funds being deducted from the soldiers pay each month. The soldiers didn't mind paying because the maids did all of their domestic chores, made the bed, swept the area around the bunk, washed and ironed clothes, and shined the boots. You know the sort of things young men really desire not to do.

Hooch maids are workers only, no touching, no hanky-panky is allowed. Besides, these women were much different from the young Saigon bargirls. They were usually older mama-sans, although a few younger girls were able to get clearance, they mostly worked alongside their mothers. The hooch maids are a good source of knowledge of what life is like for the average Vietnamese. Most of the Vietnamese language spoken by soldiers was learned from their "mama-sans", as they tried to teach each other their language in single words and short phrases. For many G.I.'s a pseudo-parental bond developed between the maid and her employer. Although there is a limit to what the two could talk about, there is always the matter of security. There had been incidences when the VC back in their village had threatened the maid's family. Unless she were to provide them with information about the goings on at the base, or to pace off distances between barracks, or other important buildings, her family could be beheaded or worse. The VC would use this information to pre-set the crude guidance for their rocket attacks on the bases. It was far simpler just not to talk with the maids other than command them their duties and learn a few words.

For the most part the hooch maids governed themselves and there was little conflict between them. After all they could have their security clearance revoked and expelled from the base quite easily. They knew not to create any disturbances and do the work they were hired to do, or else lose the financial benefit of working for Uncle Sam.

It seemed as if every hooch maid chewed the naturally grown, Betelnut, a small red wild berry that grew on bushes all over Vietnam. It provided the chewer with a mild sedated feeling, bright red lips and gums, long term use created black rotten teeth. But if you couldn't touch them anyhow who cared? Their looks only served the G.I.'s into compliance with the "no touching" order.

It's been two months now that Mitchell has been in country, and only now has found out what happened to his best friend Richard. In a letter home, Richard wrote to his family that he shook Mitchell to wake him up that morning back at the transient company in Bien Hoa. He told his family that Mitchell was almost delirious from fatigue when he finally opened his eyes. Richard felt he understood him when Richard told Mitchell where he was going to be transferred, but of course Mitchell had been so exhausted and didn't remember any of it.

Richard wrote that he has been stationed up north in Da Nang, a coastal city with a major shipping port. Mitchell was relieved at the news, at least he won't have to worry about him so much as Mitchell has been told he has been assigned a job as a mail clerk. A rear echelon job that should keep him from combat, and harm's way, to Mitchell it seemed ironic how their destinies have taken such a different turn.

Mitchell sat contemplating writing to Richard but to send him in a letter now and to explain what he had been doing since he has been in-country would only serve to cause Richard concern. Flying combat missions are all Mitchell does every day, so there is little else to write about. Mitchell decided not to write. Thus began his veil of secrecy like some sort of invisible force field. No one should ever know exactly what Mitchell has done here. Could he say he spent each day flying, hunting down the ultimate prey in airborne vehicles, and then destroying him?. Why would anyone ever ask? Would anyone really ever want to know? Mitchell wondered how he could ever tell his friends or family what he has done here. No sir, Mitchell decided no one would ever know.

Now having flown now more than fifty combat missions, Mitchell has earned another Air medal and is feeling like a pro at his job. For those unfortunate enough to be radioed in as "eligible male", the game is over. Those Vietnamese soldiers who survived must know that their time on earth is limited.

However the American Soldiers must fight hard to survive and protect the lives of fellow Americans and their allies. Combat is in Mitchell, he is a combatant, and everything else is secondary. He fights to preserve his life and those he serves with. Nothing else matters anymore, not until he goes home, alive…or dead.

While in route to the AO for the first mission of the day, Mitchell was sort of daydreaming, just gazing out over the passing scenery. As they flew along past miles of rice paddies, jungle and tributaries, he noticed a large fresh palm leaf floating in the middle of a muddy river tributary. It's bright green color in brilliant contrast to the murky water surrounding it. At first it escaped him why it caught his attention. It did seem a little odd the leaf was not the usual dried out, and brown foliage usually found floating. As they flew directly over Mitch noticed the rivers current flowing towards the Mekong Delta that would eventually lead out to sea. Small grass and debris, and the ripple effect of the currents flow on the river banks indicated the slow movement eastward. He stared out at the stationary leaf in the middle of the flowing river, a stationary leaf in a flowing current? The Taipan's flew past and as Mitchell looked back, he thought he saw the leaf move upstream.

"Hey Mr. Fleming", he called out to the pilot over the intercom.

"I think I see something suspicious"

"Wh-cha got kid", Fleming responded.

"Well, not real sure but I think there is a guy swimming under a palm leaf up the river we just flew past". He only mentioned a "guy" because he knew it was the only way to turn them back, anyhow what if it was a guy?

"You sure, where?" asked Fleming.

Mitchell indicated the direction best he could from the rear seat. They have flown well past the river by now and Mitchell's anxiety level is rising at the prospect that we will miss the opportunity to find out if he was correct to report his suspicion. How could anyone be so dumb, did that person think he wouldn't suspect a leaf going the wrong direction? All he had to do was go with the flow, and Mitchell would never have suspected a thing.

Now they are obligated to interrupt the mission at hand to investigate the intentions of this idiot. He was so sure someone was under that leaf.

Fleming has radioed to C&C to get permission to investigate Mitchell's claim.

"OK Taipan flight, check it out quick and give me a sit-rep".

"Roger, copy", Fleming banked hard right.

They found the large nipa palm leaf stationary right there where Mitchell had spotted it. Fleming also thought it was suspicious. All three Taipan's begin to circle the rivers suspect area, as the lead ship, they circle closest to the intended target, while the others circle wider.

"If there is someone under there, let's make sure he's alone", Fleming called for the wing ships to keep a look out.

They watched as the leaf moves slowly upstream, the murky waters are so dark that nothing could be seen under the palm leaf. The thick black mud of the riverbank is well exposed now due to the low water condition of the dry season. Suddenly a bare foot makes an abrupt appearance on the surface, to the side of the large leaf, and disappears again.

"Damn kid, your right", the pilot is excited now.

"C&C, Taipan lead", Fleming radioed.

"Go lead".

"C&C, we've got a possible Victor Charlie swimming underwater, request permission to fire".

They all knew that friendly's don't swim upstream under murky water, so the general conclusion is that he is avoiding detection, thereby making this target a Viet Cong. Once again, the burden of their duty falls on Mitchell.

"Taipan lead, be advised that you are in a free fire zone".

The pilot responded with, "Roger, understand, cleared to fire".

C&C responds, "Roger lead, you are cleared to fire, let me know what happens".

Fleming brought the chopper around and flew downstream a few hundred yards and then turns back one hundred eighty degrees and flies directly upstream low, and slow, very low. The two wing ships circle above, watching, waiting.

"OK kid, whenever you're ready", the pilot commanded.

At thirty feet above the water, Mitchell leaned out and took aim at the leaf. He waited until the last possible second to get in a good long burst without missing with a single bullet. Sighting down the barrel, he opened up right on target. The raging bullets caused the water to erupt up all around the intended target. And in the mist of all the upward spray, Mitchell caught a glimpse of a figure leap up from under the leaf, and out of the water to his waist. He could see the person's hands over his head, his head back and gulping in air. That reaction exposed his bare chest to the incoming rounds. With his head tilted back and mouth agape, so close now Mitchell could see his pain. In an instant, the eligible male splashed back down and disappeared under the dismal waters.

The color of the river changes to a deeper reddish brown as they fly out, banking right. They wait for any sign of Charlie to surface. The bits and pieces of the leaf have taken a more natural course downstream.

"He came out of the water so fast I thought he was going to fly into the helicopter", Fleming said.

"That stupid fucker jumped up right in front of the bullets", Mitchell responded.

After a few minutes to determine that no one could possibly have survived, Fleming depressed the microphone switch.

"C&C we've got one confirmed KIA here", he reported.

"Roger, good work, now see if you can catch up to the flight"

"Yes sir, Taipan's in route", Fleming said cheerfully.

They fly off towards the flight of slicks heading to the PZ, leaving the body of the lone male lying somewhere under the water. In three days' time the decomposing corpse will fill with enough gas to float the corpse to the surface. It too will drift downstream until hung up on a riverbank and rot away, or to be eaten up by insects and such. Likely his family will never know of his violent demise. He is for now just, "missing in action".

It was hard to accept not having any control of your own life, Mitchell no longer felt like a person, but rather a machine, like the helicopter, doing a job commanded by others who are not in control either. Every day was the same routine, up before sun light, shit, shower, and a shave, then breakfast. Out to the flight line, preflight, fuel-up, fly to the AO, Re-fuel, Sorties before lunch, re-fuel, Sorties after lunch, re-fuel, Fly back to base, Perform daily maintenance, get drunk, sleep, and do it all over again tomorrow. Maybe what Mitchell needed is that steam bath the guys are always talking about, tonight Mitchell decided, he'll give it a try.

They've caught up with the flight and have completed the usual three or four sorties before lunch, re-fueled the aircraft and now they are standing by in the AO waiting for the next mission.

At the airbase at Can Tho, the flight of EMU's and Taipan's, twelve ships in a single file alongside the runway sit motionless in the mid-day sun. EMU one-five has been called up on a re-supply mission. After just a short time on the ground, one-five took off and disappeared over the horizon. The rest of the aircrews eat lunch, play ball, read, nap and engage in other assorted past times like pulling practical jokes on each other. A favorite is the application of leaches to a sleepy crewman who has not yet learned to keep one eye open. Horseplay can turn deadly if the recipient has no sense of humor, as all are armed, Mitchell decided to mind his own business.

An old Vietnamese woman from the nearby village, is carrying two baskets, one is slung on each end of a bamboo pole. Her walk is deliberate to prevent her burden from bouncing. She has walked over to each of the choppers, but hesitates getting too close, soliciting ice packed Coca-Cola to the flight crews. As she peddles her wares, a small group of kids play also keeping their distance from the still helicopters. Mitchell took one of the bottles from the toothless old lady and paid her with crumpled up funny money. Since no coins were minted by the military, their loose change consisted of small paper currency, the larger denominations have been folded neatly into Mitchell's wallet.

VC Coke is bottled in Saigon so before opening, Mitchell shook the bottle and held it up high over his head into the bright sunlight, peering through the thick glass. As the sun streaked through the dark sugary mixture, he looked for the telltale signs of glistening particles of ground up glass. Reportedly the VC knew of Americans zeal for the most popular drink and would sabotage the liquid with ground up glass. The hazardous substance has made its way into the stomach lining of some poor G.I.'s who did not take the precaution seriously. Those dudes had their insides tore up by the glass particles and bled slowly to death. Or so the rumor had it. Hmmm, but Mitchell's Coke is as cold as it is sweet, a welcome relief in the middle of the day in Vietnam.

A little girl approaches Mitchell's helicopter, she is maybe eight years old. Her jet-black hair gleams in the sunlight. She has a cute round face with high cheekbones, lightly colored skin and large coy brown eyes. She is wearing a sleeveless white blouse and blue faded silk pants, and pink flip-flops worn thin. She is a cute child, unlike the others in some unexplainable way. Not like the other kids who aggressively beg for handouts and are shooed away. She has not said anything and has not ventured to close to the chopper. Standing alone, her eyes would dart towards Mitchell but when he looked back at her she would immediately look back down. All the while she kept her hands behind her back.

Mitchell opened the top to the water cooler, reached inside and grabbed an apple that he had saved from breakfast. It was ice cold and bright red, he then offered it to her with an outreached arm. To his surprise she smiled at him and walked slowly forward to accept the offering. She took it with both hands, looked closely at it and handed it back to Mitchell. Still smiling she climbs up into the door opening and onto the chopper's cargo deck. Suspiciously Mitchell watched her, any sudden move on her part will require instant discipline. Patting her down lightly outside her loose clothing, she had no objects that would harm the helicopter. He then gave her a nod of approval and a smile. Then she climbed up on Mitchell's jump seat, behind him. He had to slide forward to give her some room. Mitchell had to know what she was up to, maybe some kind of child's play. Her little fingers began playing in the hair on his head, she seemed to be searching for something. Damn Mitchell thought, maybe she thinks I got fleas or worse yet, lice! Then she grabbed a hair and yanked it out by the root.

"Ouch, you little brat, what are you doing", he said rubbing his scalp.

Without a word she reached around to show him the lone gray hair she found. Her tiny fingers held the single silvery strand of age. With a little giggle she grabbed the apple from Mitchell's hand and jumped to the ground mumbling something in Vietnamese as she hurried on. The removal of a gray hair in exchange for an apple, Mitchell contemplated its meaning with a smile.

Hours have gone by when the flight is called up to extract the ARVN troops from the LZ where they had put them in this morning. EMU one-five has only recently returned from their re-supply mission. Since there was negative suppression in the LZ and there have been no reports of troops having taken fire, this should be a fairly routine extraction.

The lead EMU pilot, with his finger pointed up into the air, begins to make a circling motion with is arm over his head, indicating that the flight is to crank up the birds and make ready for flight. Down the line of waiting helicopters other crew members begin to imitate the circling arm motion so that all are alerted. Slowly the crews ready their aircraft, get dressed and climb into their respective helicopters. The Taipan's know that they have a little more time as they fly at a lower altitude and do not need the time to climb and descend into the LZ. So they will be the last to take off.

Soon all the waiting aircraft are cranked and running, it's mission time. The EMU's depart Can Tho as a well-coordinated, precise flying team and form up into four vee formations of three ships each. As the EMU's reach their cruising altitude of approximately two thousand feet, the Taipan's then lift off. Only minutes behind the EMU's, they reach their low cruising altitude of one hundred fifty feet or so. Mitchell resists the urge to switch to the AFVN radio to listen to some real world music, and continues to monitor the mission frequency.

As they close the distance on the EMU flight, they are about three miles behind and below the formation of EMU's when the most fearsome call came over the radio,

" EMU one-five, going down".

Those were the last words heard by anyone outside of the on-board crew.

All eyes immediately went upward and there was total silence over the radio.

Almost at cruising altitude the flight was beginning to level off. EMU One Five heard the ringing of metal at the same time they felt the shudder through the airframe. With the Co-pilot at the control, the pilot of the predestined craft instinctively placed his hands on the cyclic stick and collective controls, then commanded the co-pilot through the intercom,

"I've got it".

The co-pilot thought to himself, "What could I have done wrong", everything seemed fine until he felt the shudder hard against his foot that had been gently pushing on the tail rotor pedals.

The aircraft nosed downward and began to slowly spiral. The pilot fighting for control knows he's lost the tail rotor and nosed down to keep the air slip stream rushing past the tail boom to prevent the main rotor torque from spinning the fuselage like a top under the large spinning blades. He manages to slow the spiral but it's a helpless situation. He will not give up and is working at a swift pace to regain control. He fully depresses the radio trigger button on the cyclic stick, first click intercom, second click transmit VHF, and announces his craft is going down. In the back seats, the crew-chief and gunner know they are in deep shit although they are unaware of the cause. The crew-chief wonders what could have caused his craft to falter, and hopes it was not anything he might have missed during the routine maintenance. Perhaps they have been hit by ground fire, he wondered. He then took a quick look out to the rear of the tail boom to see if he can get a visual on any damage. Not seeing anything out of the ordinary he turns to watch the pilot who he now relies on to save them all.

The gunner thinks about being on the ground again. He is a former infantryman and has volunteered to fly as a gunner to avoid combat on the ground. He absolutely hated having his feet wet for days at a time. Sensing an imminent crash he mentally prepares for duty on the ground, get both pilots out and grab all the weapons and ammo they can carry, set up a perimeter. While holding onto his seat with one hand and the other grabbing at the airframe, he looks around to visually confirm the location of all the weapons. His anxiety level is high but he is not scared.

The crew-chief has become aware the impact will be hard, the downward angle of the nose is extreme and the airspeed is too high. He worries about the damage to his aircraft but he also knows the helicopter can be rebuilt if necessary. He has never heard the wind rush past so loudly before. He hopes the rotor blades don't disintegrate, God, that could get us killed, he thinks. The co-pilot watches the instrument panel intently, he briefly looked down at the spiraling ground but quickly took his eyes away. He is worried that he might break his leg again as he had done in college, playing football.

From the back seat he could see the flight ahead and high above them. He unfastened his seatbelt and got on his knees on the floor between the pilot's seats to get a better view of the flight through the windshield. One-five had already fallen well below the rest of the flight. Mitchell was sure like him, everyone watching, hoped EMU one-five would recover and fly straight or at worst set down in a soft rice paddy so that they could extract the crew to safety.

The Taipan's have learned to watch over the EMU flight like a vigilant parent with little children. Keeping the EMU's safe was their job, but now they watch in horror, totally helpless. Fleming nosed over the chopper promptly to pick up some more airspeed. It was a sickening sight to watch EMU one-five spin down from the rest of the flight, spiraling, nose over tail and quite obviously out of control. The remainder of the flight stayed in perfect formation except for the void left by One-Five. It seemed to take forever for the eventual impact.

Back inside EMU One Five, the spinning has disorientated the crew, they no longer care about the ground rushing up towards them. Time has taken another dimension as they think of all the possibilities to get out of this situation. The crew-chief smiled as he thought of what he will tell of their experience back at base. Everyone will crowd around as he relays the story of today's crash. He can hear the Oooo's and Ahhhh's of fellow aviators as they marvel at his story of survival… Of course no one in the crew, never, ever thought of their eventual demise. Then mercifully, as though someone had walked into a room and reached for the wall switch, with a quick flick, the light of life went out. Death's swift hand grabbed four of them.

Mitchell's ship was not more than three minutes behind the impact, they could see only a dark rising plume of smoke.

"Grab the fire extinguisher" Fleming snapped.

Piloting the chopper he made a fast and low approach, soon they could see the impact zone, it looked bad, real bad. They made a running landing in the rice paddy opposite the wreckage and skidded to a stop. They were not more than fifty feet on the right of the burning hulk.

With the fire extinguisher in hand, Mitchell jumped out the left door before the helicopter came to a halt and ran to the wreckage to get as close as he could. It was not the heat from the smoldering mass that stopped him cold in his tracks, rather it was the scene lying at his feet. Not many recognizable parts of the aircraft were evident, the rear portion of the tail boom was twisted and buckled. Shiny metallic pieces of the rotor blades honeycomb structure scattered all about, the turbine engine was burning with an intense white hot glow from the magnesium compressor section.

The complete cargo area, where the crew-chief and gunner sat just moments ago, was a pile of hot ash. Somewhere among the whitish remains of what has burned are the gray ashes of the backseat crew. Apparently the craft impacted or flipped upside down. Feeling totally useless with the extinguisher in his hand, Mitchell glanced down at the red bottle in his hand and wondered what possible good would this do now.

Walking around to the front of the pile of debris where the two pilots armor plated seats remained intact, but were upside down, Mitchell stood frozen at the sight of the two pairs of legs sticking up from under the overturned seats. The four smoldering leather combat boots, rubber heels melted, laces burned away, sitting upside-down on top of charred and blackened bone that was seconds ago, human legs.

Looking back to his aircraft, with tears swelling in hardened eyes, Mitchell slowly shook his head with a negative response to the crew. Although anyone could see that the crash was so fierce, there could not have been any survivors. How could such a dreadful thing happen, what could have caused one-five to just go down like this, and kill four of their comrades. Mitchell never truly understood how vulnerable they were in those machines until now.

He was not aware of the other Taipan's still circling above, providing gun cover for him now on the ground. Nor was he aware of the heat from the wreckage, or was he aware of the smell, it seemed as if all his senses have shut down. With an empty feeling, he walked cautiously towards the waiting crew. The hardest thing Mitchell ever had to do was to climb back into that helicopter and fly off.

In the following months, it would be determined that after one-five returned late to Can Tho, upon completing their re-supply mission. The hungry crew-chief had opened a can of C-rations and placed it under the still red hot tail pipe through an inspection door, to heat up his lunch. This was a common practice until this incident. Also under the tailpipe is a tail-rotor shaft that connects to the transmission located forward of the engine. The shaft runs back, down the centerline under the engine and past the tailpipe and on top of the tail boom to the tail rotors. Shaft couplers and hanger bearings join together the multiple sections of shaft.

One-Five's, crew-chief failed to remove the C-ration can when they were called up to bring back the troops from the LZ that afternoon. Apparently the can vibrated over to a coupler where one of the two bolts that joined the two halves of the coupler together, hit the edge of the can. The shaft and coupler turn at more than three thousand R.P.M.'s, this caused the coupler to literally explode apart. EMU One-Five was left without the tail-rotor to counter the effect of the main rotor torque, causing them to spin out of control. A can of pork and beans destroyed a helicopter and killed four crewmen, Mitchell had concluded that bad luck, or carelessness can be just as deadly as the Viet Cong.

They fly back to Bearcat in a solemn mood, losing One-Five has put a damper on what would have been a good day otherwise. After completing his crew-chief duties Mitch decided to take the long awaited steam bath and massage. The building is located on the base, about a half-mile walk down a gravel road that runs past the flight line towards the perimeter of the base. This is a government sanctioned facility, solely for the use and pleasure of base personnel. Inside the steam bath the girl sitting at the desk in front of the curtain that masks the opening in the partition in the wall, smiles and says,

"Hellro G.I.", and then asked Mitchell what he wanted, Steam? Massage? Han-yob?,

"Say what?", suddenly realizing she meant "hand job".

"My girls do number one yob, make you come, you like"?

"Oh, that", it did not take much to understand now.

"How much for the works", he asked.

"Fou dollra", she stated holding up three and one half fingers.

"Good price for number one girl's", she took his money.

She leads Mitchell to a large shower room.

"Take showra now, then steam, I send girl for you when you finny"

Mitchell stripped naked and folded his clothes, placing them on the shelf provided for such articles. A quick and thorough cleaning to get the surface dirt, he was already feeling better. Wrapping the towel provided around his waist, he opened the heavy wood door to the steam bath. A blast of hot steam struck him upon entering, holding his arms straight out, he felt around for a place to sit. The steam was so thick that he could not see the others in the room although their voices were seemingly near. It was like breathing and drinking at the same time, but soon he became accustomed to the heavy mist and relaxed. Sitting there in the intense heat Mitchell could feel months of trapped-in dirt expel itself from the pores of his skin and flow like the muddy tributary to his feet.

Having tolerated the heat for as long as it was possible, he stepped from the bath after a quick cold rinse and was met by a young girl. She introduced herself as *Ngoc* and was there to show him the way to a cubicle for his massage. She walked right up to him and grabs the towel from his waist. Then she reached for his manhood and led the way down the short hallway. Mitchell was still in tow by his private part as they approach a small cubicle that is obscured by a curtain.

Entering, he laid down on the massage table while *Ngoc* began her massage on his back, then to the arms and legs and feet. He felt as though he could lapse into a coma. Her tiny, and strong hands manipulating muscles with the skill of old oriental teachings. She asks him to turn over and began the massage again beginning with the face. Finally she placed the towel across his abdomen and again grabbed his manhood to manually manipulate him to orgasm. He closed his eyes to imagine the round eyed beauty that he would make love to. Mitchell released and then dosed off, and *Ngoc* let him sleep for over an hour before waking him to allow room for the next lucky G.I.

I think I'll do this again, Mitchell promised himself.

After a couple of cold beers at the company EM Club, Mitchell headed back to the barracks. Inside, a hot and heavy card game of "spades" was being played on a bunk of one of the Taipan's. The four players were excitedly slapping the cards down as they trumped each other furiously. The small crowd standing around the bunk roared at each overtaking of another pile of downed cards. Mitchell stood behind one of the players and lit another cigarette. The players studied their cards while one team member tried to hint to his partner what the best suit to throw out was. Sweat poured from the players as they prepared to pounce on the next card to fall. It wasn't just a game to them it was war! Finally the victorious team had taken the invisible trophy, and loser's blamed each other for their loss. The winners and losers retired for the night.

Finally the barracks was quiet and the platoon Sergeant killed the lights. Soon after, in the darkness, a combat boot was heard to fly across the barracks. With an audible "thud", it killed the rat running along the floor and at the walls bottom edge.

The guy whose head laid next to the scene sat up in his bunk and proclaimed,

"Hey, good shot Dale, I give ya a confirmed on that one", he yelled.

Rats and the VC seemed to die without much of a fight. Maybe if I fight hard, I could just survive this conflict, Mitchell reasoned.

Dale has the honor of removing the dark carcass from the barracks. Holding the deceased rodent by the tail he makes for the door to initiate the disposal. Mitchell pulled the sheet over his head. Damn, I hate those fucking things he thought to himself.

Catching Zzz's and a little shade.

Chapter Seven

Divine Intervention

Often, he would look at the gleaming metal dog tags hanging around his neck and notice the line below the name, rank and serial number, where the wearer's religion is stamped into the metal plate. His had said "No Pref", meaning he had no preference who spoke over him should he meet an untimely demise.

Religion was never a big part of Mitchell's life prior to coming to Nam. His Mother was a Protestant, while his Dad was Methodist, neither could decide on which faith to baptize their baby. Ultimately they decided to leave it up to him. Of course they would have to wait a number of years for his decision. When the time came, he could not make up his mind either. So the time passed without taking that crucial step.

Mitchell was thinking, maybe I'll start my own church. The Church Of Combat, surely anyone who's ever been in combat is a believer. In the church of combat, you'll pray a lot. Of having heard of, and witnessed, divine intervention so often in Vietnam, gradually an awareness of some higher power is at work comes into view. And just what is divine intervention you ask, well it's anytime that you are supposed to die, but you don't!

The enemy on the ground fires his rifle at the rapidly flying helicopter overhead. A single bullet enters the helicopters plexi-glass chin bubble, below the pilot's feet. The same bullet then enters his left pant leg just above his boot on the left side. Then the round exits below the knee and re-enters just above the knee, and exits again. The same bullet re-enters his shirt, just below the left collarbone area and exits at the top of his shoulder. Then this same projectile catches the left bottom edge of the pilot's ballistic helmet, spins around inside the back of the helmet to the right side, and exits forward penetrating the windshield. The pilot who did not have a mark on him, only commented that he felt "something strange"!

In another incident, a door gunner's lip is burned by a bullet that zipped by his face as his chopper lands in the LZ.

An artillery round fired from miles away, soars through the air on its path of destruction, passes through the helicopter's open cargo doors while in flight at two thousand feet without touching crew or airframe.

A medical evacuation chopper sits down on a land mine that blows half the helicopter away, the crew is saved by the dead bodies lying on the floor.

In one sortie into a landing zone, all the slick helicopters, and two gunships are shot down in an ambush, none wounded or killed.

Or how about that grenade that Mitchell dropped on the floor awhile back, it should have detonated before he got it out the door, he was sure of that. And what about Larry's crash, it just happens that a Vietnamese medic saves his life, when everyone else gave him up for dead?

Miracles, or just dumb luck, no sir, it happens all too often to be just luck. A powerful force is at work here, something very spiritual.

Sometimes it is felt so strongly that the soul simply surrendered to it. Leaving a person with the feeling that what comes, comes, no way to change the inevitable. So with no real need to worry about his wellbeing, Mitchell felt it necessary to only think of his job.

Their sortie now, takes them into the LZ well ahead of the flight of EMU's. The mission objective is to visually check out enemy activity in the area prior to the deployment of troops. It is now, nearing the end of the dry season. This time of year the rice paddies are dried up, leaving cracks and small gorges in abstract patterns in the squared off paddies separated by the dikes, that in the wet season become the pathways for the rice farmers.

As they entered the proposed LZ, they were informed that a nearby artillery firebase has received a "fire order", to "prep the LZ", or pound the intended landing zone with a barrage of artillery. This is done to discourage anyone in the vicinity from advancing into the LZ. And what if they are already there? Boy, are they going to have a pounding headache. The idea is to obliterate the area were helicopters and troops might make contact with any booby-traps and deter any bad guys.

Again, Mitchell's ship is the lead gunship as they enter the LZ at a hundred and fifty feet, ninety knots airspeed. The other two wing ships are in trail formation, one behind the other. On the first pass over the LZ, Mitchell saw what looked like an above ground gravesite. A bamboo flagpole had been erected in the center of the grave. And on top of the pole, hanging as limp as a dead dog's dick in the still midday air, was that flag. The Taipan's bank over the top of the pile of mud and stone, sure enough it is a gravesite. After some deliberation between the crew and pilots over the intercom they determine the flag is that of the North Vietnamese Army. It had a big yellow star in the center, and divided in half, with the upper half red and the lower half blue, yes it had to be.

Unmistakably the finest souvenir any aircrew could ever hope for. Such a flag flying in South Viet Nam is almost unheard of, hardcore NVA are rare in these parts. Regimented Army's do not march in the open rice paddies, behind enemy lines. Mostly the allied forces engage the Guerrillas and sympathizers, or Viet Cong. The Cong can move about freely as they look and dress like the civilian population. Yet here is proof that the NVA exists in the Delta region.

"He must have been an NVA officer", the pilot says increasing its desirability. He surmised that only an officer would have been buried above ground and have his country's flag staffed on his grave.

"We can't just let that go without making some attempt to get it", the pilot teases.

Some deliberation occurs between the two pilots as to how to best approach the intended landing in the LZ and to keep the aircraft and crew reasonably safe.

The two wing ships will provide cover to the chopper on the ground. A weighted down helicopter, in high heat needs a lot of room to get back into the air, the pilots choose the intended landing direction.

"We should have plenty of room to clear the tree line ahead of us", the pilot is certain.

Then it was decided that someone other than a pilot should make the retrieval.

"Any volunteers to snatch that flag back there", the pilot asks?

No one could ever top this souvenir, why everyone on the base would come to see it, maybe offer lots of money for it.

"I'll get it sir", the words just seemed to slip from Mitchell's lips.

"OK, chief it's yours", "I will circle around again before going in", he says.

"It could be a booby trap, so be careful" the pilot commented.

Why in hell didn't he say that before I agreed to get it, Mitchell thought?

They continue to circle and survey the LZ, while giving more thought to the illegal task that they are about to undertake. Endangering the ship and crew would be wholly frowned upon by the higher ups and disciplinary action would be administered for sure.

"Maybe we should shoot up the area first", Mitchell commented

"No don't do that, it could blow up taking the flag with it", the co-pilot spoke out.

"Could be that grave is one big bomb just waiting for some idiots like us to grab a souvenir", the gunner says, while grinning at Mitchell.

Mitchell really thought the pilot would change his mind once he realizes just how dangerous this stunt is. Then they'll go about their job, then leave, and Artie will blow this area off the map, taking the flag with it, Right?

Wrong, the pilot begins his approach into the open field to land a safe distance from the grave, just in case the crew chief trigger's an explosion.

"We wouldn't want to damage the aircraft".

"If I trigger an explosion", Is he kidding, Mitchell was beginning to get worried?

As they fly over one of the rows of tall trees that border all four sides of the open area, the pilot announced,

"Artie (artillery) just informed me they will begin prepping the LZ in twelve minutes, so make it quick Chief".

Great, just what he needed was more pressure.

As the aircraft flares back to slow for the intended landing, the Gunner is heard to say,

"Any last wishes before you blow yourself up Collins"

"Here", Mitchell said handing the gunner his Instamatic camera, "Take pictures".

"Roger that", he responded as he reached for the small square instrument that might capture the images of glory, or doom!

They touched down on the hardened gray parched earth. The helicopters gusty rotor wash picked up bits of dried grasses and sand. In the fierce swirling draft, a foreign particle found its way into Mitchell's left eyeball. Unplugging his intercom cord, he decided to wear the helmet on this mission. Slowly he walked over to the mound half observing each careful step to where the supposed NVA officer was buried. Observing the scene with a skeptical eye, Mitchell found the telltale signs of an impending disaster.

There are fine wires crossing over the top of the grave. The top of the grave is flat, with sloping sides. At a standing height of about twenty inches the grave mound has been neatly assembled. The wires do not traverse down the sloped side, but rather are stretched tight outwards from the top edge a couple of feet and disappear into the ground. A gap in the wire is left between the sloped side and the point where the wire enters the dirt. Not much effort has gone into disguising the trap. He looked back at the waiting crew in the chopper who in turn is looking at him to hurry. With a quick rub to the afflicted eye, and a deep breath he knelt down on the ground at the foot of the grave to change the perspective of the site.

Yes, I think there's just is enough room to crawl down the side, he surmised. This is the only way to do it, I am already this far, might just as well go for it. Shit, I wish I could see a little better, Mitchell almost convinced himself.

Crawling to where the bamboo pole was inserted into the center of the packed dirt and rock mound wouldn't be all that hard. He just couldn't touch those fucking wires. He wondered briefly how many explosives there could be all around him. What fucking difference would it make, either way I'd be blown to bits, forget about it already, and just do it, he now saw this as his personal mission!

Rolling over on his back, the bright sun nearly blinded the good right eye. He got his helmet under the first wire and began to tediously inch his way forward. A small pool of sweat puddles in each of the eye sockets. Mitchell's heart rate began to climb, so far so good. Inch by inch he wormed his way towards the prize.

Reaching the point adjacent to the pole, he noticed there were no wires attached to it. Mitchell reached up to grab the base of the bamboo pole. Have to be careful nothing snags a wire, got it! He gave it a tug upward and it came free easier than anticipated. But what do I do with it now, Mitchell wondered, the pole was eight feet high. After a few seconds thought, he slid the pole at a steep angle down along side of his body until it was all under the wire with him. Mitchell began to slither his way back out with the captured prize. Having cleared all the wires, he stood up, turned and ran for the waiting chopper. The whole crew was waving frantically for him to hurry. It was then, when Mitchell remembered the imminent artillery barrage, how long did I take?

The pole was too long to fit in, so he ripped the flag off the end and discarded the pole. Climbing aboard he plugged the helmet com-cord in but hadn't yet fastened the seatbelt and the pilot pulled in the collective to get them airborne.

The chopper nosed over sharply to get the airspeed up, but the impact of the first artillery shell exploding directly off their nose stopped their forward movement. Bringing the stick back to slow the aircraft the pilot snapped his head left, then right, in effort to quickly determine an alternative escape route.

They were still watching the rising earth form a huge cone shaped torrent of dirt through the windscreen when the second eruption occurred only seconds later and was even closer. The falling debris from the first explosion began to filter through the rotor blades.

"Their walking the rounds towards us", shouted the co-pilot

With the rotor speed R.P.M.'s bleeding off, while trying to maintain the hover, the pilot kicks the right rotor pedal to swing the tail over to the right. Abruptly they turn, still just a couple of feet off the ground. And again they nosed over to get the badly needed airspeed. As they complete a left ninety-degree turn they are faced with a tree line so close there was no hope of getting enough speed or lift to clear the trees.

"Go left, go left", shouted the co-pilot.

A couple more explosions and another left turn, all eyes are glued to the far tree line that they had flown over to land. Maybe, just maybe we got enough clearing to get us flying, Mitchell prayed, that is if we aren't blown to pieces first. It's a total barrage now, God help us all if we don't make it this way out. Come on air, more air, we need air, fuck the ground I'll never step foot on the ground again if you just give us some air, Mitchell prayed mutely.

Slowly climbing out of the LZ, Mitchell could feel the shock wave of the artillery exploding behind them as they struggled to clear the tree tops. He turned to see out to the rear and witnessed the whole LZ erupting in what is now a total barrage of exploding 155mm artillery rounds. Just a few seconds longer getting out and they would not have escaped the demolition.

This is sure one elated crew as they join up with the two wing ships who have moved away to avoid the artillery. The pilot, who flew them in, and out of harm's way, turns the controls over to the co-pilot for a well-deserved break.

A celebratory photo session with the flag ensues. Taking his turn with the flag Mitchell placed the flags bottom edge between his legs and held the top corners in order to prevent the wind in the cabin from whipping the flag. He smiled proudly as the gunner snapped his picture. The pilot turned to witness the difficulty of their photography session and offered his assistance.

"Hand me up the flag and I'll hold it against the windscreen, then you can take the picture from back there". That was the last time Mitchell saw his flag.

"You know chief I am going home soon and I will never have a chance like this again" he started.

"You, on the other hand, have plenty of time to get another one"

Mitchell thought he saw the co-pilot chuckle.

"How about you let me have this one, OK"?

Well what could he do, after all he is an officer, and Mitch is just an enlisted man.

A few nights later and still brooding over his flag, Mitchell went to watch a movie that was being shown at their new outdoor movie theater. Actually it was just some four by eight sheets of plywood, painted white to make up the screen. The seats were laid down three-foot long tree logs. Their projector was a noisy antiquated reel to reel twenty-millimeter machine, but it worked. It's only been three weeks since acquiring the projectors new bulb that took four months to get. So in celebration of the repaired machine a new screen was built just a hundred yards or so from the barracks.

Mitchell has missed the few pictures shown previously as his time at the company EM Club precluded any other recreation, however tonight was different. It's the end of the month and the cash reserves have dwindled down to zilch.

"What's playing tonight", Mitchell asked the projector operator, who is a bearded Aussie mechanic.

"Well mate, it's about some of your American criminals", "Ave a seat n-we'll get started".

Mitchell sat on a log with two others, looking around he noticed the fifteen or so other soldiers whom he did not know waiting for the movie to begin.

The loud clicking of the film passing through the machine announces the show is about to start. The flickering numbers appear, 4, 3, 2, then the names of Warren Beatty and Faye Dunaway appear as Bonnie and Clyde. This could be good, Mitchell thought, he had read a preview in the Star's-N-Stripes paper that this was supposed to be one of the hottest movies last year.

Although the film is set in the 1930's, still, the background scenery is that of home. The soldiers recognized that America in the thirty's was even more developed than Vietnam is now. The movie continues as the small gathering of GIs make comments periodically about the violence, or makes sexual innuendos directed at Bonnie.

The robbers have made an escape from a farmhouse they were holed up in. When the police and deputies came to arrest the gang, a fierce gun battle ensued. Now the chase is on, it looks like curtains for the Borrow Gang, when suddenly the bulb burnt out, again!

The moans and groans got the Aussie to open the projector, only to announce that the bulb had indeed burned out.

"Didn't you get more than one damn bulb" asked an irate soldier.

"Look mate, I was lucky to find this one, might get some sleep, nothing I can do ere". The Aussie said as he pulled the plug.

Begrudgingly the soldiers slowly got up to return to the barracks. It was late and the EM Club was closed for the night, so with nowhere else to go, Mitchell too headed back.

The barracks was dark, Mitchell laid down on his bunk, then switched on the reading light. With paper and pen in hand, his letter began, "Dear Mom", and he asked the usual questions regarding all back home, "how's so and so", "hope all is well". Having got the gratuitous stuff out of the way, he tried to write some pleasant stuff about himself, you know the kind of shit you say when you can't really tell the truth. Mitchell knew she wanted to know how he was, but how was he? She needed to know what he did, but you can't blame him for not describing to her his daily routine. So what's left huh, just shit, it was a very short letter.

It is not unusual for the artillery on the base perimeter, and just a short distance from the barracks, to begin firing without warning at any hour of the day or night. Nearly every night they would fire out into the surrounding countryside. At night, Mitchell would lay on bed listening to the loud boom and wait for the faint report of the landing shell as it exploded. He tried to imagine the shell's trajectory through the air and mentally guessing the distance of impact from their base by the time elapsed. Sometimes he would wonder if there were anyone at the receiving end of the exploding shell, and just what happened to them. He could envision the eruption of dirt and foliage created by the explosion commingled with the bodies of their enemies being sent into the air. This was a nightly past time, and usually Mitchell dozed off in these thoughts.

The tremendously loud explosion that was preceded by a resounding whooshing sound overhead and the bright flash of white light shattered the reasonable quiet of this night.

"INCOMING", someone yelled at the top of their lungs.

The sound was distinctly different than that of the outgoing artillery, almost like the tremendous crack of lightning when it strikes next to you so close you felt the heat of the burnt air.

"All right people let's get in the bunkers", "Move it, Move it", the platoon Sergeant shouted as he ran through the barracks, while heading out the door. No one else moved, for the rats nesting in the bunker were far more fearful than the incoming rockets.

Turning over on his stomach, Mitchell grabbed his pillow tightly over his head and tried to get some sleep. They all knew that if another rocket came, and it had their name on it, it did not matter where you were. When the big General in the sky comes calling for you to stand at attention, he will find you no matter where you are. The single rocket attack was just another harassment action by Charlie to create despair among the troops. But it served only to piss the soldiers off even more, and tomorrow they would extract their revenge. Mitchell Collins fell asleep thinking about the little Sergeant alone in the dark bunker, steel pot on his head, flak vest around his torso, and being eaten alive by the swarm of rodents. No way would he ever go into that bunker.

Since the flight crews keep a different schedule than the rest of the company, they are always the last to get information about the goings on in the rear. So it wasn't until the end of the following day that Mitchell had discovered that the rocket that hit last night, landed only a few feet in front of the movie screen.

Observing the blown away pieces of the movie screen, it is quite apparent that all sitting there would have been killed or horribly wounded.

"It was a Chinese one-two-two rocket, probably fired from the tree line just north of the perimeter", a soldier cleaning up the mess stated.

"Looks like the bulb burned out just in time", he continued.

"What time did it hit", Mitchell asked?

"It's been recorded at nine forty five".

"How long was the movie", Mitchell was asking as though he wasn't there.

"Well it started at eight, and was a hundred and eleven minutes runtime"

"It should've ended at nine fifty two, give or take a couple of minutes".

"The movie had seven more minutes to run after the blast, would have got everyone who stayed to see the end", the soldier concluded.

Meanwhile Mitchell concluded that they would have met their maker before Bonnie and Clyde got to meet theirs.

Mitchell stood disbelieving the number of holes in the movie screen. It had been peppered from top to bottom and side to side. Most of the log movie seats had been displaced and were tore up pretty bad, and bits of wood were strewn all about. A small crater in front of the screen indicated where the rocket impacted, almost dead center of the screen.

Just a lucky shot, hardly, Mitchell thought! Someone had paced off the distance for Charlie. But how would they have known about the movie times. Mitchell could only wonder.

That bulb burning out again for no apparent reason, yes sir, that's what they call divine intervention in the church of combat.

Captured NVA (North Vietnamese Army) flag from a grave of an enemy officer: A highly illegal maneuver to snatch this flag in the Landing Zone of the next combat assault. A prized possession, this flag belonged to an Officer in the NVA, which was rare in the Delta.

Chapter Eight

Experiencing Vietnamization

After every two hundred fifty hours of flying time, the helicopter went into a periodic maintenance inspection. A type of thorough inspection that grounds the aircraft for at least two or three days, depending on how many replacement parts are needed and their availability. All the major components are looked at, the turbine engine, transmission, ninety-degree and forty-five degree tail rotor gearboxes, plus main and tail rotors. In truth this is the most important aspect of keeping the helicopters flying. Combat deaths caused by mechanical failure are rare given the number of hours flown. In the 135th, the Aussie's in charge of helicopter maintenance are very meticulous in their operations. The maintenance section knows that the flight crews are flying into extremely hostile territory and that the machine's reliability is paramount for their survival. Everyday maintenance has to deal with damage due to hard landings, tail rotors dipped into the mud from flaring to hard, component failure, and bullet holes that tear up everything in its path.

On one past mission when the flight went into a hot LZ, and was ambushed, every craft had been hit. Some were torn up bad, the repair crews often worked through the night so that all the ships would be mission ready the next day. These operations included engine replacement, main rotor replacement, hydraulic and avionics replaced. Any component could be exchanged or repaired. It was only when there was extensive damage to the airframe that the chopper was scrapped or sent stateside to Bell Helicopter repair facilities in Texas, for a major rebuild only to return months later for more combat. Given the intricacies of the mechanics of a helicopter with its numerous components and systems, Mitchell had to say that he is impressed with the reliability of the Huey and the people who maintain them.

Crews are assigned to the helicopters, the crew-chief's own the aircraft. It is signed for by the crew-chief, and care for the aircraft becomes his responsibility. Down time is rest time, when the bird can't fly, neither does the crew, unless of course they are temporally assigned to another aircraft. To prevent himself from becoming too well known by the rear echelon personnel or the duty officers, Mitchell would volunteer to fly anybody's aircraft, as a crew-chief or gunner, in a slick or a gunship. It didn't happen very often but this way he would avoid those who were always looking for someone available for work details, a/k/a shit duty.

Besides evading laborious work in the heat of the day, it was a good idea for Mitchell who never flew slicks prior to becoming a gunship crewman, to experience the flight habits of the slick aircrew and to get a slick perspective of the mission. It also brought closeness with the slickies that encouraged the protective nature of the gun platoon. Of course there was always the normal animosity between the Taipan's and the EMU's, but not like it was with the folks in the rear, those non-combatant types.

It was somewhat unnerving for him to be on the ground in the LZ, even if only for a few seconds while the troops loaded or unloaded. A helicopter is a large target. The feeling of being vulnerable to sniper fire as well as RPG's attack was not unfounded. Many a slick crewmember fell victim to an enemy in the tree line at the edge of the rice paddy or hidden in the tall grass during the wet season. A well-camouflaged VC could remain undetected in the LZ if he did not shoot at the gunships looking for him prior to the slicks arrival. But once he made his position known, all were relentless in their pursuit to destroy him.

On the approach for landing into the LZ orders from C&C, who had conferred with his Vietnamese counterpart, as to how volatile the LZ is passed on to the flight crews through the AC's (aircraft commanders), then to the back seat crews. A "cold LZ" meant that the landing zone was deemed not to have the enemy present. On the other hand a "hot LZ" meant that there was the possibility "Charlie" was lurking somewhere close. The order was either to go into the LZ under no suppression, or full suppression. All guns fired if full suppression was ordered. Under the rules of engagement, anything in the LZ was fair game, I repeat, anything!

The slick's machine guns were mounted on a ridged post that was affixed to the airframe, and were somewhat restrictive compared to what Mitch was used to. Mitch could fire up about forty degrees and down ninety, and side-to-side almost a hundred eighty degrees, however shooting between the skids and under the tail-boom was not possible. But none of that mattered on his first full suppression into the LZ.

With nine choppers ahead of them, and the two other behind, they prepare to enter the LZ. The flight pattern is approximately forty-five degrees to the clearing. The EMU's tighten up the in-line, or trailing formation while bobbing up and down and weaving slightly, but he still found it remarkable how close they could fly without chopping each other up. All the slicks continue to descend into the LZ. On the final turn and at one hundred feet the order to begin full suppression is given.

The ARVN troops sitting on the floor at the opened cargo doors also began to fire their M-16's, popping sporadic rounds at the tree line. With the last fifty feet of altitude Mitch began shooting at the only hooch in the LZ. A good place for Charlie to hide so he kept the fire up. The troops sitting close to him at the door noticed his tracer's path and began to share the target. As the helicopter neared the ground they are abreast of the hooch door. A bamboo door made of poles all tied together, was closed. They knew that most hooch's had built into the structure, a bunker made of alternating mud and logs. If people were inside their bullets could never penetrate the bunker, but neither could they come out and fire at them, hence the suppression.

A few more tracers pierced the now splintered bamboo door, when suddenly a Vietnamese potbellied pig came bursting out the opening. His legs moving faster than his bulk would go. First it ran directly towards the landing helicopters, then must have realized where they were and quickly turned away. Mitch decided it could be a VC pig and fired at it. He missed the little porker, and the VC meal turned to run away along the side of the hooch. He kept firing and a tracer hit it in the right buttock, the bullets passed through its body and blew the right fore leg off. The porker kept up a three-legged run and disappeared. Yea, a VC pig for sure.

The first insertion goes smoothly after that. The slick flight headed back to pick up the second load of ARVN's for insertion and to join their counterparts on the ground. Hopefully those in the LZ now will make contact with the real enemy, before they return. At least they'll know what to expect returning to the LZ. Mitchell hated surprises.

He could just imagine himself crashing, just before going into the LZ, Charlie has the perimeter sealed, and the ground troops are pinned down in the open paddy. Would he survive the impact only to be captured and tortured to death? It is widely known that any flight crew member has an open bounty on his head, Charlie can make a year's pay with proof of an American kill. That last two hundred feet going in, landing or hovering, and going out of the LZ, made him very nervous. Taipans flew low but at least we were always moving, and moving targets were harder to hit.

Mitchell's ship was on the ground now and the Taipan's buzzed overhead and begins to fire rockets into the tree line on both sides of the flight. He quickly looked out to the rear and saw a Taipan diving onto the tree-line spitting rockets and machine gun fire. From his ground level perspective, the helicopter gunship firepower must be an awesome fright to the enemy. He continued his suppressive fire at the base of the trees. But for Mitch it is a welcome sight to see the effectiveness of the rockets in a heavy tree line. The sight of all that armament unleashed, just to keep "Charlie's" head down!

"Yea boys, go get-em", he uttered wishing now he were up there too.

The slick lifted to a hover then nosed over for airspeed, but then Mitch noticed something wrong, one of the ARVN troops has not exited. AnotherThe crew-chief has already warned Mitch that the ARVN's sometimes did not want to get out, but that none could go back to the PZ.

"Shove'em out if you have to" the chief had said.

The helicopter lifts even more, five feet high now. Mitchell cursed under his breath, that chicken shit lazy bastard does not want to get out. He knows he can't go back to the PZ with us. The ARVN just sat there with a death grip on the troop seat support, looking down as they gained more altitude. Twenty feet now, so with a swift boot to his backside, Mitchell propels him outwards into the tall grass before they got any higher. He had to kick him hard enough to cause him to release his grip on that pole. The airborne soldier emitted a high pitched blood-curdling scream as he fell away from the aircraft. Mitchell looked out to see him land into the tall grass and disappear, he should have been ok, probably just scared the crap outta him. Then Mitchell thought what would cause him to scream out like that, maybe he was afraid of heights. He sat back pondering the ARVN's outburst.

Mitchell soon noticed something on the pole at the edge of the troop seat closest to the door opening, where the ARVN had hung on to, afraid to leap. There, it appeared to have his shriveled up and dismembered pinkie finger stuck to the troop seat support by a ring pull attached to a pin that holds the troop seats together. He probably got his finger stuck in the small metal ring and could not undo his finger, so that's why he did not jump when he was supposed to. Why didn't the stupid bastard say something, shit that had to hurt? With a look of disgust, Mitchell pulled the mutilated appendage free with his gloved hand and quickly tossed it out.

Vietnamization was the term given to allow the South Vietnam government to fight for their own country without benefit of allied forces. These insertions are part of that plan. U.S. troop reduction is already underway, but for those who stay the war gets more intense.

This conflict has become very unpopular back home, and there is increasing demand to bring an end to the war. Of course they all wanted that too, but once you become acclimated to the situation, you begin to feel a sense of pride in your job, and wish to see it through. Mitch never really thought he was fighting for "Vietnam", or for the "American way of life", but rather for the preservation of his American and Allied troops. As long as Americans had to be there, he wanted to be there to be a part of all their survival.

Problem was, the ARVN forces did not seem to be very dedicated to the preservation of their form of government. The ARVN's are young, like Mitchell, and by virtue of having reached the age of nineteen, they must serve into their armed forces. Their background is simple and most come from small hamlets and villages that dot the countryside. The GI's tried to understand that the ARVN soldiers that have just been inserted into the LZ, have lived with war of some kind or another, for all of their lives. It is reasonable to suppose there is a kind of complacency towards war if you grew up with it from birth. To be totally honest about things, the general attitude of the American soldier is they all had a little more respect for the North Vietnamese as fighting soldiers.

The NVA were a different breed of fighter. Recruited at the age of sixteen into the Ho Chi Minh Communist Youth League, he is born into poverty and raised in his village that was his whole world. He likely was one of five children raised by and through an extended family that included several generations of his immediate family as well as collateral relatives. He would have resented outsiders and even his own people if they had come from the city. Having been drafted at the age of twenty into the Army, or PAVN, (People's Army of Vietnam), he never had more than a fifth grade education. His limited schooling made it difficult for him to cope with his life in the MilitaryArmy since he had so little knowledge of technical things in the modern world. He has never learned of the outside world beyond his village not even other parts of Vietnam. His family and religion has impressed upon him the importance of collective strength and he would never question that or any order given to him by a superior officer. Non-materialistic, he got along easily on the bare essentials and regarded simplicity as a great virtue, a fortunate coincidence since he received little reward for his service, with a month's pay he could afford about a dozen bottles of beer.

His trust in the PAVN lead him to believe that he would be treated fairly while in service and that in the event of his death his family would receive compensation. Although not politically conscious, much of what he knew of politics consisted of slogans he was obligated to learn even though he could only dimly comprehend their meaning.

Having been given limited military training, he was survival orientated, tough, disciplined combat fighter, who persevered with stubborn determination, and more often than not against hopeless odds. This young soldier could be stubbornly hostile even rebellious without regard to consequences. He knew little about military strategy or tactics, but believed that warfare consisted largely of careful planning, meticulous preparation, and then sustained and intensive mass attack. Illiterate and driven, he was to be feared, and respected.

In the lower half of the country there are the southern Army personnel who did little to encourage, or motivate the U.S. troops to assist them in their way of life. The ARVN certainly had a resource advantage and really only lacked the will or the drive to win. To the American fighting man it was all too obvious that the ARVN was not the disciplined soldier that they were. Their leadership lacked any kind of fortitude and was corrupt beyond belief. Their deficiency in education along with the arrogance of dictator military leaders usually spelled disaster for the ARVN soldier in battles. Sure there were those officers who had been educated, more likely to have come from one of the larger cities. Some had even attended school in the U.S., and became officers who drove hard their peasant subordinates. Unfortunately there just was not enough of them.

Most wondered, what was Tricky Dick, (then president, Richard M. Nixon), was thinking when he thought these guys had a snowballs chance in hell to combat the communist aggression coming their way. It was a good laugh for all believing the ARVN was going to win the war for themselves. For now, the American troops were in "survival mode". They won't be allowed to win the war, and the "Police action", will be soon over, so might as well live to fight another day.

The slick crews had to be especially watchful when transporting ARVN troops. On occasion an ARVN would leave part of his battle gear behind in the chopper to avoid having to carry the extra weight around while on mission in the LZ.

A couple of weeks ago an ARVN left a claymore mine under the troop seat in a helicopter belonging to another Assault Helicopter Company. He found it on the mission later that day and decided to take it back to his barracks. A claymore is an anti-personnel mine with a large explosive device and a hand held detonator, or "clacker", when the clacker is squeezed, an electric charge is transmitted to the explosive via a wire.

Back at the barracks the crew-chief inserts the detonators trigger wire into the claymore. A fellow bunkmate happens to walk by and notice the new found play toy and inquiries about it. They both sit on the bunk presumably trying to figure out what to do with it. The bunkmate hands the deadly device back to the crew-chief who takes the explosive in one hand and the clacker in the other. In an instant of forgetfulness the clacker is squeezed and an explosion results, killing the crew-chief and several other unsuspecting bunkmates in the barracks. With so many ways to die, just living becomes quite a challenge.

A call comes from C&C to medivac wounded from the LZ where they have put the troops in this morning. Seems the ARVN's have encountered the enemy and have taken casualties. Only one slick ship is needed for this sortie and they are it. In minutes Mitchell's chopper is airborne and in route to the LZ.

There won't be any gun cover on this mission, the ARVN's have suppressed the enemy when they made contact and have three of their wounded to evacuate to show for their action.

On arrival to the LZ a violet smoke is popped to indicate where they are to land. The pilot makes a rapid decent to the smoke and touchdown in tall grass. But now there seems to be some sort of delay getting the wounded on board. Apparently no one on the ground wants to carry the wounded through the tall grass the sixty feet or so to the helicopter. The time on the ground has become critical and the pilot has ordered the gunner to go and assist in bringing the wounded to the helicopter, "so we can get the hell out of here", the pilot snapped.

Mitchell stayed aboard to man the machinegun, just in case. The gunner unplugged his helmet com-cord and swings the boom microphone out and away from his lips. Then he jumps down to the ground and ran straight out towards the wounded lying unseen in the high grass.

While four of the ARVN's finally picked up two of the wounded, the gunner has reached down to pick up the other. The gunner is carrying his wounded man cradled in his arms. As they drew nearer, the gunner has made several gestures by bending over forward so far his human cargo nearly fell out of his arms. The wounded man's head is resting on the left shoulder of the gunner, but his head did not move when the gunner leaned forward. Mitchell helped the other two wounded onto the floor of the chopper, noticing that neither has been shot, but suffer from shrapnel wounds. Although not seriously wounded, they are bleeding and appear to be in some pain. Mitchell looked up to see the gunner with his injured man still cradled in his arms like a baby.

When the gunner was at the cargo door Mitchell could see that the wounded man the gunner is carrying was shot in the right eye. With a large portion of his right side of the face blown away, a deep gaping hole was left. When the gunner picked up the ailing soldier, he lifted him high on his chest. When the soldiers head flopped over towards the gunners left shoulder, the gunners microphone which had been turned out away from his mouth, went into the wound in the right eye of the injured, and had gotten stuck deep into the man's face. Unable to detach the microphone from the hole in the soldier's head, he tried leaning forward while carrying him to the chopper. The gunner waited for Mitchell to take the soldier into the helicopter. Mitchell could swear he heard a slurping sound when they finally freed the gunner's microphone from the bloodied face. The two of them gently laid the last of the wounded on the cargo floor, and hurried to their seats.

Once inside the pilots lifted off before they were buckled in their seats.

Mitchell was in his seat and plugged in his com-cord first, then buckled up. The gunner was shifting the wounded around to allow him room to get back to his seat. Mitch heard the pilots talking to each other saying that they were not happy about the time it took to get the wounded aboard and would ask the gunner something about it.

Then the Gunner was finally back in his seat he buckled up and then plugged in his helmet com-cord. At that same moment, the pilot turned to look back at the Gunner and sternly asked, "What the fuck took you so long", he shouted.

The gunner nervously swung his microphone back to his lips to reply to the demanding officer and then suddenly realized just where that microphone touching his lip had just been. A look of total disgust came over the gunner as he wiped his mouth of the bloody wet goo, and the pilots broke into roaring laughter. Evidently the pilots saw what was happening and planned the event to stir up the gunner. Mitchell had to admit that the gunner fell right into that one. Mitchell looked away trying not to laugh. He was glad to see the slickies had a sense of humor.

Heading to a field hospital, one of the wounded by shrapnel and sitting closest to Mitchell, looked at him with tears in his eyes and mumbled something in Vietnamese. Not understanding what exactly what it was he was trying to say, because of all the ambient noise and the fact that the only Vietnamese Mitchell spoke was a few cuss words and such. He surmised that the wounded ARVN was asking if he was going to die. Mitchell always tried to stay detached from any kind of emotion regarding the missions, but it seemed safe to give the injured boy soldier a reassuring pat on the head with a smile and a quick nod in the universal language to the affirmative.

Looking around the floor of the chopper, where two of the wounded were sitting, and the other motionless and sprawled out flat on his back with half his face shot away. Mitchell wondered about the experience of Vietnamization and how long these little guys would last if left to their own accord. And who was going to fly all the helicopters needed to lift out the dead and wounded.

Arriving at the field hospital minutes later the partial faced ARVN died, or was dead when they got him in the chopper. The other two were delivered alive. A medical corpsman and five assistants, with wheeled gurneys met them on arrival at the field hospitals heli-pad and carted off the dead and wounded. Mission completed, they head back to the A.O.

After a day of flying slicks with the EMU platoon, dealing with the war up close and personal, a new revelation comes to light. You needn't be a fortuneteller to know that the Armed Forces of Viet Nam, solely assuming responsibility over their country's protection or "Vietnamization", simply is not going to work, at least not from a combat point of view. The soldiers in the north were much more determined towards their ultimate goal. How else could they face such insurmountable odds behind enemy lines and continue a war for years with so little resources.

The North's fighting style is "Guerrilla warfare", and here in the South we are fighting a "Conventional warfare". Our resources seem unending, munitions, transportation, intelligence, food, even entertainment. But our enemy has but his will and determination. It appeared to Mitch it is despairing for him to continue, but then he realized that the ARVN has already been fighting for a lot longer than the one year he will have in country. And what of the NVA, from the looks of things he can't win unless the American's all go home. But for sure when they are gone the North will come in and take over. It will be only a matter of time.

Mitchell could only hope that he is long gone before that end comes.

The hazards of flying night time Hunter / Killer missions…tree's!

Chapter Nine

Birds of Prey

A young crew-chief unbuckled his seat belt, and without any word to the others in the flight crew, he leaned forward out of his seat, away from the door opening and into a two- thousand foot swan dive into the terra firma below.

On the day before he received a "Dear John" letter. You know, one of those heart crushing letters that inform you that your loved one back home has dumped you. Either for someone else, or maybe just because she believed you were never coming back, or perhaps she became a hippie anti-war protester, and now thinks you are a baby killer. Whatever the reason, the result is painful. But doing yourself in hardly seemed like an appropriate response. The way Mitchell saw it, why help the Viet Cong who are trying to eliminate you, by eliminating yourself.

There are so few connections to the home left behind. Every object becomes very important, like the letters from home, your photographs, and your civilian clothes that hang in your locker. To lose any one, is to lose a piece of your real life. It's all there is to connect you to reality, and to the real world.

Mitchell wondered what his girlfriend was doing back home. But what difference would it make anyway, he was in Vietnam, and she is eight thousand miles away in the real world. He tried hard not to think of those things he has no control over. Maybe Mitchell thought, he should write another letter today though, just in case.

It is now July 2nd, in two days he will be nineteen years old. A big parcel came today for him at mail call, his mother has sent a "care package", a cardboard box, filled with popcorn to protect the contents inside. A birthday card, some chocolate candy bars, a cup cake with a candle, and plastic toy soldiers to give to the Vietnamese kids. The candy bars had melted and looked like brown soup, the cupcake was hard as a rock, and the popcorn was stale, but edible. Holding a heat warped wax candle, Mitchell thought, Happy fucking Birthday to me. But he did appreciate the gesture.

Mitchell discarded the toy soldiers into the latrines cut steel drums to be burned away with the rest of the crap. To offer them to the young kids here, create "little beggars", does more harm than good. The military has educated the troops on the results of being generous to Vietnam's young. Even made the comparison of the soldiers of previous world wars who generously gave candy and such to civilians, but they were assured this situation was different. He saw no reason to doubt their declaration, therefore he disassociated himself from the Vietnamese kids, with the one exception. That little girl in Can Tho, for whom he still brought cold fresh apples in exchange for the removal of a gray hair or two!

Now, on his actual birth date, Mitchell was not allowed to fly. It is some kind of military regulation. He guessed the military in there infinite wisdom figured that it would be quite difficult to tell a soldier parents back home that their son or daughter was killed on his or her birthday. So at least he has a real day off. It felt a little odd that this was not only his birthday, July the fourth, but also a national holiday back home as well, yet there will be no celebration today. Funny thing that with all the real hardcore fireworks he has seen lately, what the hell would he do anyway, light firecrackers? For the first time in his life he preferred not to hear any loud noises on this day.

Having found two other Taipan's to share his day off, it is decided to go on a visit to the USO in Saigon. It had taken several hours to get there and Mitchell was anxious to begin his celebration. While the three of them were walking down the street towards the USO, they witnessed five children mug an Army officer. The snot nosed, dirty little criminals ranged in age from about eight to maybe twelve years of age. The attack came as the Officer was walking on the opposite side of the street from them, and facing towards the three. As they came abreast of each other they saw the Major who had crossed an alleyway that connected to the street.

First, two of the younger Dink brats approached the officer to beg for money. The Major who was probably in his late twenty's declined. The beggars continued, meanwhile three of the others joined the first team. They began by pulling and tugging at his arm all screaming "G.I. money plez, G.I. money plez". The tall thin Major, dressed in a short sleeved Khaki uniform, neatly pressed, with spit shined shoes, and gold oak leaf clusters pinned to his collar attempted to walk away.

By now two of the kids were clinging with arms and legs wrapped tightly around each of his two legs, while one of the older ones tried to remove his watch. The Major made a flimsy attempt to push off his attackers. Those hanging on to his legs were now reaching into the back pocket to remove his wallet. The Major did not have enough hands to keep all those little hands at bay. Soon they had him face down, on the sidewalk. Three jumped on top of the Major before he could roll over. Hands and arms were flailing everywhere in what could only be described as a well-coordinated attack.

The Major never called out for assistance and succumbed to his attackers. Mitchell and his buddies stood in awe at the spectacle, knowing that their assistance would have resulted in the death of one or more of the muggers. He realized too that they, the muggers, did not attempt to molest any other G.I.'s on the street.

Like the hungry Lion in the jungle, in search of weak prey, those young muggers knew the Major was new in country, and to Saigon, and sensed little resistance to their attack. In reality, Mitchell thought he was apprehensive to hurt the tiny criminals. They retreated to the alley from which they sprang their deed. Meanwhile Mitchell and the others scoffed at the Major for his lack of aggression, and allowing the little VC victory in that skirmish. They walked on, laughing and talking of how they would have handled the situation, by smashing in their little faces and worse.

Of having walked in, and out of the USO, because the round-eyed women they were promised that would be attending the coffee and donuts were in fact slant eyed Vietnamese. Again Mitchell found himself in a Saigon bar, with his new acquaintances and guzzling down Beer 33, the best of the local brew.

Close acquaintances are like friends except that they are brought together by circumstance rather than personal cognizance. They are none the less important at the time, but somehow you know the relationship is short term. When all you have for family is your short time buddy's, you tend to treat them like close friends. They drank until they all felt the closeness of their new relationships. And in those few hours, there in that foreign drinking establishment, Mitchell found the warmth of security in knowing that it was all for one, and one for all.

There was no warning for the fight that broke out. Even if there was, Mitchell was already too drunk to see it coming. A hurling body collapses against the back of his chair causing him to fall forward unto the table, that in turned scooted several feet across the floor. The chair slid away and he ended up on the dirty tile floor. Mitchell rolled over to see the white uniforms of several Navy personnel punching it out with the olive drab uniforms of the Army soldiers.

An instinctive reaction to protect his friends overwhelmed him as he jumped to his feet and then to leap atop one of the Swabbies. Locking his head under his left arm in a half nelson hold, Mitchell punched his face with the right fist. Then a crushing blow to the back of Mitchell's neck that caused him nearly to black out. The Swab got away as he went to the floor again. Mitchell's legs sort of just gave out and ended up sitting motionless on the dirty and beer soaked tile.

With the noise lessening and the blurring beginning to subside, he could make out four really huge guys in Army uniform pushing the remaining troops away from the center of the action. They were wearing the maroon colored berets of the Special Forces. Undoubtedly they were the badest dudes on the block, and just as quickly as the fight started, it was over.

One of the Special Forces guy's shouted, "we should be fighting the Dinks, not each other", and with that one enormous statement they all shook hands and went back to their serious drinking. With a throbbing pain in the neck Mitchell raised his glass to a blubbering toast, "Here's to Independence Day, and happy fucking birthday to me"!

The following day Mitchell was back in the sky. The morning air was unusually cool, almost chilly, as they flew south to a new Area of Operation. The sun had just peaked over the horizon, and a light low lying mist covered the ground. The palm trees below and dark green vegetation faintly peering through a purple, pink haze that had an almost surreal appearance. Mitchell looked out over past the gunner to his left to see Taipan Two Five, and One Four in formation. Some days flying was just too beautiful to be involved in a war.

It was a longer than usual flight to the first refuel point at Vinh Long, most days the flight refueled at My Tho, twenty-seven miles or so to the northeast. Today they are working an area unofficially called Snoopy's Nose, named for the shape the river made when it carved its way through the thick jungle. Flying over the perimeter of the base at Vinh Long, it seemed much like Bearcat only bigger and with more people and buildings, and a long PSP runway, a kind of snap together corrugated metal "instant runway", laid out flat for over a mile. Generally it is used mostly for larger fixed wing aircraft to keep their tires out of the mud, but it could be seen everywhere there were aircraft.

After refueling, the flight of EMU's is told to shut down to await further orders. Then the Taipan's lifted off to check out Snoopy's Nose. A bright sunny day prevails as they entered the Nose. The area is heavily wooded with tall palm trees with smaller brush covering the rest of the ground. A lone American advisor on the ground, working with a company of ARVN long-range patrol, or LRP's, has asked for assistance. They had been taking small weapons fire from an unknown number of Viet Cong who are "dug in" underground, into what is referred to as "spider holes". The Cong have managed to resist the advance of ARVN's into their territory.

There was great difficulty in observing the friendly troops on the ground, who had managed to get in close to the enemy, and was keeping a low profile. They had to mark the target area so that they did not inadvertently shoot the wrong Vietnamese's or worse, the American. So it is decided to mark the target with smoke. Mitch will "pop" a red smoke and trail it, he held it in hand, until ready to drop, the advisor will tell them via the radio when they are over the target. At that same moment the advisor will ignite a yellow smoke to mark his position, and then the air strike can begin.

They have made several hi-speed, low-level recon passes over the area without taking any fire. There is a sense that the enemy resistance has left the area without the knowledge of the ARVN's, but they decide to play along anyhow. If the Cong were still in the area the helicopters should have been an irresistible target. The terrain below is thick with low shrubs amongst sparse tall palm trees. The spider holes are impossible to detect from the air. The gunships could only catch glimpses of the ARVN troops lying on the ground. Their weapons all pointed in the same direction, toward the unseen bad guy's.

The advisor transmits them a direction he would like the Taipan flight leader to approach him at, so they start a low-level bank to get set up for the smoke run. The radio crackles with the voice of the advisor directing the flight path.

"Come left twenty degrees" the advisor requests.

"Ready red smoke, chief" the pilot say's to Mitchell.

Then came the voice from the radio on the ground below, "OK, hold that course for a half click".

They continue the flight path towards the advisor at a very slow airspeed. Mitch anticipates the drop and prepares to trail the smoke. The pin is pulled, and the spoon is released a loud pop is heard when the smoke grenade is ignited. The VC on the ground also heard the "pop" and thought the gunships had begun firing at them. That triggered quite an unexpected barrage of return fire. Bullets ripped through the floor all around Mitch, he let go the smoke to cover his head with his hands.

"Damn, all I did was pop a smoke".

The bulletproof vest lying under his canvas seat was not large enough to protect his whole body, although he tucked up his legs into a ball to try. The pucker factor was at the max. He keyed the mike, "RECIEVING FIRE", Mitch screamed.

But the pilot was already banking hard to avoid the enemy's ground fire. Once away, Mitch grabbed the M-60 off his lap, and began firing to the rear spraying lead where the red smoke rose up from the ground. As the advisor communicated over his radio, they could hear the bullets from their guns zipping through the trees, the sound coming from his microphone. Man he was close to the action Mitch thought.

An intense ground battle ensued for nearly twenty minutes before the ARVN's withdrew, only to allow the Taipan's to use their rockets. They flew fast orbits behind the action to prevent a retreat by the VC. Now they had trapped the Cong from retreating, the ARVN's in front, and the river to both sides. Next they climbed for altitude to begin the air strikes. Rockets and mini-gun ammunition were totally expended into the wooded area where the red smoke that started this whole mess has long faded. Small fires burned on the ground. A tall palm treetop is smoldering and many of the large leafy stems hangs torn and tattered from the rocket impact. The area being devastated by eighty or more rockets and thousands of M-60 rounds penetrating the earth, trying to reach an enemy buried six feet down into a two foot diameter hole.

C&C ordered the gunships back to Vinh Long to rearm and refuel. On the way Mitch recounted the horrible feeling of nearly having been shot to pieces. He thinks this was the most scared he has been yet, or maybe it was just the hangover or the still throbbing pain in the back of his neck. But for that brief instant he really felt what it must be like to be torn up by those AK-47 bullets, a sickening feeling swelled in his gut.

On the ground they find four new bullet holes in the ship but no vital parts have been compromised, so the mission continues. Mitch momentarily wondered what his mother might think should he go home all shot up?

"Well hell, it isn't gonna happen today", he decided angrily.

They head back to the Nose, flying low and fast. A radio communication has informed them that the shooting has subsided and the ARVN's were once more advancing into the previously held VC territory. A number of the Cong have already been eliminated from the big game.

"ARVN (3), NVA (0)".

The Taipan's approach from the south at the bottom of the Nose, the rice paddies on the opposite side of the river are a strong contrast to that of the Nose and its jungle like wooded interior. Just as they charge towards the edge of the tree line, a crewmember on one of the other ships calls out an "eligible male". Taipan's swing to the west a bit and see the man wearing black pajamas, and straw hat walking slowly across a rice paddy dyke towards a hooch less than a klick away. The lead gunship converges upon him from the rear, coming up on the right side. On the low-level pass Mitch can see he is an old man, with a long thin and graybeard. In his right hand is a walking stick, and a little girl in the other. They circle the two like giant birds of prey.

The old man and the little girl walk on, hand in hand very slowly, moving straight ahead and not looking up.

"C&C this is Taipan One Six, our eligible has a little girl with him, over", begins the radio communiqué.

"Roger One Six, standby"

C&C has decided to confer with the American advisor on the ground with what to do with the eligible male.

"Ahhh One Six, you have clearance" C&C's voice was barely perceivable.

"Charlie Charlie, One Six, can you say again", the lead pilot asks.

In the back seat Mitch and his gunner listen intently, there can't be any mistake here.

"The advisor said he has taken fire from across the river and believes your eligible to be Victor Charlie", he say's louder now, "You are cleared to fire".

What! Mitch stomped on the floor mike button.

"I am not shooting that fucking kid", he announced over the intercom that only his crew could hear.

But Mitch also knew that if called upon to do so, he had the instrument, and the duty to follow orders.

"Roger Charlie Charlie, but what about the girl" the pilot asked solemnly.

"One Six, standby"

Already He could not believe that this is going to happen. Jesus, they couldn't really want me to shoot a little kid, he wondered.

It was not unusual to fire on someone who was unarmed, often at the first sound of the helicopters the VC would hide their weapons to blend in with the farmers. But kids were another story.

"Ahhh One Six, can you separate the two with a warning shot?" asked C&C.

Thankfully they are at least trying to save her.

"Roger, we'll try that, standby"

With that they rolled in close,

"OK chief whenever you feel ready fire to the front of them".

No way he was going to hit that kid. Mitch squeezed the trigger and the upwardly surging dirt, thirty feet in front of the two warned of what was to come. The old man let go of the little girls hand, but she in turned reached up with both hands to grab his arm and continued along his side. They walked on along the rice-dike, towards a mud and straw hooch about seventy five yards ahead.

The ship behind them rolled in and gave a second warning. Mitch watched just to be sure the wing crew-chief did not hit the two. His was a short burst also, and a bit closer. It had to be obvious, even to a peasant dirt farmer that these were warning shots. At this altitude they could shoot rabbits on the run between the eyes. Good, the old man knew the right thing to do, he reached behind the girl a gently pushed her forward.

"Charlie Charlie, we have a lone eligible male in sight"

"Roger One Six, you are cleared to fire when she is well clear".

Although Mitch could not hear what was being said between the two below us, he still knew. The little girl with her long shiny black hair, picked up her pace and moved ahead of the old man. In turn the old man slowed his pace. Several times she turned to see if the old man was still following her, and probably to reassure herself that he was okay. They waited a long time for her to clear the area, as they circled the slowly moving eligible male making small strides with his cane, neither of the two looked up to us to visually confront their aggressor.

The little girl was just in front of the hooch now as they circle around the target.

"OK, chief let's do it" the pilot say's.

Mitch opened up with a short burst on this pass, his aim was intentional and accurate. Banking around he looked back to see the little girl some distance away, safe, but she heard the gunfire and turned to look. The old man waved frantically at her to continue into the hooch. Shortly she disappeared behind the bamboo door. The old man stopped walking, stood bent over, and supported himself with the walking stick and looked on towards the hooch straight ahead. Then he slowly went down to his knees, his hands sliding down the stick. Mitch has hit him, and he is mortally wounded. At close range the bullets pass through a body so quick that he may not have even known he was shot. As cruel as it is, his demise will come either by bleeding to death, or a direct hit on a vital organ.

The wing ship rolled in with one long burst that brought the old guy down. He laid there on top of the rice dyke on his left side, almost in a fetal position. His hat and walking stick lay on the ground next to him.

As they made a second pass to the left of the still body Mitch looked through the left door, the gunner opened fired on the body. The bullets impacting at such close range caused the corpse to jerk grotesquely sideways along the ground with each penetrating round.

"Do ya think he's dead now", Mitchell asked the gunner sarcastically shaking his head in disgust.

"Our bloody job done, our job done bloody", it was time for them to retreat to someplace else, another time, another place, another planet.

"Charlie Charlie, we have one KIA here"

"Roger, good work boy's" the commanders voice was relieved.

No one asked of the girl's fate, but Mitch hoped someone would find her and console her. Deep in the recess of his conscience, he knew if he could have, he would.

The American advisor on the ground reports he has four Viet Cong KIA's, and one wounded ARVN, who does not require a medivac. There is no way that the dead old man would not have known of the Viet Cong's activity in this area. He should have left when told to do so. He was in all probability a village elder. For whatever the reason he became a VC sympathizer, and probably orchestrated his village's fate! All of these operations are preceded with warnings to the villagers many days prior. There is no distinction between a VC sympathizer, and an enemy soldier. Either would kill you as to look at you. Mitch just could not understand why he would risk that little girl. Well if she had no previous cause to hate the Americans before, she sure does now, and will probably grow up a VC also.

Later that day ARVN soldiers recovered the corpse of the old man and found papers on the body that proved he was indeed a Viet Cong sympathizer and chief of the local village. It is not hard to imagine his participation in matters that would cause harm to ARVN and/or more importantly, American troops.

They followed the Co Chien River northwest, back to Vinh Long to begin the days insertions of ARVN's into the LZ. It's going to be a long day.

The EMU's lift off, and they all go right to work, one lift then another. A few hours later, they have a chance to shut down and wait for further orders. The day is mighty hot and sometimes it is quite boring just lying around in the chopper trying to keep the mind occupied. The pilots have taken the shaded spot under the fuselage for a nap. Some of the other crewmen have gone in search of "short time girls", those local village girls usually found on, or near any high traffic airfield and prostitute themselves.

Mitch leaned back on the floor inside the chopper, propped his head up on a chicken plate and closed his eyes. The midday heat is suffocating and saps the energy from within. Sleep preserves the needed strength to continue the day's missions and be alert. Naptime was a precious commodity and interruptions were rarely welcomed.

He could recognize the sound of almost every aircraft in the military arsenal, and some that were not. The loud buzzing sound awoke him. As the buzz drew near, Mitch could picture in his mind the bright silver Polatus Porter fixed wing airplane, with its turbine turning the large four bladed props. The plane was commonly used by the Air America organization that was reputed to be CIA. The buzzing was at its loudest, when he propped open one eye to see why the deafening noise did not continue down the runway. The Polatus was hovering into the wind about six feet off the runway, when he turned to look, one of the pilots was looking at him lying there. Must have a very low stall speed to be able to hover in that light wind, he thought. Finally the plane touched down, rolled about five feet and stopped. A remarkable feat for a fixed wing, Mitchell was impressed with the craft.

The plane turned off the active runway and parked on the other side of the airfield. There it was met by a small group of soldiers that began to unload bodies. Mitch decided to take a walk.

Arriving at the plane four American Air Force servicemen and two civilians had unloaded the bodies of four Viet Cong. They laid them all side by side and face up. The deceased had been shot up pretty good. One had the top left corner of his skull shot away leaving his brain exposed. Another had so many holes in him he looked like he fell face down on a bed of large nails. Turning to another one of the servicemen about the same age as Mitchell, he asked,

"Are these dudes from around here?"

"Yea, they shelled the base here last night with mortar fire" he responded as he scrutinized Mitchell.

"Army sent out a patrol to secure the area and found these guy's".

"Why did they come in Air America?" Mitch asked knowing Air America didn't land in the boonies to pick up this load.

"Not sure, something about one of them was working for us", "hell of a way to get fired" he said grinning.

A short jaunt down the runway, Mitch came across a deuce and a half truck filled with more Vietnamese's squatting down in the bed of the truck. Upon closer examination he could see that they were all Vietnamese males, dirty and disheveled. Obviously they had been in the rice fields as their feet and legs had dried mud crusted on them. Many looked like young boys, even younger than he did. All were wearing black silk short pants and a few had black shirts to match and their hands were bound behind their backs. Mitch stepped up close to get a good look. Some of the men in the middle stretched their necks to get a look at Mitchell and then smiled. While some of the others mumbled under their breath in Vietnamese.

One made a gesture that he wanted a cigarette. Mitch reached into his flight suit for the pack when an American Sergeant, whom he thought to be standing guard on the truck, came around the back of the vehicle and told Mitch not to hand them anything.

"Sure Sarge, why these guys getting punished", he asked

"Their POW's" the sarge replied.

"VC?", "Charlie?" not believing them capable of more than planting rice.

"Captured this morning", he said.

So, this is what they look like up closely. One of them smiled his toothless grin.

Face to face now with his enemy Mitch was not intimidated in the least. He may even feel a little sorry for the little bastards. Sure, they had been captured and stripped of their capability to inflict harm. But who knew of their recent deeds. Recalling why they are here and those who won't be leaving alive, his feelings changed quickly. Mitch supposed the oddity went both ways as they stared at each other before he finally blurted out "fuck you assholes", and presented them with an indignant middle finger.

They seemed glad to have been captured, perhaps it was better for them to be out of the field and out of the action for a while. Surely, they did not have a barracks to return to after a day of fighting, nor could they enjoy the Saigon bar scene. At least now they will get three square meals and a dry place to sleep.

Certainly, they are better off than the four of their counterparts on the ground next to the Air America's Polatus, or the old, man lying in the rice paddy with a hundred holes in him.

A Taipan escorts the EMU flight into the Landing Zone.

Chapter Ten
Way to Die

The cool morning air is inescapable in a helicopter flying at a thousand feet with no doors on it. Mitch unbuckled the seat belt to sit on the floor behind the pilot's seat, back to back, looking rearward. At least there is not so much wind here. Tired from the night before, they stayed up late to watch TV.

"That's one small step for man, one giant leap for mankind", came the voice of astronaut Neil Armstrong as he stepped foot on the surface of the moon. They sat watching the television newscast live as it happened in the recreation room along with most of his unit comrades. A sense of pride swelled as he realized America was capable of more than conflict, a lot more. The war would be over for him someday, and he could look forward to doing anything he wanted to do, even become an astronaut.

In a news segment following the landing of Eagle One, a film clip of the clean up after the 1969 TET offensive in Saigon, GI's in body bags, VC corpse's laying scattered in the street, smoked out and burning buildings. A captured Viet Cong who has just brutally murdered a family, including children, is shot in the head on live TV by Saigon's Police Chief. When the bullet is fired the man's face grimaces, blood gushes from the exit hole like a fire hose, and the body collapses in the street like a sack of potatoes thrown from a third floor window. Then again this could be all there is for the rest of Mitchell's life, if he died here in this country. No more terrible a fate for a young man can be imagined. He needed to think ahead of this place, never give up, and get his ass back home.

In the Nam, to be short does not reflect one's height, but rather it is a measurement of how many remaining days before rotating out of country and head back to real World. The days are counted down like a slow countdown launch of a space rocket. Today Mitch is two hundred and twenty four days short. In the past months, sometimes he would forget to count a few days and was surprised to find himself shorter than expected. In the beginning he did not record the remaining days, it was just too many to care. These days it is a staunch ritual.

For now though it is enough to think of his impending R&R, (rest and recuperation) in just a couple of months. Mitch gave a lot of thought to where in the world he wanted to spend six glorious days and nights. The Army has generously offered the R&R to all U.S. service personal in the Nam for a period of six months or more. He would receive airfare to any free country in the world. Yea, you know, what a deal, right?

But how would he act among real people? His transformation into a combat soldier has metamorphosed him into an animal-like humanoid, instinctive and vicious. He did not even talk the same, speaking in a vulgar variation of English mixed with military superlatives and all joined together by the word "fucking". Believing he should be locked up, and not sent out among the general population to wreak his havoc on good people. He was not sure he could trust himself, just look at the kind of things he has done already. He never would have believed himself capable of the kind of destruction he has perpetrated thus far. These past months he changed, reacting to instinct not thought. He has mechanized his actions and set aside emotion. His actions are foreign, even to him. But he had to know if this is a permanent change or will he be able to find himself again. Maybe someplace not so different from Vietnam would be all right.

Hawaii is the most popular spot for the married soldiers, as they usually meet their wives for the short reunion. Although he had heard some horrific stories by returning soldiers because they forgot how to treat real people from the world. Imagine trying to have a short second honeymoon with a soldier who just came out of combat carrying the baggage of the brutality of war. Wives often saw a side of hubby they never knew existed.

Some of his fellow Australian comrades have graciously offered their homes to Mitch should he decide to go there. He gave that idea reasonable consideration. But after much deliberation he decided that if he saw, even one round-eyed woman he would fall in love out of desperation, go AWOL and never return to the Nam. He could not chance a court-martial he might then be shot before a firing squad as a deserter. So he decided it would be best to visit another oriental country.

A returning GI from his R&R in Bangkok Thailand told Mitch of his experiences there. The people were friendly towards the American soldiers and prostitution was a respected profession. That sounded good to Mitch, Bangkok it is then, even the name holds promise.

A U.S. Navy Seal Team patrol on a special op's mission has asked for, and received an insertion of ARVN's into an area where they believe a heavy concentration of VC exists. The 135th has been asked to insert the members of the ARVN, 9th Special Forces into an LZ designated by the Seal Team. The mission was a surprise attack on an enemy stronghold. Higher ups, a/k/a top ranking officers, with the 135th planned the insertion to best give the ground troops the element of surprise they desired.

The landing zone was close to a main tributary, and if not for the rice dikes, probably would have been completely flooded out. The whole flight of nine slicks and three gunships flew at low level, below the tree tops over the murky water. Higher up decided that a low-level approach into the LZ would keep the noise down of the arriving flight and they could catch the enemy by surprise. So the flight, in single file, snaked its way down the winding river, EMU's leading, Taipan's in trail. C&C still flew at three thousand feet or so to observe the operation and call to out any obstacles ahead of the flight. The unusual flight approach added an element of additional danger, but at the same time broke the monotony of our daily mission pattern.

Tall thin palm trees lined each side of the river, as they were winding down the river below the treetops, there were not enough of the trees to visually conceal the flight. But their speed and silence made up for that. Soon they were opposite the intended LZ. The plan is for the slicks, loaded with their cargo of Seal's, to pop up over the trees, a hasty ninety degree turn to right, then drop right back down in the LZ. The key element here is to do it quickly. The slicks would barely touch the earth, while the human load bailed out and dispersed in all directions to create a secure perimeter.

C&C gave the flight the order to come up over the trees,

"OK EMU lead, execute approach, keep it tight"

The EMU's pulled up on the collective, bringing the birds up and over the tree line. From the rear of the formation, it looked like the back seat of a roller coaster ride, except made up of helicopters, winding all around, rolling up and down.

As they came over the treetops the lead slick was making his flare to slow the ship down, C&C gave another order.

"Hold it there lead, do not go any further", commanded C&C.

The lead slick flared even harder to stop the forward momentum, the EMU's were tight on one another, so when lead flared hard so did the second ship, and the third and so on. There was no time to pick a good landing spot, everyone had to put down where they could without piling up on the chopper ahead.

Mitch figured there are more ways to die here than any other place on earth, so he was not so surprised when the killer mud claim another victim. The early rains from another monsoon season have begun to soften the Earth's hardened parched soil

When the fifth slick in the line, landed in the LZ with a full load of ARVN's, the right skid sunk deep into the mud. That pilot had to touch down and land because he had flared too hard, and stuck the tail stinger into the mud. And therefore had no room to nose over forward and keep the ship out of the mud.

The ailing bird heaved to the starboard side until the blades barely struck soft mud. The pilot rolled off the throttles, then bailed out as the load of ARVN's jumped to the ground through the left cargo door that was still high. The circumference of the rotor disk took up the same angle as the helicopter, cocked over, left high, right low, but with the slowing blades striking dirt on every counterclockwise and downward pass.

They flew almost directly above when Mitch saw the last of the ARVN's with a white chicken in his arms, poking his head out from the low side of the downed bird. The ARVN and fowl looked up to see them through the spinning blades then he stepped out unto the mud. The feathered creature was not unusual cargo for the Vietnamese's to carry into combat. The midday meal was often supplemented with fresh fowl.

The soldier crouched down, seemingly to observe each time a rotor blade swung around past him. "Come on get out of there" Mitch thought. He assumed briefly that the trapped soldier would realize that the blades were still turning to fast for him to exit to the right and he would simply leave the aircraft the way the others did. As they hovered to the right side Mitch could see the Vietnamese soldier more clearly in the cargo door.

Mitchell could see very distinctly that he is young man with a pure white chicken cradled in his arm. He is wearing a bright red scarf around his neck that is a symbol of the Special Forces unit to which he belongs. He has lost his helmet, and Mitch thought if he tries to run out on the right side he will wish he had his helmet on when the rotor blade strikes him in the head. With that, he saw him pick up the chicken under his chin, both arms huddling the creature close into his chest. He then leans forward to charge outward to the right. Mentally, Mitch screamed "Stop, you can't go that way".

They have slowly passed overhead now, and Mitch had to look straight down past his landing skids to see the wreckage fifty feet below. The soldier hesitated momentarily, maybe he heard Mitchell's menta scream. Then as if he were a football player with the chicken tucked into his body as though it were a ball for winning score of the game, he charged outward.

Ohhh bad play, the rotor blades turned much to quickly to be passable between them. Almost in slow motion, the blade caught him just above the right shoulder as he charged headfirst through the blades. The chicken that was under his chin exploded, sending a cloud of white feathers into the air like it was shot out of a cannon. The ARVN soldier's head disappeared in the cloud of feathers, while the headless body slammed to the ground, never crossing the goal line. In disbelief at what he had just witnessed, he stared in awe. When the feathers settled down on the surface of the mud, the body still had the red scarf tied to the neck just below where the head had been. But there was no trace of the man's head, or his chicken. Mitch could only imagine the total disintegration of both. He pondered his passing with the question, was it the mud, or the act of trying to save the chicken that caused this death. No, I think I'll chalk this one up to stupidity too, Mitch decided.

"Dear Mom,

Today we flew over beautiful rice paddies and inserted a company of ARVN (The Army of the Republic of Vietnam) soldiers to look for and capture "if possible" the enemy. They are fighting hard so we don't have to. All part of the Vietnamization plan, so I can come home soon"...

The reality is there are only three ways out, One, rotation (the preferred method), Two, get wounded serious enough to be shipped to Japan (usually loss of a limb or two) then home, and Three, go home in a body bag (last resort).

But first today's missions must be completed. With one chopper being air lifted out of the LZ by a Chinook helicopter, a heavy military cargo chopper capable of hooking up then lifting and flying off with a Huey. It looks like an over grown shoebox but has two main rotors and two engines. All the while another chopper from Bearcat has been dispatched to complete the insertions and should arrive in an hour or so.

Back in the pickup zone, there are seven ARVN troops per load, per chopper. So that nine slicks carry sixty three fully geared soldiers into the LZ, per lift. Today's plan calls for a total of three lifts into the LZ. The troops waiting in the PZ (pick-up zone) line up down the runway in separate groups spaced apart so a chopper will land opposite each group with just enough space between groups for the other choppers without crashing into each other.

But now for the moment the slicks are shut down and lined up down the PSP runway. The ARVN troops are huddled in their little groups sitting or lying on the ground awaiting the new arrival from Bearcat.

The Taipan's are called up into the air to beat it for the LZ, where the downed chopper and the headless corpse have been removed. The first load is still there, and has not yet advanced outward into the surrounding tree lines yet.

The mission has been halted again due to increasing tension on the ground. The previously inserted ground troops have discovered evidence that a large number of enemy either has been in the area or is still there. A request for a napalm air strike by the U.S. Air Force's, Phantom F-4's has been issued and the Taipan's are standing by for word on the attack by the "fast movers". Meanwhile they continued their tree top search for the enemy below.

Soon a single voice comes up on the mission frequency and breaks the long radio silence. It is the voice of the pilot flying his Cessna L-19A Bird Dog, a high-wing, twin-seat tail-dragger that seems awfully out of place in combat with the exception of the four 2.75 inch rocket tubes under each wing. Mitch looked up through the rotor blades to try and catch a glimpse of the escorts to the "little brother" that were always nearby.

For the most part the little airplane scout is defenseless and can be shot down quite easily. But if you reveal your position to the bird dog, he will mark your position with a white phosphorus rocket. The "fast movers", or "big brothers", hanging out above twenty thousand feet will surely see that smoke. They will dive down onto the white smoke with their nearly invisible forward profile. Screaming towards the earth, you won't see them until they have rained holy terror down on you, 20 mm cannon fire, five hundred pound bombs and that most terrifying, Napalm. If you survive the initial onslaught, you just might hear the roar of the afterburners as the first jet climbs to altitude faster than a speeding bullet can catch him. But don't get to comfortable with his departure, because the next one is right behind him, and now your ass is cooked.

The Taipan's have been asked to fly out of the immediate LZ area to make room for the "big show", obliging they climb to a safer altitude and out of the way. Mitch watched the bird dog dive in to a low orbit to hunt his target. Like a true bird dog sniffing for prey, the little plane banks and cranks searching. Soon he calmly reports,

"Ground, this is little brother, I have three Victor Charlie on the run".

Hey what's this, first of all, the three gunships with twelve pairs of eyes didn't see anything in the LZ when they flew as low or lower than he. Secondly why would they run now from the bird dog?

"Marking the target now" the bird dog pilot reports.

A single rocket is fired when the nose of the fixed wing drops and then rises again sharply. A large plume of white dense smoke rises with streamers blossoming outward from the center, trailing their scorching bits of phosphorus.

"Ground control, be advised I have three confirmed KIA"

"What? Is he kidding, imagine trying to claim three confirmed kills with just one "willie pete" rocket, who the hell is that guy bullshitting".

The Taipan's have switched to the alternate frequency to discuss this outrageous claim by the Air Force pilot. They saw no evidence of enemy troop movement in the LZ, then the scout shows up and with but one pair of eyes he sees a whole fucking Army of bad guys, yea right. The Taipan's decide to get into the LZ just as soon as the "fast movers" are out, to verify the allegation.

The show continues when the F-4 Phantom jets roll in on the marker. They have been orbiting to the left, when Mitch noticed the pilot looking over his right shoulder, straining to see the incoming jet. He looked quickly over his shoulder as the jet boogied past so fast that Mitch missed the aircraft's approach to the target and caught only his flame shooting from his afterburners as the jet climbed high and to the right. At the same instant the ground erupted in a huge fireball and rising black smoke from the Napalm. The whole damn length of the tree line is fried in an instant. Then came the second fast mover, in another earth shaking blast, the flame rose and seared black all within its domain.

They had to agree it was a good show, but how impersonal it is to drop in like that and not look your enemy in the eye before you blow him to smithereens. They know they are killing people but yet they are detached from witnessing their destruction. From the helicopter, their eyes are all too keenly aware of the death and dismemberment caused by their actions. The Taipan's supposed now they will claim a whole Army of KIA's.

Show's over in minutes, and the Taipan's roll in for the confirmation, but the bird dog who moved only a short distance from the drop zone and has beaten them back into the area.

"Ground, this is little brother",

"Little brother, this is ground, go"

"Ah roger, be advised the target area is completely destroyed", the radio crackles again.

"The KIA's are cooked and gone"

So with no positive confirmation the little bird dog pilot is credited with three confirmed kills.

"Roger that little brother, understand three confirmed" reports ground.

"Pleasure doing business with you, call us again when we can be of service"

"Roger, ground out"

The whole rest of the day, as they completed their mission, they never made any contact, or saw any of the VC claimed by the ARVN ground forces, or the U.S. Air Farce.

It's the last refueling for today, so they can make haste back to Bearcat. Thinking ahead, he hope they would get back soon enough so that he may submit his requisition for R&R to Bangkok.

Pulling out the fuel nozzle from the fill tube and closing the locking cap, he then prepared the ship for the flight back. Sliding the ammo can up against the bulkhead, M-60 laid to rest. Then pulling out the chicken plate from under his seat, Mitch would use it as a pillow for the impending nap so desperately needed.

A quick pee under the tail boom before taking off, then stamping his foot down to shake off the excess yellow liquid from his boot before climbing in. The turbine exhaust combined with the rotor wash had blown the weak stream of piss all across his muddy boots.

The gunner took up a position on the floor near the center. Mitch sat with his back to the door post between the pilot's door and the cargo area facing aft, with his left leg hanging down to let the rush of air dry the remaining wetness off his boot.

He stared out as they flew over the countryside. The topography below past slowly at high altitude, trees, then rice paddies, then trees and an occasional village, more rice paddies, then trees. The ambient noise of the helicopter began to fade. Sitting motionless while more terrain passed, soon the noise disappeared.

As he was engrossed in thoughts of home, the music playing into the helmet seemed to enhance his mind's vision of days before, when life was whole lot better. At the oceans edge on a hot and sunny day the water was clear and cool. There were images of white sandy beaches, where the six-foot waves formed perfect curls on top and could be surfed for hours on end. A brand new Gordon Smith surfboard heavily waxed and ready for the big ones. There were pretty blond girls in skimpy bikinis, excitedly scream out about the wave a surfer just caught. The girls shriek at another surfer when his toes hang over the front of his board as he "hanged ten". Mitchell's long, and sun bleached hair feels wet and salty. An exposed naked back and shoulders reddened by the sun's rays, he could almost feel the stinging of his sunburn.

He day dreamed of a future in the real world, a day when he would be home with family and friends. Mitch could see himself driving a fast new car, sporty with big tires and low profile. The images were vivid and seemed so real, he tried to reach out to feel it. Reaching, reaching for the images to confirm the reality that he needed so badly.

Mitchell's nerves all jumped in unison at the sudden shock of returning to helicopter gunship, the loud noise filling his ears again. The gunner had forcefully grabbed his arm to pull him back in the aircraft. The gunner was still lying down on his back, half-asleep, when he opened one eye and noticed that Mitch had begun to lean out towards the door. He watched him briefly, as he was not sure what Mitch was doing since his eyes were wide open.

"But you looked like you wuz in a daze", he said.

The gunner finally reached over to pull Mitch in when he was sure he would fall out into the void.

Mitch gave him the dirtiest look he could muster up for bringing him back into the helicopter and reality.

"Man, you were going to fall out, I am tellin ya."

"I wasn't even sleeping, asshole" Mitch said.

"I know, that's why I watched you for a while" he continued,

"You was like in a trance or sumptin, then you just started to go"

He nodded his acceptance of the gunner's account, deep down inside he knew he was right.

Back on the flight line, the senior pilot told Mitch that he had heard other pilots speak of losing crew members before.

"Not sure if they jumped or just fell asleep and rolled out the door"

"But you can be hypnotized by the moving terrain, it's like target fixation".

Yet another damn way to die, Mitch thought.

"He probably saved your life, best you keep your seat belt on when we are in the air".

Mission disrupted, a gunship pilot receives injuries during an air assault.

Chapter Eleven
No Prisoners

One morning in the schoolyard, during recess, when I was nine years old, George Davies, the class bully shoved me hard from behind. I fell forward into another bunch of students knocking a little girl to the ground. She began to cry, but honestly, I think it made me the angriest because I knew I was going to be in big trouble for hurting her. Turning to face George, I felt the rage of real anger probably for the first time in my life. We began to fight as I tore into him like an animal. I can't really explain how I managed to get the better of George, as he was a much larger kid than I. My anger clouded my careful consideration of my reaction, however I ended up on top of him, and pinning him to the ground. My knee's dug hard into his shoulders as I sat on his chest. The other students quickly gathered around us. In unison they began to chant, "hit him, hit him, hit him". I had never fought before in anger and did not want to hurt George. But I had to show him it was over as far as his pushing me around. I closed my eyes and turned my head away to the side. Clinching a tight fist and raising my hand over my head, I sharply brought the hand down to where I thought his face would be. The resultant pain in my knuckles indicated a direct hit. I looked down to see George's bloodied lip. Having seen the damage caused by my anger, I felt horribly guilty of perpetrating such a violent act. Carefully I let him up as I expected retaliation, but we had had enough. He succumbed to the beating and I swore to myself to never hurt anyone, ever again.

In a new area of operation with several nearby villages nestled in along the edge of a thick jungle, two of the Taipan's have been asked to fly over today's intended LZ "Quebec Tango", for a reconnaissance mission. On arrival they notice small muddy fields. The open area was not as large as a rice paddy, and there are patches of knee high grass. The area is heavily wooded to three sides and the fourth is at the edge of a thick triple canopy jungle. The area looks hot, too many places to hide, could be plenty of Viet Cong here.

There have not been any U.S. operations here for a long time, too much green vegetation and no bomb craters. It seems almost peaceful. Mitch leaned out to look behind the ship, seeing their wingman in close formation. The gunner and crew-chief are to the limit of the seat belts that have been loosened to allow half of their body to be outside the aircraft. With one foot on top of the rocket pod and the other pressed hard against the doorpost pressing their backs into the rear bulkhead to keep them in the seat in the event of a sudden maneuver. Their M-60's are at the ready, "locked and loaded".

With helmets on, and the dark visors down over the eyes, they are faceless hunters. Scanning downward, they continuously survey the terrain below, forward then aft, searching for the elusive enemy.

The area is a designated, "free fire zone", no friendlies are said to inhabit the area. Mitchell always liked the free fire areas, as he did not need to fear shooting the wrong people. Here everyone is the right person!

The pilot in command today is new to Mitchell, and this is his first time in this ship. He has been flying CA's, (combat assaults), for nine months and has three months left in country. His experience is evident by his radio skills and command of the aircraft controls. Actually Mitchell felt very confident in his ability, he has learned to tell the difference between a good, or a great pilot. Fortunately for the back seat crews there were no bad pilots. Having a veteran pilot at the controls should increase his odds of survival on the mission.

The Taipan's continued their search, buzzing from one open field to another. Like giant bumblebees in search of particular flower filled with sweet nectar.

Down at tree top level, cranking and banking, if one area is deemed uninhabited they flew to another. It was not long before they easily spotted three individuals wearing those round conical hats, the light straw color in stark contract to the dark gray muddy field. Walking across an open field they traversed the oozing earth, a short distance behind them was another river. As they approached, the pilot noticed that the three persons far ahead and below them now, were carrying "something" over their shoulders. Still a few hundred meters out, the pilot keyed his mic.

"Charlie, Charlie, Taipan lead, over", called the pilot.

"Go lead, this is Command", answered C&C.

"Ah roger, we have three eligible males, possible weapons, three klicks east of LZ Quebec Tango, over".

They flew closer to the trio, extending his neck to see over the pilot's shoulder, Mitch saw they are carrying what appeared to be rifles over their shoulders. An adrenaline rush enables the senses to prepare for what looks like is going to be an exchange of gunplay with the enemy. All eyes watch intently as the helicopter approaches the trio.

"Lead, what are they doing at this time, over" asked C&C.

"Wait one for a sit-rep, over"

The pilot nosed the chopper over to pick up airspeed and flew directly at the three males.

"Fire, when fired at back there, OK", spoke the pilot on intercom.

"Roger that", responded the gunner.

"Got it," Mitch said while adjusting the ammo belt over his left forearm to help feed it smoothly into the breach of the machinegun. He stuck his right shoulder and head out to see ahead. The wind rush caused his flight suit to flap rapidly, the collar whipping at his neck. Lifting the heavy gun into his shoulder and taking aim he was prepared to fire if one of the three made any aggressive moves.

It is the Standard Operating Procedure for the AC (aircraft commander) to take the controls of the aircraft while in the LZ, co-pilots fly to and from an AO. If there is going to be fighting the pilot always banked right so he could see the playing field unobstructed! While banking right, the left seat gunner is looking at blue sky. The chief is the gunner that nearly always fired offensively, but both are defensive gunners.

They over-flew the three males and banked hard right. Looking straight down at them, they seemed to rotate on the ground as the helicopter tightened the turn. They all were pretty muddy up to their knees. Two wore black silk shorts and had no shirt on; the other was dressed in all black. All three had digging tools over their shoulder, one a pick, the other a shovel, and something like a garden hoe. None dared to look up past the brim of their hats directly at the circling gunships as they loomed overhead. Although the straw hats obscured their faces, they still looked as though they are guilty of something. They walked abreast of each other slowly forward picking their feet up high to take another step.

"I don't know Pete, what do you make of it" the pilot spoke to the co-pilot.

"Maybe they are burying a cache of weapons out here" he responded.

"Yea, they sure aren't farmer's way out here," said the pilot.

"I am coming around again to get another look," he said again

"Charlie, Charlie, Taipan Lead",

"Go, Lead",

"Ah looks like they are burying a cache, all three have digging equipment or…shovels",

"Wait one for clearance" ordered C&C,

"Roger C&C, coming around",

"Roger, Lead".

They came around onto the original flight path, and flew directly at them again. The airspeed slowed to fifty knots at an approximately altitude of ninety feet. Now almost right above them the call from C&C came over the radio.

"Taipan Lead, you have clearance to…."

Going weightless in the seat belt without warning, the ship nosed over sharply to a point that allowed the pilot to fire a single rocket nearly straight down. The rocket exploded under the aircraft sending up a deluge of mud and debris. The helicopter stalled in flight and fell to about twenty feet above the ground, the craft yawed heavily right, then left before the pilot was able to regain control. A hard bank to the right was felt as Mitch snapped his head left into the cockpit to be sure everything was OK. He looked towards the co-pilot in the left front seat. As they banked hard, the horizon tilted sharply as Mitch saw the blue sky past the co-pilot and in his right peripheral vision he saw only the ground.

Then he witnessed one of the conical straw gook hats as it climbed past the left windshield, it was on fire and soared straight up past the windshield and continued above them. It was flipping end over end, while burning yellow flames covered nearly all of it. Then a few chunks of the gooey mud splattered over both windshields. Never had they fired a rocket so close to the ground, Mitch's first thought is that they might have damage somewhere.

As they came around, still circling right, the wing ship behind, has flown over the explosion area without firing. The falling debris was still settling down to earth. In a matter of seconds they were back near the crater left by the rocket. They looked down to see two decimated bodies, one body was intact with most of his clothes blown off, and covered in blood and mud. The other has been torn into pieces by the blast. One arm there, another over there, and legs over on the other side of the dike, and his chest and head without limbs, lay next to the crater. With so many parts scattered about, he looked like a doll that some child, in a fit of rage had pulled off the arms and legs.

The third man had remained standing, he had been the man in the middle of the three, yet somehow remained alive after the explosion. Mitch thought it had to be impossible for him to live after that. They had all been walking in stride, side by side through the mud, close together. How could one have survived such an incredible explosion? Mitch thought of that flaming gook hat. Either that hat was propelled really high, or they had fallen really low. In any case it was a sight never before experienced.

The persistent survivor put both his hands over his head in typical surrender fashion. He bled slightly from a wound in his shoulder. It was too late for him to surrender now, a gunship does not take prisoners. The extra weight of another person would not let the aircraft get airborne again. He is still the enemy and the rules say we can't let him go, so the only option is for him to die. They had admired his luck in surviving the blast, but it was to no avail. He managed only to prolong his agony. There is no hope for him, If Mitch did not do it, the crew-chief on the wing ship will. The dead man began to walk slowly forward.

"OK chief, I'll come around again, we got to finish this",

"Coming in low and slow", the pilot continued.

"Gunner you keep a sharp look out in that tree line over there",

"If you miss, wings chief wants the shot, OK?"

Mitchell keyed the microphone, "I won't miss", he said with the confidence of a seasoned gunner.

He did come in low, very low, twenty-five feet. And he was slow, maybe twenty knots or less. They were nearly hovering to the remaining eligible male and the pilot kicked the tail rotor pedal with the right foot so that Mitch was looking directly at the target. He waited until he was a few feet from the edge of the diameter of the rotor blades.

With both hands still raised in the air to surrender, the dazed VC walked towards the aircraft. The enemy with shiny black hair covered in mud, and bleeding from small shrapnel wounds, looked at Mitchell like he wanted help. Shit, Mitchell thought, he thinks we are coming to pick him up. Suddenly something felt terribly wrong.

There is no emotion of hatred, nor did he have any personal feeling towards this individual. He was here solely to complete the mission. He has separated himself from the human being that he used to be, to the military weapon that he is now.

Mitchell had hesitated not really wanting to fire. The pilot spoke up,

"Wa-cha waiting for Chief, fire back there", the command came sharply.

When he pulled the trigger, the first few rounds hit him in the belly, went through him, and kicked up the mud behind the male target. Shooting down at him from their hovering position he did not flinch, and he took another step towards the aircraft. Mitch squeezed the trigger again and held it.

He saw the tracers disappear in his chest. Again he took another stumbling step. Mitch needed to expeditiously end his suffering and finish with this horrific scene. He raised the gun barrel upward, walking the tracers towards his head. A round caught him on the left side of his neck, blowing out a portion of flesh. His hands came down to grab at the open wound, but he never touched it before he collapsed to the ground.

The helicopter nosed over to regain airspeed. Mitch sat in silence while the crackle of noise on the intercom gave the situation report to C&C.

A twinge of fear bolted through Mitchell when had shot at the individual, it took too long to end the ordeal. Thinking the machinegun was not very effective at close range, Mitch worried, what if I can't bring them down instantly, then surely the risk is greater that he could be killed. He did not understand how the enemy could have survived so many bullet and shrapnel wounds. The ship and four lives depended on him to be able to dispatch the enemy quickly and efficiently. That single rocket should have ended the mission. It was almost like he wasn't supposed to die.

He wondered about the tools they were carrying. It was the tools that killed them all, it is what had initiated the mission. Without the shovel, hoe and pick, they might have gone about their business unharmed. Surely they had to be burying weapons. And what were they going to do with those weapons? Kill American Soldiers! Mitch was sure that if they had been given the chance they surely would.

Haunted all day by that mission, nothing felt right about the event of the morning, as hard as he tried to forget, the thoughts came back. Over and over the scene played out his head, sometimes even producing a nauseous effect in his stomach. Shooting him at such close range seemed unnecessary. Why did he live so long? Burning questions that had no answers, Mitch was uneasy, but he remembered his training.

"A soldier does not think, he obeys orders", and so he tried not to think of it anymore.

Although he did ask the pilot why he had fired the rocket from such a low altitude,

"Going home soon, could be my last chance to get some confirmed kills", he stated with a big grin and slight chuckle.

Suddenly he realized the pilots desire to accrue a KIA count was greater than their safety. This is known as "short timer's guts". When you have survived long enough in combat you begin to feel like you are invincible and begin to take chances. This is when you are the most dangerous to yourself and others.

They went about the day as usual, but something felt different within Mitchell. When he closed his eyes to nap after they had shut down for lunch, he flashed back only see the confused look on the face of the Viet Cong when he pulled the trigger. What did he think we were going to do with him anyhow? Did anyone tell him it was ok to kill the American's, but he couldn't get killed? Mitch had felt he looked dazed and confused, but why?

The Taipan's were down a long time for lunch, going into the second hour, the flight crews are getting jittery. Not because they are not secure in the PZ, but because flying is what they do. Sitting on the ground is for slicks but not the gunnies.

A hundred yards away is thatched hooch in an open rice paddy. Mitchell's gunner and him, and the crew-chief from their first wing ship, decide to investigate the little shack to see how the pheasant farmer lived. The three of them grab their M-16's and walk off. Although they have not seen anyone from the hooch since they landed, it would not surprise them if a family of Vietnamese were hiding inside. For local residents, it was safer not to been seen when an operation had commenced. Locals in these remote villages were not accustomed to having a dozen helicopters parked in their rice paddy.

Approaching the front entrance, they began to speak a bit louder so that any occupants inside are forewarned to their arrival. The smell of a burning fire emanates from inside. Sliding the M-16's off their shoulders, the gunner who is a former infantryman and who spearheaded this expedition went in first. Carefully he pushed the bamboo door aside with the barrel of his weapon. He peaked around the corner and stepped inside. Mitch hesitated to follow, thinking this was a crime of forced entry, but then thought, "what the fuck, we're soldiers on a mission", then followed him into the darkened structure.

Inside was a family, an old man lying in the only bed in the one room, seemingly unable to move. Standing beside him a younger woman, perhaps his daughter, and on the floor were two children, a boy and a girl. The infants have dirty little faces, and big brown eyes sucking in every detail of the intrusion. The live-in pig and chickens didn't seem to mind them at all.

A fire burned on one side of the hooch, and candles burned on both sides of the bed set up on empty tarnished brass 105mm Howitzer casings. An odor of incense permeated the air inside. The room was about one hundred eighty square feet, had one window opening that was closed and remarkably few belongings. A straw chest, one bed with raw wood posts and head board, blankets, some pots, a couple of floor mats strewn on the straw and dirt floor. Opposite from the fire used for cooking, along the back wall, a large woven straw container of freshly husked rice is filled to the brim. The container was three feet high and about four feet in diameter. Mitch stuck his hand deep into the grains to feel for hidden objects, like weapons.

Without being able to fully communicate with their unwilling hosts, they smiled a lot to let them know they meant them no harm. But the crews were concerned with their security as well. The gunner poked around under the bed while the other crew-chief checked out the chest and folded pile of old blankets. Mitch found an old piece of canvas hanging curiously from the wall alongside the stored rice. Lifting it he discovered the entrance to a bunker. Stepping to the side he shoved the barrel of his rifle into the small hole before looking in. It was very dark inside, having appeased himself it was empty he turned to the gunner to ask if he knew anything about the bunkers.

"All these hooch's have them, it's the only protection these people have from us when the shooting starts", he spoke while he continued searching.

"Made of mud and logs, first with small bits of wood then packed with mud, then larger logs and more mud, all criss-crossed until it's about five feet thick"

The crawl hole in the center was their refuge in the event of an artillery barrage, mortar attack (ours or theirs), or our gunship rockets.

"Not much will penetrate to the core of one of these", he said.

"How about a five hundred pounder", Mitch asked.

"Maybe, if it's a direct hit".

The whole family crawled into the core that was a foot and a half high and barely two feet wide by ten feet deep. Personally Mitch thought it looked like an instant grave.

Having satisfied their curiosity, they left the hooch unmolested. Mitch took a quick look around the side of the hooch to see the exterior of the bunker that extruded from the outside wall.

"Always thought that it was a fire place or stove" he said to the gunner.

"Damn good place for Charlie to hide too", the gunner responded.

With his new knowledge Mitch will know to fire into the hooch near the side with the bunker to keep Charlie's head down while in the LZ. But he really wanted to find a way to penetrate that bunker. If "Charlie" used it then he would escape their onslaught.

Meanwhile the flight has been called up in their absence, and they are forced to run the hundred yards back to the choppers. The pilots have just begun to fire up the turbines and they see the blades beginning to slowly turn. Mitch wondered if the pilots are pissed that they were not there.

That being the first time inside a farmer's hooch, he was glad to have explored the dwelling, and now has a personal mission to find a way to get into those bunkers. In the past they have burned down the hooch and those bunkers always remain unscathed.

The Viet Cong entering a village would terrorize the local peasant farmers, if U.S. discovered them, or Allied troops, certainly they would make good use of those bunkers. If that's where the bad guys are going to hang out, then they needed a way to get them while they are in there. Only problem he could see is how to know whose inside, friend or foe?

Thinking about the bunkers kept his mind off the morning's mission and put some purpose into his continued existence here. It allowed him to think of something no one else seemed to realize, that is the need to be able to destroy those bunkers from the air. Mitch could save American lives with a solution to this problem. And that is what this really was all about anyhow, but how to do it?

Upon returning back to base, and as he entered the barracks, another Taipan crew-chief, lying on his bunk, sat up to plant his feet on the floor to make his announcement.

"Hey, I hear your wasting the friendlies now", he started,

"They don't count as confirmed KIA's shithead" he continued.

"What the fuck are you talking about" Mitch asked scornfully.

"Your three KIA's this morning, that's what", "Friendlies", he said with a smug look on his face.

"Bullshit asshole, they were Cong for sure, burying a cache of weapons".

"Not according to the C.O. (commanding officer)", "they was dirt farmers".

If he wanted to start some shit with Mitchell, this was a good way to get a lot of it.

"First of all dick breath, the pilot did the two with a rocket", "I took out the wounded gook, who was probably already fucked", Mitch retorted rather defensively.

"Besides, we had clearance", "who the fuck told your ass anyhow", he demanded.

"C.O.'s clerk, got the report in when I was in his office", he lay back on the bunk and continued.

"Said the three had just buried one of the gooks wife, who just died", "you dick-heads wiped out the whole fucking funeral".

Mitch knew he was right, he just fucking knew it.

"And how did the fucking clerk find out" he asked still defensive.

"A report from the ARVN troops they put in there after you guy's left, one of them found the papers in one of their fucking pants pocket".

Now Mitch was really pissed, but at the higher ups in command instead of the bearer of the bad news. Besides he wasn't making accusations really, it was just his way of telling Mitch that they had made a big mistake today. There is no way for the aircrews to know how higher up determines where or when to order clearance to fire on individuals. But today the system failed.

He tried to reason that perhaps the three strolled off to bury a loved one in an area they were not allowed into, even if it is their country. It was hard enough to deal with the actions of his duty, but at least he should not have to deal with agonizing over if the people he was shooting at were friend or foe.

All that can be said about the guy, whose finger was on the trigger, is that he followed orders. Somehow, Mitch supposed, I will have to learn to live with that.

H.U.D. [heads up display], used by the aircraft commander to guide the 2.75" rocket to the target.

Chapter Twelve

Bangkok Butterfly

In some ways we are all products of our environment, at least up to a point of intellect where we decide if the environment is a good thing, or a bad thing. For some changing the environment is an overwhelming obstacle. For others the change comes naturally with increased awareness of a need for change. Still others have their environment changed for them through circumstance. Such as it was when I joined the Army.

Up until that first day at basic training, everyone associated with our induction into military service had been so pleasant. With a friendly smile the recruiter spoke of an "all paid education" that they could not get anywhere else. And a career learned that he'd be able to use when back in civilian life. And of course, travel opportunities, foreign countries like Germany, France, or if he was, "man enough to accept his duty as a U.S. citizen, and join the conflict in Nam". To the Barber who shaved their heads when they asked for a little trim off the sides, responded with a warm "sure kid", and then proceeded to run his sheers at the closest possible setting, right down the middle of their heads. Or the Quarter Master who provided them with new uniforms and boots.

"What size shoe do you wear"?

"Ten and a half".

"Ok here ya go"!

"But these are eleven's".

"You'll need the extra room for heavy socks cause you'll be doing a lot of marching", he would say with a grin.

"Gee, thanks sarge", it sounded like he was genuinely concerned.

A bus full of fresh recruits in olive drab uniform fatigues that included a baseball cap to hide their freshly shaved heads, the military's objective to make them all look equal. A duffel bag full of miscellaneous soldier stuff was also distributed to each.

The bus came to a stop at an old, white two story wooden barracks that will be their home for the next nine weeks. The bus door opened and a drill instructor stepped up into the front, next to the driver and said, "Grab your gear troops, and fall into formation outside". They were all exhausted from the long trip and hoped that a rest would have been more appropriate. The drill instructor did not seem to be a very intimidating sort, with his round, "Smokey the bear" drill instructor hat, and those thick black rimmed eye glasses, but boy was Mitchell wrong to judge too soon.

After a few moans and groans, and the comment "hey Sarge when do we eat", the DI marched down the center aisle, stamping his feet down hard towards the back of the bus, he was at a fast pace screaming.

"GRAB YOUR GEAR AND GET YOUR ASSES OFF MY BUS YOU SLOBS", spit sprayed from his lips.

"MOVE IT, MOVE IT, MOVE IT", he yelled at the top of his lungs.

"YOU DOG FACES AIN'T SHIT HERE, I AM GOING TO BREAK YOUR ASSES TILL YOU CRY FOR YOUR MOMMA"

"NOW GET OFF MY DAMN BUS, MOVE IT, MOVE IT".

Outside the door of the bus, another Drill Instructor barking orders on where, and how to fall in line. A mass confusion ensued, new recruits bumping, stumbling into each other, DI's screaming at the top of their lungs. A new recruit picks a fight with another, who had just stepped on his foot.

Yep, he was beginning to think he had been deceived. No one ever spoke of verbal abuse, or getting his ass broke. But Mitch decided to hang in there and follow the crowd because he needed to see what would happen next.

His tour of duty in Vietnam, during this conflict, brought him into an environment that was, for a young man, very strange, and extremely hazardous. He has learned to do things that no man should ask a son to do. Mitchell also learned to survive.

He had no fantasies about wearing the Army Uniform. It was not for the sake of girls who liked men in uniform that drove him to enlistment. But while he was in uniform, he knew he was a soldier and acted accordingly. Although Mitch resisted the typical brainwashing of the drill instructors during basic training to "kill, kill, kill", especially on the bayonet course, he did respect the fact they have trained them to survive as well.

In a foreign country, in a strange and hostile surrounding, and in a military uniform, one has little recourse other than to conform to the standards set by the environment. Mitch became for the most part, a product of war. There was only a short time each day when he, was himself, the real him. It was during that time the brain held together the internal struggle of the two personalities.

In the past six months, the lessons were fast presented and had to be fast learned. Now it is time to take a break from this upside down World and learn to be anything other than a soldier.

Mitchell's request for R&R, to Bangkok, Thailand has been granted. With orders in hand, and one-month's pay in his pocket, all three hundred and twenty dollars, including hazardous duty and flight pay, he hopped aboard the three-quarter ton truck for the bumpy ride.

Leaving Bearcat, for Ton Son Nhut Airbase, to catch a Military Airlift Command jet, his feelings for taking a "vacation" just now are ambiguous. He wanted to go, feeling like he needed a break from the action, but he worried about his crew and helicopter.

Landing in Thailand is not so unlike landing in the Nam. Tall palm trees, rice paddies, oriental people and of course, soldiers. This is exactly the kind of place he would feel the most comfortable in.

Upon disembarking the aircraft, an ice cool beer was offered by an attractive Thai lady, and graciously accepted. A twelve ounce'r, with an alcohol content more than twice what he was used to. Aaahh, a few quick gulps and he had a buzz going already.

They sat in the processing center with perhaps, fifty other R&R serviceman of varied ranks and service. A female host in a traditional red Thai dress with a wide piece of material draped over her shoulder and gold embroidery, has welcomed them and now desires to explain to the group, some of the customs and laws regarding her country.

"It is an insult to touch the head of any Thai person", she began.

"It is also an insult to point the bottom of your feet at another", she added,

"Keep your feet on the floor where they belong", spoken with a beautiful smile.

They are warned of the illicit trade in drugs, such as Heroin and Opium.

"If you choose to indulge yourselves in such activity, I can assure you that you will not have a very good time in Thailand", she warned softly in perfect English. With a knowing smile, her eye's that had been heavily outlined in black seemed to search out any potential culprits. Maybe, this won't be as much fun as I imagined, Mitch worried.

Given a list of hotels that cater to American Servicemen, Mitch chose the Diamond Hotel, because it sounded like a classy joint. A van transported them to their respective hotels. Once they arrived, he checked in at the hotel lobby desk.

"Will you require a driver during your stay, sir", asked the clerk.

"How much is that", after all, he is on a budget.

"Let me get you a driver and you can negotiate directly with him". The clerk raised his hand to summon a man sitting at a table near the front entrance with four others. The desk clerk introduced a driver who would be his personal chauffeur for the week, for a fee of course!

Another GI standing at the desk, waiting for his room key, overheard the introduction. Mitch recognized him as another who rode in on the van with him. He asked to share a driver, saying they could save money if they split the cost. But Mitch had already made up his mind to go solo on this trip. He needed to forget about being a soldier for a while. If this guy tagged along, they would both end up talking about the war that he was trying to forget. So Mitch politely declined his offer.

Mr. Ying Prayoon was short in stature but was not the usual skinny, bone-protruding oriental that Mitch was accustomed to. His large smile and rounded cheeks made him seem to be a cheerful sort. With an enthusiastic handshake he looked at Mitch with his dark eyes.

"I am here to introduce you to Bangkok and to be sure you have berry good time", he began.

"First, we must find for you a bootiful lady to take care of you", Ying said.

He seemed to be very wise to the needs of American servicemen.

"Deal, how much", Mitch asked.

"Six days, sixty Baht", he said referring to his local currency. Negotiations over, they shook hands, and Mitch turned and headed for the elevator and his room.

After inspecting the room for booby traps, and changing into his civvies, he returned to the lobby to meet with Ying. Together they drove off in his little white Renault. Driving through a section of Bangkok's "red light district" where Bars, nightclubs and strip clubs are in abundance, Ying pulled up to a well-lighted club and instructed Mitch to go inside. Ying parked the car, while he entered the dance club. He was not sure that he wanted to dance with a lady, at least not vertically, but he trusted Ying to accomplish his mission. Mitch was seated by the cordial matre'd at a table close to the elevated dance stage, the music was loud and the disco lights flashed bright.

Soon Thai ladies and girls were parading around the stage, some gyrating to the music others just smiling and caressing themselves. They marched from one side of the stage to the other. They wore numbers around their neck, a dark colored disk and large white numbers that hung on a chain, and could be seen from anywhere in the joint. Ying finally joined Mitch and told him that if Mitch liked one that he saw tell him the number. Then Ying would arrange to have her to come back to the hotel with him, for a fee of course!

Nervously he scanned the crowd for the best looking, hey, he knew they were not getting married, this was just for fun, but still Mitch had his standards.

"Just tell me what numba you rike" Ying insisted.

"Well Ying, maybe I should see them all first", he replied.

"Not possible, too many girl, take all night." he replied with a grin ear to ear, his head bobbing up and down.

Mitch scanned again, too old, too ugly, too skinny, damn can't even get laid in a whorehouse!

"Maybe you rook at some pic-chaw's?" he said.

"Huh"

"You know, Fo-toes"

"Oh yes, that could help"

A waiter bought another round of beer and a black leather photo album containing a hundred pictures of scantily clad females.

Feeling the pressure of having to make a decision, Mitch gave Ying a number.

"Berry good, berry bootiful gir, I go pick her up, take her to hotel, you have drink with her at bar, you like, you keep, OK?"

"OK"!

Back in the hotel bar Ying introduces him to Karra.

"Nice to meet you Kar-ra" Mitch says.

She giggled and said "not Kar-ra, my name is Carr-raa"

"Oh", he said slowly, trying to imitate her vocals, "Carr-raaa"

"No not Car-raaa", she says still smiling, "Karr-raa"

Maybe the machineguns and exploding bombs has affected his hearing, but it still sounded the same to him.

"Could you spell it for me" he asked, but by now he really didn't give a shit.

"C-A-R-L-A"

He wondered why this poor girl's mother would name her something no one in her family could possibly pronounce properly.

Maybe it was her attitude or maybe her looks, everyone looks better in a one-dimensional photo. In three dimensions she was lacking.

Mitch supposed he was trying to fulfill a fantasy, that being to make love to a girl who looked like the half-French and half-Vietnamese whore in Saigon. Although he hadn't seen her in six months, she had made an indelible impression with her beauty.

"Well Carla I suppose we should get the business out of the way", not knowing of any delicate way to put it, he asked, "What do you charge".

She began with all the nice things she would do for him, take him shopping and make sure the vendors don't rip him off, show him the best sights in Thailand and of course make love to him like no other women could ever do.

"All that sounds nice Carla, but how much?"

"Six days, One hundred American dollar", he did not recall telling her how long he would be in Bangkok. His mind began racing, four dollars each visit at the steam bath, times six equal twenty-four dollars. A Saigon hooker, seven dollars, times six, equal forty-two dollars. Six divided into one hundred equal…about sixteen fifty.

"Carla I'll give you twenty five dollars for just one night", love does not come cheap.

What the hell, he had enough money to last the six nights at this rate. He has no intention of going back with money in his pocket anyway. Well Carla wasn't too happy about the arrangement but she accepted his offer. Perhaps she thought she could change his mind during the evening's escapades. But by morning she was gone and it was just Ying and him again.

Feeling somewhat relieved he decided to do a little sightseeing and shopping with Ying. They drove to TIMLAND (Thailand-In-Miniature-land), where native peoples demonstrated Thai culture, Thai Kick Boxing, sword fighting, cock fighting, and of course a demonstration of elephants dragging teakwood logs out of the jungle. All very interesting but the real excitement came when he met the Boa Constrictor. The snake was ten feet long and weighed over seventy pounds. Its owner began to wrap the reptile around his shoulders and neck. Nervously Mitch asked if it had been fed recently. He was assured

"she", would not want to eat just yet.

"So why is she squeezing me", he asked nervously.

"She likes you"!

With a photo taken by Ying, it took two to un-coil the serpent creature.

But by far the best was the solid gold Buddha, fifty tons of gleaming yellow metal. The big guy housed in his own private temple on the outskirts of town, he smiled at all who came to see him from his reclining position. Mitch wondered if they would miss his big toe?

The next few nights went according to plan, a new girl each night until he found the right one. On the fifth night Ying and Mitch revisited an old club where he had met the more attractive ladies of the night. There he found someone to keep the testosterone flowing, nicest one yet. He asked her to be his date for the evening and to his astonishment she rejected him.

"What!" he exclaimed, "Why, don't you like me?"

"You Ok, but you berry big Bangkok butterfly."

"What do you mean" he asked flabbergasted.

"You fly like butterfly, all over Bangkok, from one girl, to another girl"

"Oh, I see, I have a reputation"

"But sweetie, I was only waiting for you", spoken as smooth as Thai silk.

She smiled, seemingly to accept his excuse. A bit more prodding and she conceded, besides most of the other GI's had already left with dates. He did promise however, to keep her until he left Bangkok. After all she was the best in five days of searching.

They went on a date to the movies. He resisted at first but conceded only after she informed Mitch that, waitresses inside the theater served beer and wine. Then they did some more night clubbing, and finally ended back at the sin bin.

In the hallway from the elevator to the room, sweetie and he came across another GI who was not doing too well. He had his arms around two escort ladies who were in fact supporting him as he tried to walk to his room. His head bobbed up and down, as he stumbled along.

"Is he alright", Mitch asked the girls out of concern for a fellow GI.

"He take too many drugs, bean like diss for five day" one of the girls said.

His escorts and Mitchell's spoke to each other in native tongue, then Sweetie said he will be fine, smoked too much opium, probably won't remember it, or Thailand!

After double bolting the door, they quickly went to it! Sexually she was fine, but afterwards Mitch felt he was being treated like a "John", her heart was just not in it.

The following morning the three of them were having breakfast in the hotel cafeteria. Ying and Sweetie excused Mitch as he went to the Men's room. He strode out into the lobby and down the hall. Upon his exit from the relief station, he came face to face with an absolutely gorgeous creature applying a fresh coat of lipstick in the mirror that hung between the two bathrooms. He recognized her as an escort by the black lace mini skirt, spiked heels and teased hair tastefully done. She obviously was not at the hotel alone. Mitch summoned up some courage.

"Hi, Ahhh I hope you don't mind my saying so, but you are wasting your time with that"

"Oh, why you tell me dat", she said turning to face him with a notable smirk.

"Because you're already the most beautiful woman in Thailand"!

The smirk turned to smile, "I am in", he thought.

"Are you with someone" stating the obvious.

"Yes", she said with a shrug, "But he not so nice like you", her eye's scanning Mitch from head to toe.

"Are you with someone", she asked turning back to the mirror.

"Yes, but she's not so nice either".

After quickly devising a plan to rid each of them of their excess baggage, he returned to the table and instructed Ying to take Sweetie home with an ample cash gratuity. This was surely going to feed the fire of his reputation, but with one day left he still had a mission to accomplish. Namely to bed down with someone who excited him as much as, well you know who!

They met for dinner at 6:30 pm, Ying had gone to her home and brought her back to the hotel. Then we were off to a fancy restaurant where the matre'd pulled the chair out for his date and himself. It was now he realized that prostitution is a respected profession here. This girl is treated like she was his wife. They ate, drank and watched an elaborate stage show, and drank some more. She was beautiful and getting more so by the drink.

At dinner, he worked himself into a frenzy thinking of having sex with this very young and beautiful creature. Ok, so maybe it was the booze, but whatever it was, he was ready. Soon it was time for a romp in the sack. He opened the hotel room door and led her into his short time palace.

Mitch tried a clumsy attempt at small talk but all he could think of, was wild and passionate sex. He made his move towards her.

"No wait" she exclaimed.

"I want to take your clothes off you very slowly"

Oh shit, this is great, she's sexy too!

She began with little nibbling kisses to the neck and face. Then the shirt buttons one at a time, slowly kissing the exposed areas as she worked her way down. With her tiny hands she released his belt buckle and pulled the pant zipper down to the stop. Noticing the sweat beads on his forehead she asked.

"You like me to kiss you here", she asked with grin.

Not being able to speak, he nodded affirmative.

After removing all their clothing, he took a long look at his new love goddess. Her petite frame reminded him of a very young girl, almost too young. Somehow her breasts seemed smaller than before she removed the lace bra. Her skin is flawless as she stood naked in front of the dresser mirror and applied fresh lipstick to puckered lips. Mitch assumed it was a Thai tradition to have sex with colored lips. Then she turned and slid under the covers while turning out the light.

For the next several hours they fornicated in the bed, on the dresser, on the bathroom counter, the floor, the chair, no place in the room was sacred. Lights went on, then off, then on again. At one point he had removed the dresser mirror to position it on the chair next to the bed so they could watch themselves. This of course was done at her request. She knew more positions than did the Kama Sutra. Not one part of her silky soft body went untouched by hand or mouth, and vice versa. Whenever he would become flaccid after an explosive orgasm, she would massage him back to full erection utilizing muscles in her vagina, with him still inside her! She was without a doubt, the best sex he had ever had.

He laid in exhaustion on the bed trying to catch his breath when his "little sugar flower" enthusiastically went to her purse to extract her silk scarf with which she would show him "something new", that she had learned.

"I like you, no extra charge for this", she spoke sincerely.

She sat at the edge of the bed with her left leg tucked under the right leg that dangled over the side but too short to reach the floor. With her black scarf she began talking of her past life, before becoming a hooker. She began in a small village far north of Bangkok. Her father was a poor farmer with many children and had sold her into slavery. She talked as she held the delicate silk by one corner between thumb and forefinger, letting it hang down and gathering the material together to form a long black line.

At one point she had been kidnapped and taken to Greece, where she was first forced into prostitution. There she learned how to make Greek love. She continued as she wrapped a portion of the silk around petite fingers to form a simple knot.

"I was stolen by a competitor, a very bad man, and taken to France".

"There I learned how to make French love". She tied more small silk knots, each a perfect distance from the other.

"My French boss traded me to a Spaniard, who taught me how to make love to Spanish men".

He wanted to yell BULLSHIT, but he was curious as to where she was going with this story, so he simply asked how she ended back here.

More knots now, that the scarf begins to resemble a black beaded necklace.

"Well I escaped from the Spaniard cause he beat me"

Another knot tied.

"I knew people in Bangkok, so I returned here, there are many soldiers who need me", she added, "like you"!

"There, all done"

"What are you going to do with that", Mitch inquired.

"I am going to put this into your butt, leaving this little bit out" she stated a matter of fact.

"Then I am going to put Mr. Turtle Head into my mouth", his surprised look seemingly going unnoticed.

"When you ready to have orgasm, I will pull fast the scarf out", she demonstrated with a quick motion of her arm, "at just the right moment and I will drain you of all your love juice", she smiled proudly.

No fucking way!

"You won't be able to perform orgasm again for one month", she said with an ear to ear grin.

Mitch's head was racing at the thought of not being able to have a climax for a whole month.

"Turn over baby".

"Are you fucking nuts, you ain't put'n that up my ass".

"You like, you see".

So, having missed the opportunity to be drained dry of all his love juice and unable to have intercourse for a month, he opted for another round of missionary sex. At some time in the wee hours of the last morning in Bangkok, Mitch had passed out from sheer exhaustion.

He first heard the water in the bathtub running before realizing that he had but hours left before returning to his unit in Vietnam, a place that he truly did not think about for six whole days.

Perhaps one more romp in the bathtub before I leave the love goddess and Bangkok, he proposed to himself. He threw back the sheet and marched for the bathroom. Entering, he saw her in the tub playing with the water. Noticing a black, longhaired wig placed on the toilet tank lid, he turned to see his love goddess in a sober light.

"Come sit with me" the little girl said.

He wanted to ask her what happened to her big sister but knew that this nubile nymphet was in fact his love goddess. He stared at her inquisitively as he stood looking down at her trying to clear the fog in his brain.

"How old are you", Mitch asked, hoping that he hadn't broke any laws here.

"Sixteen"

Lowering himself into the hot water and facing her, he looked hard to see any resemblance of the mature, experienced courtesan that had pleasured him to exhaustion.

"What happened to the older girl I was with last night", he asked searching for an answer to why he did not recognize his lust interest.

"Oh, you did not look at me so hard", she replied.

"You did not see my wig, or my put-on eye lashes, and I have a padded bra", she spoke like the little girl she was.

"You tricked me", he exclaimed

"You did not care before how old I was"

"But I……", it was no use to argue.

She washed his legs chest and back, he would not let her touch him anywhere else. Then she began to giggle.

"What's so funny", he asked.

"Mr. Turtle Head goes inside"

"Huh" looking down between his legs, "Oh that", feeling somewhat embarrassed.

"You want to make love some more", she asked softly.

"No, I gotta go".

As he dressed he began to feel nervous about returning to Vietnam. Would this little girl be the last he would have to make love to?

Suddenly he thought of his girlfriend back home. He wondered, if she was doing the same things that he had done.

"Better write a letter home as soon as I get back".

Mitch tipped Ying generously after dropping him at the airport and thanked him profusely. He really got to like him and hoped to see Ying again.

"You're not so far away Ying, after the war maybe I'll come to see you again"

"I hope you can do dat" he replied, handing him his business card.

Now Mitch's mission was accomplished, no money in his pockets. He picked up the duffel bag and walked towards the terminal.

Sitting on the plane he stared out the window as they flew along at higher altitudes than he was used to. Soon he would be back in his helicopter flying just above the trees.

Still not quite ready to think of returning to combat he tried recalling events of the recent past. The thoughts appeared, and swam around inside his head of the six glorious days and nights in Bangkok. And his love goddess, perhaps she told the truth about her sexual plights. After all where else could she have learned all those wonderful tricks?

Returning felt so very different, he supposed it was because he was now a veteran of the war, having completed half his tour of duty. He was much smarter now, maybe too smart to return to combat. He thought of going AWOL briefly but quickly discounted that option after all he was still in Asia somewhere.

The plane touched down at Tan Son Nhut airbase, it looked quite different from the first night they landed in country. From the small window porthole he could see hundreds of people going about their duties in the sweltering heat. With aircraft parked on the ground of every description, being prepared for missions.

Well I've made this far maybe, just maybe I can make it all the way, he surmised.

Bangkok has already begun to fade in Mitchell's thoughts, still one thing is certain, he will miss the experience, all of it, even his dubious reputation as the "Bangkok butterfly".

Again, the doors of the plane opened filling the cabin with a surge of superheated air and that smell that Mitchell knew all too well.

Sunrise over the delta, an EMU heads into the sun, passing over the Saigon River.

Chapter Thirteen

War is Hell

Returning to Tinh Bien Hoa Province where Bearcat was situated was like never having left, nothing's changed. It still looked, and smelled the same. Mitchell began unpacking the duffel bag of the new clothes that he had purchased in Bangkok, and those clothes that he had brought with him from the real world. His civvies were his connection to the real world even if he could only "feel" like a civilian for just six days and nights.

All too soon the recognizable sound was heard of the platoon Sergeant's boots on the wood floor. The Sergeant approached Mitchell's bunk area as he neatly folded a pair of new silk pants. Walking down the center of the isle with a clipboard in his hand, the Sergeant's eyes were glued on Mitchell as he came near. Mitchell kept his head low in hopes that the Sergeant would not recognize him and just keep on walking by. Stopping to talk directly at Mitchell, he informed Mitch, with a cynical grin that he was back on the duty roster. He would be back in the air by the following morning. Great, he thought, I go from a civilian lover, to aerial combat soldier in less than twenty-four hours.

With everything unpacked, and little else to do, he decided to head over to the club for a drink. Mitchell's next goal is to find out how the missions went the past week in his absence. He wanted to get a "heads up", to see how many helicopters, or crewmembers have been shot up. Like Mitchell said before, "I don't like surprises". He needed to know if the flight was working in any new AO's, or hot LZ's. Mental preparation is half the battle you know, it's when you're caught off guard that mistakes are made. One mistake here may be all you will ever get.

At four in the afternoon the Monsoon rains came like clockwork. A heavy torrential downpour, that occurred each day, for about an hour. It rained so hard you could not see the fifty feet or so to the barracks next door. The rainfall on corrugated metal roofs pounded loudly as the water ran off the sides like a mountain waterfall. Soon it would end, leaving everything soaked and the ground all muddy.

Dodging the puddles, and jumping over the more gooey parts of the terrain, Mitchell made his way to the recreation room and bar. Nothing has changed here either. The room was filled with the stench of sweaty, alcohol-laden soldiers, cigarette smoke, and an occasional fart. This commingled with the sounds of loud rock-n-roll music, poker chips falling on wood tables, and conversations loaded with "fuck this" and "fuck that". It scared Mitchell that he is growing comfortable within this life style. He felt strangely at ease here in his familiar surroundings.

"Aye ya bloody bastard you", came a familiar voice from the bearded Aussie who bellied up to the bar from a table a few feet away.

"How's yer R-n-R", he spoke as he brushed the beard with one hand away from his lips.

"Bangkok, right mate"

"Yea, too short, but I had a fucking good time", Mitch replied.

Bennie, was the kind of guy who was in the know about everything that went on in the company, he talked a lot with everyone.

"Hey Bennie, anything going on that I need to know about, I am scheduled to fly tomorrow, and I could use a briefing".

"Right Mate, not much doing here, no worries", he said as he raised his hand to summon the barkeeper, "Ave a big drink-n float the boat", the Royal Australian Navy personnel have their own language. So with little going on Mitchell gulped down a CC&7, at least he'll sleep a little better tonight.

If the truth be told, he was anxious to get back into the air and flying combat assaults. He missed his regular adrenaline rushes. Daily multiple near death experiences can make you as high as an opium-den caretaker. Anything else is boring, and to be bored is a torturously time expanding, and a mentally cruel state.

It was difficult to get out of the bunk the next morning, a little extra sleep might have made all the difference with his disposition which seemed to be sinking. Maybe it was the platoon sergeant waking Mitch in the midst of a beautiful dream about some lovely girl, whose face he had not clearly seen. But he could feel her warmth and passion as he embraced her tightly. Then as he looked to see into her eye's, to verify whether she was round-eyed or slant, he was jolted from the deep sleep. The impact of waking up to the ambient surroundings left him feeling empty and very lonely.

Bangkok now seemed like a hallucination that he had long ago. As Mitchell sat looking out over the passing terrain his chopper was on the way to the AO. So early this morning, it felt like he never left this place. The helicopter's noise and radio communications have heightened his senses to a point of awareness, that all else has faded. Mitchell was a weapon again, somehow he thought it would have been harder to return to the hostilities.

The slicks are waiting back in the PZ, while the Taipan's did an aerial survey in the LZ. Negative suppression was ordered when the flight arrives, even though there has been recent enemy activity. The flight was on alert to avoid shooting anywhere near the village that lies to the southeast several klicks away. The village is empty now, but the villagers want it back in one piece when the troops finish the operation here. A single stray tracer can start a hooch on fire which in turns starts the others burning. And if the wind is right the whole village goes up in smoke. The gunships circle the LZ wide and begin closing in towards the center of the LZ on each completed three hundred sixty-degree turn.

"I've got two possible in the tree line that we just flew over", Mitchell reported to the pilot. The pilot then keyed his mike to transmit to the wing ships.

"Taipan's, lead, two eligible in the tree line, anyone else got-em"

"Negative, report", the wing ship called out.

"You sure you got something", asked Mitchell's pilot.

"There look", Mitch said pointing out into thin air.

"You see-em, crouched down, hiding behind those bushes", he spoke loudly into his microphone to overcome the wind noise.

Mitchell knew his voice sounded excited, but he tried to speak clearly and distinctly. They were nearly on top of them by now. Definitely two, one appeared to be a woman with her conical hat covering her chest. Was she hiding a weapon also? It did not matter that one was a female. In combat if you take up arms against your enemy you are eligible for termination. Both were hiding low behind a bush that bordered the front of the tree line. A few steps back and they could disappear into the thick tree line.

"Ahhh, Charlie-Charlie, Taipan Lead"

"Go Lead"

"We've got two possible eligible ahhh in a tree line at the edge of the LZ", "What do you want us to do with them, over"

"Stand-by lead".

They tried hard to see them again more clearly, but the bushes obscured the enemy. In the crouched position it was difficult to know whether or not they had weapons. The Taipan's got as close as they could without becoming a clear target themselves. A few seconds elapsed and then the call came.

"The slicks are inbound, lead, can't take any chances, get-em outta there", radioed C&C.

"Roger, cleared to fire"

Mitchell didn't really need the pilot to tell him when to shoot, "clearance", meant "cleared to fire when ready", and he was ready. Mitch squeezed the trigger and let fly the tracers that pointed to the two in the tree line. A long burst with accurate aiming. Damn, he felt good that he still had a steady aim! They flew at an angle across the front of their position, firing all the while, and then breaking left, ninety degrees, just before over flying them. Mitch looked back under the tail boom to confirm his KIA's.

Tran Le Tam, and her little sister *le Yen* had listen to the elders read the pamphlets that had been circulated through their hamlet. There was to be a military operation in their vicinity in three days. All inhabitants were required to vacate the immediate area. *Le Tram's* brother had been recruited into the Army of the Republic of Vietnam some eight months ago. Upon hearing of the operation she immediately assumed that her brother was coming home and she desperately wanted to see him again.

After convincing her little sister that their eldest brother was going to be in the operation they devised a plan to visit a cousin in a neighboring village before the operation began. Then early on the day of the operation they would sneak back to their hamlet and wait for their brother. *Le Yen* wanted to know if they would get in trouble if they were not supposed to be there. *Le Tam* assured her they would hide until they saw their brother, after that she didn't care what happened.

Both girls heard the loud popping sounds of the machine that flew and breathed fire. Their hearts pounded as they ran to the rear of the hooch along the path that ran parallel to a tree line towards the sound of the air machines. Entering a thick brush Le Tam whispered to her sister to keep low and don't move. Overhead they saw the air machines drawing nearer *Le Yen* became scared and wanted to run as the noise from the flying dragon grew louder. Her older sister shouted at her to stay still but *Le Yen* was too nervous and jittery. The machines flew circles in front of them and *Le Tam* felt secure in the thought that they are well concealed. *Le Tam* reached out to take *Le Yen's* hand when she heard the strange sound of impacts all around them. At the same instant she heard rapid zipping noise through the brush, and a dull thud, and sudden jolt of Le Yens hand that she had been holding. She quickly pulled her sister's hand closer but did not feel any weight on the other end. Le Tam looked down to observe her sisters detached hand cradled in her own hand.

Wing one was in position to fire just as the slicks returned and began their approach into the LZ.

"Hold your fire, Taipan's", commanded C&C.

"We'll let the troops get your eligible's if their still there",

"Cover the flight".

The Taipan's broke off their engagement and followed Taipan lead. Rolling out, they banked right towards the arriving flight. One of the Taipan's would hold back behind the flight just in case the VC in the bush came out firing. With enough altitude he was ready with rockets.

The slicks are but seconds in the LZ, the troops have disembarked and the slicks lift off again to return to the PZ for another load. Meanwhile, the Taipan's got back to the tree line where the two targets have been suppressed. They find nothing, they're gone, and that usually meant they got away unscathed, or other enemy not seen has carried the bodies away. Mitch looked for signs of blood, no luck, no body count, two confirmed here would raise his tally to more than a dozen, but the gruesome score card went unchanged.

It would be a few more minutes before the flight returned with another load. The Taipan's buzzed the treetops of the tree line closest to the advancing ground troops. The thick foliage of trees and shrubs was not very wide, it was more of a border between the rice paddies. As they passed over the other side Mitch saw two forms walking away from the tree line on the opposite side into the adjoining open paddy. He readied the machine gun as they flew closer.

The two have stopped when they heard the approaching gunships. The pair of VC's turned slowly around to look up and confront the airborne predators. Mitch looked for, but saw no weapons. Then he muttered, awe shit, shit, shit, shit, as he could now see they were just two very young females. One looked in her late teens, or early twenties, the other ten, twelve. They continued to walk while the older girl held up one of the arms of the younger girl to show them the missing hand of her right arm. Blood trailed down the little girls arm, over the hand of her companion and down the side of her white blouse. Mitchell knew it was him that had shot the hand off this poor little girl. He was after all, the only one who fired at the enemy ready to ambush the flight in the LZ. Or so it had appeared.

A call went out to the ground troops to try to recover the two girls for medical attention. But the troops were too far away and the girls continued to walk briskly towards the abandoned hamlet. Mitch knew the possibility of loss of blood or infection would kill that child without proper medical attention. Her fate now left to others, he wondered what would happen to her. But how could he find out? He knew he would never really know for sure, ever.

Haunted by what he saw, he reasoned the system did not fail here. This was circumstance, stacked against the two girls that had stupidly tried to hide in a restricted area during an operation that was forewarned. It was circumstance that did not allow the time to check them out more thoroughly due to the arrival of the slicks. No way to let them stay there while the flight was in the LZ. Especially not knowing if they had weapons or not. And it is circumstance that does not allow the flight to turn back or circle the LZ to wait for confirmation. Once the mission has commenced, it continues until accomplished. Far too risky to have the choppers fly around in hostile territory with a load of troops. Finally it was circumstance that allowed Mitchell to be there in the chopper. One more day in Bangkok with that cute whore would have saved this child her agony. At least they were both alive, for now. So why didn't he feel a little better?

After the last insertion of troops all the choppers returned to the PZ to shut down, and wait to extract the troops out from the LZ later in the afternoon.

Three Taipan gunships roar overhead as they flew out past the PZ to secure the landing area where all the slicks have landed and begun to shut down. They stayed in the LZ after the last insertion to ensure the troops didn't get into trouble. After a time when no contact with the enemy was made, the Taipan's were released to join the EMU's in the PZ. It was time for a break, consume some C-rations, and if time permitted, a nap.

The two-lane road ran straight for almost eight klicks between two large Hamlets in the Delta, and was surrounded by water filled rice paddies. It was decided to have the flight shut down on the road. The troops of ARVN's that had just been inserted had been trucked to this point, and then airlifted into the LZ. The area is wide open with the only tree line a couple of klicks away.

A high speed, low level, flyby of the tree line, revealed nothing. The Taipan's returned to the paved road where the slicks landed and shut down the engines. Some of the slick crews have already stripped their shirts and are lying down on the cargo deck escaping the mid-day sun. The two-lane road, is the only "dry" place around for miles, but is bustling with traffic going to and from Saigon some forty miles to the Northwest.

On the landing approach people are walking, riding scooters, and a few scarce automobiles traveling back and forth over the road. The slicks are lined up in single file, down one lane of the highway restricting the traffic flow. As Mitchell's ship slowly converts from flight to a hover at approximately twenty feet, the strong rotor down wash of air nearly blows a few pedestrians into a flooded rice paddy adjacent to the road. An older woman has had her straw hat blown into the water as she cusses the landing helicopter out from under her breath, but moves on regardless. Vehicular traffic has been temporally halted until the entire flight of chopper's shut down and all the rotor blades have stopped turning.

On the ground, Mitchell stayed in his seat to observe the pedestrian traffic that apparently did not seem overly concerned by the presence of fifteen large helicopters sitting on their highway. In fact they hardly gave them a second look, preferring to pass the long column of aircraft expeditiously without looking.

It was now when Mitch truly realized just how upside-down life here in the Nam. Back in the States this scene would cause quite a commotion, all these choppers on a public highway would have attracted large numbers of gawkers, and a heavy police presence, possibly television cameras, and the like, yes sir it would be quite different back home.

He stayed in his seat until the rotor blades came to a full stop, then exited the aircraft to align the blades with the fuselage by hand. With the blades out of harm's way from passing traffic Mitch turned to speak to the pilot whom was writing something in his notepad.

"Fuck man, I really feel bad about the little girl's hand".

"Not your fault chief, there was nothing else to do, we couldn't let unknowns hang out there in the LZ", he said trying to reassure Mitch.

"I know, but this is fucking happening too often".

The pilot stopped writing for a moment and turned to Mitchell.

"War is hell, ain't it", he said with a large grin.

Mitchell reached into his pocket for the Zippo lighter that he purchased in Saigon with the custom engraving that said *"Vietnam 69-70"*, on the lid, and the slogan,

If you kill for pleasure,

You're a sadist.

If you kill for money,

You're a professional.

If you kill for both,

You're a Taipan, is engraved on the lower case. A platoon's slogan that had a ring of truth, we did kill for the pleasure of knowing an American life is saved with each enemy dead. And the Government did pay us for what we do here. And, yes we are Taipan's. But he hoped this was meant only for the duration of his tour of duty! He lit the cigarette dangling from his lips pondering his future with his acquired skills.

He took a long hard drag on the smoke while looking out over the terrain. Mitch felt a little bit nervous sitting in the open like this and having the Vietnamese civilian population passing so closely to the aircraft.

"Who's fucking bright idea was it to shut down here", he asked the pilot.

"Look around man, there ain't no other place else above water" the pilot responded.

"What if one of these fucking gooks wants to toss in a grenade or some shit", was his immediate response.

"Then shoot any mother fucker who gets too close", the pilot commanded.

A little more at ease now with his permission to fire on any enemy who tried to earn him or herself a paid vacation from Uncle Ho, (Ho Chi Minh, the North Vietnamese leader), or a few extra piaster for the folks back home, up North. He crawled under the helicopter with his M-16 rifle to nap in the shaded spot provided by the fuselage. A sniper in that tree-line, far away would have a difficult time getting him here.

About an hour later, THUMP-WHOOSH, and instantly following was felt the impact of the exploding mortar in the flooded rice paddy some six hundred yards away as the water and mud rose up. The slick's gunners who were providing guard duty while the flight was on the ground all began to scream "INCOMMING", while running to their aircraft. Everyone scrambled to get into the air as rapidly as possible. Mitch rolled out from under his ship to see that all the civilian population has disappeared or was in hiding. They were already cranking up the turbine as the second round exploded, THUMP-WHOOSH, not far from the previous one. They must be firing from the limits of the mortar range cause they can't seem to get any closer.

In what seemed impossible in such a short time, were the slicks lifting off. No one performed the pre-flight checks, nor was any start-up procedures followed. The only thing that mattered was to get airborne, now! Some pulled into a hover, kicked the tail over ninety degrees and lifted out. They flew out in every direction away from the incoming explosions. There was no coordinated departure, it was every aircraft for themselves. There would be time later in the air to organize if you made it out. Pilots at the controls with no helmets on, some had no shirts on either, it was truly a Chinese fire drill and free for all to save the aircrafts.

Mitch's ship had to wait on the last slick that was just ahead of them. They finally lifted out to the right leaving a clear path. The Taipan ship was weighed down with armament and needed more runway, or in this case highway, to get airborne. From a low hover the pilot nosed over and began a running takeoff when the turbine's whine began to decrease and down they bounced on the pavement two or three times before the landing skids came grinding to a halt.

Both pilots looked at each other and shrugged their shoulders, the aircraft commander began the restart procedure with no luck. All the other aircraft were airborne now. They are alone on the road, like a sitting duck. The two airborne Taipan wing ships have headed towards the tree line to suppress the mortar fire.

Maybe we've been hit", the pilot announced, "Chief, take a look"

Mitch jumped to the ground and ducked under the tail boom to inspect under the cowling of the left side facing the tree line. Not finding anything unusual, he opened the engine cowling to inspect the engine. Nothing, he went to the co-pilot to see if they figured out their problem.

"Seems like we're not getting any fuel", he said, "But the fuel level is good".

With that statement, Mitch remembered something from helicopter school that an instructor had said while they studied the fuel control system. The fuel control was designed by some genius, who according to the instructor, "went crazy" upon completing the complicated mechanisms that control the fuel at various barometric pressures.

"Don't ever touch it", he warned,

"You guys are too stupid and will only fuck it up"

There was this only one screw slot on the side of the fuel control to make some kind of adjustment, but Mitchell couldn't remember exactly what it's for. What the hell we aren't going anywhere this way he thought to himself, and then asked the Gunner to hand him a box of C-rations. Reaching inside the box for the flat, P-38 folding can opener and removing it. He went back to the fuel control and using the can opener, fitting the flat end into the slot and turned a quarter turn to the right.

Giving the thumbs-up to the pilot he began to restart. He waited to hear the igniters tick, and the transmission, and turbine begin their ascending whine before latching down the engine cowling and returning to his seat. The engine rpm's increased normally and the blades were soon turning at full idle, then at full rpm for liftoff. Slowly he pulled into a hover and held steady to test the bleed off before trying to go airborne. Soon they nosed over, and lifted skyward.

"Well I'll be dipped in shit, I got us flying again with a fucking P-38", Mitch said out loud. Although he had no idea what he did, he decided not to tell anyone just in case something else got fucked up.

The flight flew thirty minutes to a friendly U.S. Navy base that had a moderate airstrip and shut down again. Once there the pilots exited the aircraft and after a few congratulatory pats on the back by the pilots, one of them asked Mitchell,

"So what did you do to get us flying again"?

"I adjusted the fuel control", sounding like he knew exactly what he was doing. Fortunately in flight school the Army does not teach pilots anything about the fuel control system either, other than it is automatic and don't fuck with it. Mitch thought they were impressed with his knowledge of nothing.

Remembering the strange disappearance of the civilians during the mortar attack in conversation with his gunner, the two concluded that the civilians had been forewarned of the attack and knew to stay away from the helicopters sitting on the road. The fact that none of them advised any Americans to the potential disaster made them believe that all of the Vietnamese civilians were VC sympathizers. Maybe Mitchell's uneasiness was not so unfounded.

After a few minutes on the ground, a Navy helicopter armament specialist approached the ship and introduced himself. Curiosity brought him to the ship to compare his Navy aircraft to their Army ships. As he and Mitch talked, the naval aviator noticed, and inquired about the M-79 grenade launcher that lay on the cargo floor. Actually it belonged to the gunner who got it from a slickie, who got it from a dead ARVN that he medivac out of the field when he flew with the slicks.

"The M-79 fires a single 40mm grenade, one at a time and loads like a break-a-way shotgun", Mitch explained while demonstrating to the specialist. He said that he knew of one of his gunship commanders who would give anything for it.

"Whatcha got", Mitchell asked with peaked interest.

"Well how about a 50 caliber machine gun",

"The same kind used from old World War II bombers", he continued.

"Sounds cool, but where could I get ammo for it".

"I'll throw in a case of Incendiary rounds, a case of H.E. (high explosive), and a case of A.P.'s (armor piercing)", he offered.

Mitch promptly asked, "The A.P.'s, can they penetrate a gook bunker".

"Fucking A, they'll even go through a six inch steel plate", he asserted.

"Look man, whatever you fire at with this baby, you send to hell".

"And if you need more ammo, I'll get it for ya", he said begging.

"Deal, go get the bitch", he said, glad to have a new toy to play with.

Then Mitch had to make a deal with the gunner to allow him to fire the big gun sometime, but he was as excited as Mitchell was for the new instrument that would be as unique as anything seen in the Nam. As far as they knew, they would have the only Huey gunship with a fifty cal.

The Specialist returned a few minutes later with three other Navy personnel.

Two carried the machinegun, and two humped the two wood crates that contained the 50 caliber rounds that would set hooch's on fire, pierce the bunkers and kill its occupants, and wipe out a tree line with high explosive rounds. Now they have the tool to penetrate those bunkers, no one can hide now. The swabs laid the gun on the cargo floor along with a special door mount to be installed by our maintenance people back at base.

The rest of the day Mitch stared at Bertha, the name he gave this big beautiful black instrument of destruction. The long fat barrel, with two wooden handgrips, and dual triggers, he couldn't wait to hear her sing.

It would be days before maintenance would complete the installation of Bertha, but soon he had his first opportunity to test fire the big gun.

Mounted on a pedestal attached to the aircraft's frame, the entire gun was mounted outside the aircraft. In the stowed position, the barrel pointed straight down. When Mitchell pulled her back towards him to fire, the cocking lever that had to be cocked twice before firing, was more than an arm's length away. He leaned way forward to cock the gun, she was now ready to sing. Pulling in on the trigger produced the sweet music, POW, POW, POW. The tracers signifying the path of what appeared to be flaming red golf balls towards the ground below. On impact the earth erupted in mud and debris. Mitchell swung the barrel forward to fire ahead of the ship to test the range of motion Bertha had, and to confirm the gun stops prevented him from shooting up his own bird.

Firing straight ahead now, POW, POW, POW, the muzzle flashed so bright he had to look over the end of the barrel, POW, POW, POW, the long barrel extending towards the front of the chopper, POW, POW, POW. The big guns kick is felt through the airframe, and her boisterous report rings in the ear like standing inside a huge church bell being given rapid strikes. He let up on the trigger to hear, FUCKING CEASE FIRE, YOUR BURNING ME GODDAMMIT, shouted into his helmet. Mitch had not realized that the length of the barrel reached all the way forward to the pilot's door opening, as there is no door. When he fired, the muzzle flash had burned the side of the pilots face, that, and the noise was deafening in his right ear. Ok, so he just would have to fire out to the side, and that was ok with Mitch.

After a couple of weeks of banging away on Bertha, finally came an opportunity to test the bunker resistance against the 50 Cal armor piercing rounds. Two VC have been spotted by the Taipan's, and took up running. One is killed by the crew-chief in the lead gunship, in a clearing surrounding a hooch that the two were heading for. It was known to be vacated because the ARVN troops had already passed through this area and radioed in the vacated dwelling. Somehow they missed the two enemies who probably felt it was safe to move after some time the troops passed. The remaining VC ran into the vacated hooch of a local farmer. The farmer's water buffalo is tied to a nearby tree, chickens scurry about on the ground and a pig nervously runs in circles around the hooch.

The helicopter is now at strike altitude and noses over to begin the rocket attack. The first misses, exploding forty feet from the hooch and leaving a hole in the earth. A second is fired, missed, striking a palm tree behind the hooch, sending the whole top clump of leaves and stems crashing to the ground. The third hits the rear left corner of the hooch sending a large section of the straw roof skywards, exposing the interior.

The gunship banks out to the right at fifty feet, circling the structure.

A look inside the hooch revealed a bunker on the opposite side of the hole. Still it is no problem for Bertha. Mitch held his fire until the rocket attack ceased so the pilot could fire his rockets without Bertha frying his face. As the ship dove down towards the ground, they were ready to go to work. Waiting to come around to the large hole in the roof, Mitch took aim and pulled the trigger. Round after round of AP's penetrating the bunker sending up debris in rapid succession until finally the bunker collapsed. If the enemy had tried to take shelter within the bunker he has surely regretted that decision now. Mitchell finally realizes he has a tool that works now so there is no hiding for the enemy.

Unfortunately there were no ground troops available to go back into the hooch to confirm or deny the remaining enemy's status. They could only speculate his demise. Taipan's claim one KIA.

Back at base camp Bearcat, Mitchell was bragging about Bertha's performance to another crew-chief when the TI, (tech. inspector), came to his aircraft to inspect the gun mounts. With a dental mirror and flashlight he crawled under the fuselage. After a few seconds had passed, the TI's voice rang out.

"Ahhh haa, just as I thought", he exclaimed!

"What, what's there, what's wrong", Mitch questioned.

Hey, when the TI says "Ah ha" about a machine that he flew in every day, he needed to know what the tech "Ah ha'd" about.

"This birds getting stressed out", he said.

"What, what do you mean", Mitch asked inquisitively.

"The fifty cal is putting too much stress on the airframe", he explained.

"There is metal fatigue damage, small cracks in the airframe"?

"Here, I'll show you" he said as he bent down with his flashlight.

The TI had been keeping a close eye on Mitchell's bird, which was standard operating procedure for any experimental equipment added to any aircraft.

Sure enough Bertha's recoil was busting up the old bird and would have to be removed right away.

A victory for the VC, yea that's what it is, with the Fifty Cal. gone they could once again escape the wrath of Bertha. Mitch felt as though he had to win the war with one hand tied behind his back. How could we be expected to win like that? Now how is he going to get into those bunkers, he thought? His M-60 is going to feel like firing a peashooter now!

"Yea, war is hell", Mitch mumbled.

Not all missions go according to plans.

Chapter Fourteen

Bad Vibes

It had been a long day of flying missions, and they had returned to base late in the afternoon. After performing the helicopters daily maintenance Mitch dragged himself over to the ammo shed where a section alongside the steel container was set up for the gunners. Makeshift plywood overhang and table, with a steel drum cut in half lengthways filled with solvent, made up the weapon's cleaning station. Mitch was helping the gunner clean the guns so they could all eat before the chow hall closed down for the night. Cleaning the guns was a messy job. The combination of gunpowder and cleaning solvents left the cleaning area saturated in black oily muck. The odor was strong and permeated the skin on the hands, the fingernails were always black and nearly impossible to get clean again. The M-60's were broken down into their smallest parts and each scrubbed meticulously clean, then thoroughly inspected. The guns bore had to be perfect and straight. It was possible for a barrel to become so hot that it could warp. This time consuming procedure left little time for anything else but a quick shower after the meal, so they ate with dirty and smelly hands.

With the passing of the afternoon's monsoon rains, the air was left with a chill. In Hell, even seventy five degrees can feel chilly. Mitch stepped out from under the showerhead and quickly drew the towel around him. After brushing his teeth he hurried out of the shower building, flip flops flapping against bare heels as he climbed the stairs to the second floor taking two steps at a time. Then off to his bunk to make ready for a good night's sleep. It seemed he always slept better in the cool of the night. The afternoon naps in the heat of the day served only to drain more energy. Besides, who could really sleep in the midday heat and humidity? It was tough enough for him just to breathe.

Mitchell drew back his camouflaged nylon poncho liner that served as a blanket. It was very thin and lightweight but comfortably warm when needed. Still, he has not become accustomed to the three-inch thin mattress that separated the weight of the body from the flat springs that lay beneath. But tonight he simply did not care, he was too exhausted to feel anything. Mitch kicked off the flip-flops and slipped in between the blanket and top sheet.

Mere seconds later, Mitchell was immersed in another one of his erotic dreams, they were having a vigorous sexual romp. There was nothing but the two of them, naked, hugging, and kissing passionately. He opened his eyes to look into her big blue round eyes and beautiful face. A feeling of ecstasy overcame him as the two of them fell through space in slow motion upon a thick pile of bear skin rugs, still embracing each other. Then with their passion appeased, they laid in bliss fondling each other gently. Her arms were around his neck, silky soft hands lightly touching his back. Mitchell stroking her shoulders, his feet are rubbing the cozy hide of the bearskin. Oh yea, he thought, that feels so nice, the thick silky hair. His toes continued to rub the fur as she began to slowly fade away, like a slow lifting fog she would soon fade in oblivion. But it was of no consequence since Mitchell was totally satisfied now. All he felt is the fur on his feet, which he continued to caress ever so slowly with his toes. She was gone now but the fur that he was feeling was still there. As he gradually became aware of the reality of his true existence, he hazily wondered why he could still feel the soft fur on his toes.

In a flash, the heart rate soared, Mitchell's eyes popped open like a lightning bolt and he threw back the blanket with such force that he was exposed from head to toe in an instant. He lifted only his head to see. Even in the black of night he saw the large rat that hovered at his feet. Its dark dimensions in ghostly contrast to the white sheet. His courage wouldn't allow him to scream outwardly but he silently panicked.

The creature shrieked and hopped as it scurried along the side of his left leg, up past the torso and leaped off his shoulder and jumped to the floor below. It happened so fast that Mitchell was frozen as it soared past his head. He could swear he felt its slimy tail smack his cheek. The rodent was long gone before Mitchell signaled a reaction as though he had been attacked by a hoard of those furry grotesque creatures. Kicking and flailing with his arms in quiet desperation to keep away the unseen.

Following his rapid heartbeat and profuse sweating the breathing became laborious as he tried in vain to fall back into repose. Looking around the barracks all the others were sound asleep, he wondered how many other of his platoon mates were having similar dreams that would end in near horror. Like Mitchell, no one would confess in the light of day, his fear of the rats. To admit to having fear, was to show weakness.

The following morning Mitchell marked his short timer's calendar, one hundred and fifty six days short today. It didn't sound like such a short time to rotate back to the world, but at least he was over the halfway mark. Mitchell has been here long enough to become numb to the experience and now only desires to get it over quickly.

Mitch felt really drowsy this morning, last night's encounter with the bearskin rug left him unable to return to slumber. His nerves shattered by the possibility of having his nose chewed off by a filthy carnivorous rat, as did another unfortunate GI who passed out drunk only to wake with a partial nose. At least that was the rumor du jour.

The missions started late this morning, the ARVN's were slow to get organized, seemed there was confusion everywhere. There were ARVN officers with riding crops whipping young soldiers into submission. Nice, he thought, hell of a way to command your troops. The subordinates all had rifles, Mitch believed he wouldn't have whipped anyone with a weapon. Still the confusion persists until finally C&C gave orders for the EMU flight to crank up. Taipans did not need a command from C&C because they went anywhere the EMU's went.

The Taipan heavy fire team lifted off ahead of the flight. The three gunships were in the vicinity of the LZ a scant ten minutes later. Approaching the LZ the lead Taipan pilot got a visual on a gathering of more than a dozen persons. As they neared he noticed they were all wearing black silk shirts and long pants. The group walked along a rice dyke in single file, one behind the other. But wait, there's something else, they have round khaki pith helmets and are harnessed into tan belts that cross over both shoulders and around their waist, and they carry AK-47's.

Holy shit, hardcore NVA soldiers in the open, marching! Surely they heard the thundering reverberation of the approaching fire team coming but there was nowhere for them to hide. The pilot apprised C&C of the situation.

The column of enemy soldiers have picked up their pace walking away from the fast approaching helicopters. Only a half a klick away, it is too late to hide now. The lead ship dove unto the column of enemy, both wing ships in trail. Running parallel to the enemy and approaching from the rear. Knowing that they knew of the impending exchange they have retained their composure for the moment. Possibly they thought the helicopters would not suspect them if they did not run. Taipan lead furiously worked the radio to establish clearance before the enemy decided to take the defensive.

The lead gunship overshot the column before "cleared to fire", was received by C&C. The first wingman's crew-chief opened up on the congregation scattering them like angry ants on a disturbed mound. Mitchell's pilot spoke anxiously as he reminded the back seat gunners to shoot first anyone who raises their weapon towards them. The NVA took off in every direction but there was no place to hide or take cover. Three ran straight ahead down the dyke, others took off across the rice paddy slowed by the waters depth and soft earth bottom. So determined to save their own lives none of the enemy seemed to even think to fire a weapon at them. Possibly, if they had they all raised their AK-47's in unison, they could have shot down at least one of them. Taipan's bank right, anxiously Mitch waited seconds for the trail ship to clear out of the way before he opened up with his machinegun. He heard the pilot say something about wanting to use rockets, to score himself some KIA's, but they were already much too low.

Shooting ducks in a pond, it was the first time they had caught so many in the open. The radio voices were as excited as school children in the play-yard. Everyone wanted in on the action, gunner's unfastened seat belts so that they could slide their ammo cans to the right door to take their shot at some of the ducks. Both gunners firing out the same door opening with one shooting forward the other aft, nothing could be missed, nothing was.

Mitch didn't have time to count how many fell on the first volley of fire but some lay motionless faced down in the now agitated shallow waters of the rice paddies. The flight continued the right hand orbits. Three full orbits were all it took until the entire congregation of enemy had been dropped in what seemed like seconds.

The carnage left the area covered in blood and debris. Bodies torn and twisted in every which way, helmets floating in murky water, unfired weapons scattered, and the personal belongings of people now expelled from service to their country lay dispersed.

Having done the dirty work for the ARVN's saved them from assaulting their own kind. With the exception of their politics, and their uniforms, they were indeed, the same! Mitchell couldn't help but to wonder how many of those young ARVN's would have been killed in a skirmish with these highly motivated and well-equipped individuals.

The EMU flight arrives moments later with the troops whose responsibility it was to search and destroy the enemy that now lay motionless in the shooting gallery. Collecting the bodies is all that remained for the young ARVN soldiers who live to fight another day.

In all, fourteen NVA were killed, none escaped the onslaught. One had been an officer and had papers on him indicating the possibility that there were many more of them in the area on a major campaign to control the area's peasant farmers. Probably to secure ample supplies of rice for the upcoming dry season to feed their troops.

Returning to base a "Successful Mission Fly Over" was called for. The Taipan's entered the traffic pattern in offset trail formation, trailing smoke from both sides of the aircraft. Then buzzing in low over their company area, a hard cyclic climb pointed the nose of the chopper skyward, to near zero airspeed. Then, at approximately three hundred feet of altitude, the pilot kicked the tail rotor pedal hard right. The nose now pointing nearly straight down causes the crew to go momentarily weightless in their seats as they dive back towards terra firma, thus completing the "Cyclic Climb, and Pedal Turn" maneuver.

On the ground and back to maintenance duty the cycle repeats once again. If not for the day's missions where anything can happen, the boredom of the routine shit would be unbearable. Taking their time, as today they have returned earlier, some of the chiefs and gunners gathered together on the flight line to bullshit about today's mission. No one "shook hands", or "congratulated" themselves, but they did comment on how stupid the enemy had been for not turning their weapons on them. And they did talk of how many each had killed, or at least thought they had. If all truly had killed as many as claimed there should have been more than fifty of them. Still in some way they felt sorrow for the poor bastards who were probably new to the Delta region and had been ill advised by their commanding officer. Never should have tried crossing those open paddies in the light of day.

The bullshit session had lasted longer than anyone would have liked and the sky had begun to turn dark. Mitch returned to his ship to button up the cowlings and finish straightening the cabin. Butch had approached him from behind,

"Hey man, how's it going" he spoke slowly. Mitch was suspicious of his tone and turned to face him.

"Cool man, what's up", he asked knowing there was more than casual conversation coming.

Butch is a surfer, who hails from California, he wore a beaded necklace and wristband and frequently partook in high-grade wacky weed. His blond hair was curly and he had a thin blond mustache. When he smiled his teeth were perfectly straight and he giggled like a little kid. They were the same age, nineteen, and had become very good acquaintances and hung out together when off duty.

Talking of home and the future was a favorite pastime. He was an EMU crew-chief and often complained about the ARVN's being lazy and that they "stunk up" his ship. Many times he would provoke the ARVN troops into an angry mob while in route to the LZ, in hopes that one of them would turn a weapon on him, "so I can have an excuse to blow his shit away". But instead they just thought he was crazy and did not pay much attention to him. Butch wanted to be in the gunship platoon very badly, saying that they got to "kill a lot more fucking gooks" than he could with the EMU's.

"Hold out your hand dude", Butch's request was very suspicious.

"Why, whatcha got there", asked Mitch hesitatingly putting his right hand out, palm up. He trusted Butch, had no reason not to, but he was also leery of practical jokes. It was dark by now and there are no lights on the flight line, so it is very dark. Butch laid the object in his hand, and he promptly closed his fingers around it.

"What's this man, I don't smoke cigars"

"It's not a cigar", he said grinning his perfect smile and a little giggle.

"I can't see it, what the fuck is it", holding the article closer to his face.

"It's some motherfuckers little finger".

In disbelief Mitch continued to hold "it".

"Where the fuck did ya get it man", he asked thinking someone left it somewhere where Butch could find it.

"I got it from one of those gooks you guy's wasted this morning", he continued.

"We were the ones who evac'ed the KIA's out"

In total disbelief, "You're fucking with me, come on where did ya get it".

"I am telling ya, I cut the son-of-a-bitch off", he said still giggling.

Suddenly Mitch felt bad vibes, this just did not feel right, not the finger mind you, something else.

"Why Butch", he asked.

"Going to send it home, cool souvenir huh", again he started with the giggle.

Then Mitchell realized this is just got to be some big joke,

"Naw, you're shitting me".

Butch had no way to cut anybody's finger off, even if he had a pocketknife, it would be quite difficult to get through the bone. So sure he was right he then asked Butch,

"So how the fuck could you cut it off, and with what", thinking he had him now. Butch leaned in close towards him almost whispering even though they were the only people in sight.

"I used needle nose pliers", "you know the little wire cutters at the end", he continued,

"Wasn't easy though, I had to cut and pull-n-twist the fucker off", he spoke and authenticated with his hands. Mitch took the pinkie finger with the three fingers of his left hand and closely scrutinized it. The little fingernail convinced him that it was genuine. He handed Butch back the hacked off appendage.

Butch took the finger and held it by the exposed piece of the bone protruding from the cut end and then with his other hand pulled on the tendon below the bone that was also exposed. By pulling on the tendon Butch was able to curl the finger as though it had a life of its own. It was a morbid moment to watch this severed human finger flex and curl at Butch's will. Playing with parts of someone's body just doesn't feel right. After all how could one know if you were pissing off the deceased, and what, if anything, would they do about it? Mitch knew that he did not want to find out. Really bad vibes man!

This was a different side of Butch than the one Mitch knew, somehow, something must have changed within him. He was always a happy sort and talked of surfing, girls, and cars, which is exactly what they had in common. He spoke too of his parents and older brother whom he always thought very highly of. He wore colored beads on a leather necklace representing the hippies of the peace movement and love. And he was always quick to put up the two fingers to flash the peace sign. But the environment here did not allow them to have that peace or to feel any sort of love. So perhaps without those positive feelings, what is left is the negativity of the war and that was getting to him. Butch had seen a lot of death, of that which he caused, and that he witnessed. Whatever it was Mitch hoped it would not happen to him. Butch put the pinkie in his top pocket and walked with Mitch back to the billet area. They only ever did spoke of that finger once again.

Over the next few days they returned to the AO where they had surprised the ducks in the shooting gallery. Battalion had wanted the enemy cleared from that area. It was up to the Vietnamese soldiers to take control of that area through their search and destroy missions. Unfortunately the NVA had kicked their asses when confronted and the ARVN would withdraw from the engagement. It was the Taipan's that would extract their wrath on so many of the enemy. Day after day for a week solid, they returned and "in support of" the ARVN's and engaged the hard fighting NVA.

It was difficult for them, in the flight crews, to really know if we were actually making any difference in the war effort. They did not have access to any sort of statistics to gage their score. The truth was they didn't really care. Theirs was to serve one year, three hundred and sixty five days doing whatever was asked of them without reward. The only compensation was the plane ticket home if they won. And if they lost we still got the ticket, but instead of a seat in the cabin of the plane you flew home in a wooden box in the cargo hold. So they tried to be careful with their life so that they would get the better seat on the plane.

It had been a few days later when Mitch stopped by to see Butch in his barracks that was just across the way from the Taipan platoon. It was also the newest building constructed by the hands of the 135th personnel. They had utilized many materials that they had stolen from the Navy base where a re-supply company received bulk material for distribution to other Navy bases throughout South Vietnam. The EMU slicks spotted the pallets of lumber and sheets of plywood the day before then they returned with a sling. After hooking up the load of ill-gotten goods, the two EMU's flew off and returned to base with enough wood to build the barracks.

He found Butch sitting on his bunk writing a letter. Butch had received a letter at today's mail call from a former girlfriend. She wrote that she had regretted their breakup just prior to his leaving for Vietnam. We talked about their past relationship and he commented that he felt he should try to get back in good grace with her when he returned home. His spirit was up and said that he wanted to go "smoke a big fat one". He opened his wall locker and rummaged inside for a bag of weed. As he searched he produced a bottle of rubbing alcohol, turned around to hand Mitch the frosted plastic bottle.

"No thanks, don't need any", he said.

"No dummy, look inside", Butch said grinning.

"Why, what's in it", Mitch asked, thinking he already knows.

"This is how I am going to get it home".

The preserved finger lay at the bottom of the container obscured by the frosted finish.

"They will never think to look inside", he said with his toothy grin.

"Who ya going to show it to at home", Mitch asked.

"I don't know, probably just some friends, they'll think it's cool"

Somehow Mitch just could not envision a scenario where you were hanging out with your civilian buddies and announce, "hey guys, you want to see something cool"? But butch had a grandeur vision, only he would know what was right for him. Mitch could only hope his friends had a strong stomach.

Walking out with Butch to the flight line, there it was as black as a well digger's ass. He fired up his fat joint, took a couple of hits and passed it to Mitch. Up until now he has had very little experience with the stuff and had not attempted to get high in country. Mitch took the weed and drew on it not inhaling, held it in his mouth and blew out.

"Good shit, man", he said.

"Not bad", Butch said eyeballing him with suspicion.

The next morning Mitch had the day off, well not off, just off from flying. He had been scheduled for Guard Duty on the base perimeter, a twenty-four hour shift, four on, and four off, for twenty-four hours. It was very tiring but it was not something that he had to do very often. The sergeant of the guard posted him in the tower on one corner of the base. From his elevated view he could see across the three hundred yards to the tree line. The tree line was so dense that one could see only ten feet into the wooded jungle. All along the Berm which is the perimeter, is a raised mound of dirt about eight feet high that completely surrounded the base and bunkers were positioned approximately twenty yards apart. Bearcat was miles in diameter and so there were hundreds of bunkers. Since the base was shared with many other American units, as well as some from Thailand, all the enlisted men, representing all the units, shared the responsibility of securing the perimeter. The separate units were responsible for their own sectors of the perimeter.

For the most part guard duty was boring, nothing to do but look out across the eight rows of concertina wire. Divided in the middle, between the fourth and fifth rows is half buried fifty-five gallon drums of Foo-Gas, a flammable concoction made from fuel into a gel like substance to create a wall of fire also capable of surrounding the base. If the enemy made it past that they encountered the next line of defense which was the claymore anti-personnel mine field. If they got past that there the M-60 machineguns would mow the enemy down. Regularly the largest problem was the monkeys that tried to sneak in search of food and tripped a flare at night. That in turned caused trigger-happy guards to start firing, which in turn started everyone else firing until all the field phones started ringing for a cease-fire. Sometimes it was all just too comical to believe.

Several days later Mitch still had not seen Butch. He went to his bunk area several times. He searched the Enlisted Man's Club each night for days. Finally He asked Bennie if he had seen Butch.

"A-vent ya err-d mate, he's down with Malaria", Bennie said with a look of concern.

"No shit, where's he at now", Mitch asked concerned.

"I spect Ee's in the field hospital at Bien Hoa".

"Any idea how long he'll be there", he responded

"Shouldn't be long mate", he fiddled with his beard for a second and added,

"Usually a week cures'em".

The following day the missions had gone fairly uneventful. Mitch returned to the barracks tired and dirty as usual. As he was getting himself ready for a nice long cool shower, the platoon sergeant was in the barracks and had stopped to talk with some of the other chiefs who bunked at the other end of the building. As he made his way towards the end where Mitch was he stopped and had words with each platoon member that was present. Mitchell tried hurrying to get the hell out of there before he made it to his end of the barracks. But the instant he spotted Mitch hastily gathering his shaving kit and towel, the Sergeant rushed directly towards him. Oh fuck, he thought now what kind of shit detail is he going to have me do. The platoon sergeant had a solemn look on his face when he spoke and asked,

"Have you got time to attend Butch Haggard's funeral tonight".

It took seconds to open his mouth to speak but nothing would come out. He handed Mitch a pamphlet with Butch's name on it and some prayers. His mind swirled in thought and weird emotions came and went so fast. Finally he nodded, yes, and the platoon sergeant turned to leave. Then suddenly his voice came back,

"You mean Butch with the EMU's", he just had to be sure it was not someone else.

"Yea, the kid from California"

He looked at the pamphlet and stared at his printed name and thought how could he die from Malaria when he was a combatant. It was just so shocking.

Forgetting about the shower for now, he went in search of Bennie, he needed someone to explain how this could have happened. Why hadn't he taken the anti-malaria pills that were issued in the mess hall?

Outside of the barracks where Butch used to live were some of his platoon mates. Mitch approached and asked if they were going to attend the funeral. All said, "yes", so then he asked if they knew how he contracted the malaria. Almost in unison they denounced that claim.

"He was fucking shot man", one had said.

"Don't know who started the damn rumor but it was bullshit all along".

In his quizzical investigation Mitchell learned that Butch had indeed died in combat while on a mission. It had happened the day that he had reported for Guard Duty. Butch took a bullet in the chest while they were in the LZ just as his helicopter was unloading the troops. One shot, one bullet, one dead. On the way out of the LZ the co-pilot noticed him slumped over, they broke from formation, and flew directly to a field hospital. He was alive on arrival but was in a coma and had been on life support for all the missing days. There did not seem to be any conspiracy regarding the Malaria rumor, just the usual tight-lipped military allowing for speculation rather than fact.

Wondering whether an ARVN had enough of Butch's prodding maybe he turned to fire the fatal shot as he disembarked from the helicopter. Or perhaps the enemy had indeed found an arbitrary target. Thinking of it made Mitchell kind of ill. He entered the base chapel and took a seat in a third row pew. The first thing Mitchell saw was Butch's black combat boots, all polished up to a high shine and standing side by side. Above the pair of boots his helmet sits atop his rifle butt, barrel pointed down and the bayonet stuck into the wood step that lead up to the Alter. An Army Chaplain read some scriptures, said a prayer and made the sign of the cross. Observing and hearing all this did not distress Mitchell so much as did the melody of the trumpet slowly playing Taps. He thought of Butch's Mom and Dad, his big brother, and of the girl that Butch wanted to renew his relationship with. Tears began to roll down Mitchell's cheeks, he turned his head to one side so no one could see him wipe them away. The ceremony was followed by a twenty-one gun salute that jolted his nerves. Leaving the Chapel, it was too soon to return to the barracks and face the others. He didn't think he was ready to talk to anyone about the incident. Mitchell decided to go for a walk alone on the flight line. There in the darkness he looked around to be certain no one was nearby. When he was sure he was completely secluded, Mitchell sat down right there on the edge of the runway and had a good cry.

That night sometime in the middle of the night Mitchell awoke for no apparent reason. He sat up in his bunk and put his feet on the floor. A very strange feeling was prodding at him, trying to say something, asking him, begging at him for something. A cold chill overcame Mitchell as the image of the finger in the alcohol bottle came into view in his mind.

Oh my God, what if they send his personal effects, including the alcohol bottle, home for his parents to discover the appendage? Mitchell could almost feel the heartbreak of Butch's parents as they wondered about the object. Would they think it belonged to Butch, or someone else, and why was it there? No, Mitchell knew he couldn't let that happen. He had to tell someone about the bottle. After all Butch was gone now, what more could they possibly do to him. Don't worry, Mitchell assured himself and the voice reaching to him, I won't let your family know what you did Butch, I promise.

The aftermath of B-52 bomber strikes shows the impact on the environment

Chapter Fifteen
Hardships

Taipan three-seven had just completed their sortie providing air support to a medivac ship lifting out the dead American infantrymen that had been ambushed the night before. Our ground troops encountered the enemy as darkness settled in and a firefight broke out lasting several hours. The area had been so hot that it took all of the previous night and most of today just to get a chopper in to extract the dead. The grunts were outnumbered three to one during the night but killed so many more of the enemy. Into the LZ, Taipan three-seven did not take any fire but they did see the results of the firefight. Dead Vietnamese piled high and the body bags of our G.I's laid out side by side, Three-seven stated that one of the bags looked only partially filled and "shook like a bowl of Jell-O", when it was loaded into the evac chopper.

Three-seven's crew-chief was the second senior chief in the Taipan platoon. Jean had already served one full term and reenlisted for another six months of combat. He received a nice cash bonus and increased his pay and rank. But the real reason for returning was because he "missed killing dinks". Seeing the body bags of the Americans had pissed Jean off to no end.

Jean's home in Spokane, Washington had been repossessed by a Bank foreclosure and his wife sued him for divorce just prior to his arriving home. Mitchell thought he had a kid also, but really he did not speak of that near as he could recall. His life as a civilian was a mess. But Jean was a mess personally too! His black greasy hair was never clean, and a day old beard always shadowed his lower face. He had a really black scraggly mustache that curled into his mouth whenever he spoke. The cookie duster hanging below the long and bumpy nose was not enough to hide his crooked yellow teeth whenever he would smile, usually when he talked of killing people. But Jean was a good crew-chief and mechanic. Most pilots seemed to like him others just feared him. But no one really ever knew when he would just go off.

The pilots knew he could keep them alive or get them all killed depending on his attitude du jour. They had flown together for many months and have become accustomed to each other. Jean often pushed the limits of his authority, mostly because he was older than nearly most all of the pilots, calling them "a bunch of fucking kids". Mitch presumed that a form of complacency derives from crews working together, day in, and day out for far too long.

Three-seven passed at low altitude over a remote village on their return to the PZ, to catch up with the rest of the Taipan's. Jean spotted three Buddhist Monks walking along a dirt road. The Monks were shaved bald and wore loose bright orange robes that draped over them. They walked onward with their arms folded in front of them, chitchatting away. The brightly colored robes caught Jean's attention and his brain just clicked into kill mode. He raised his M-60 and waited for the helicopter to just barely pass over them so that the pilots could not see what he was firing at. At the appropriate time and shooting from the hip, he fired a short burst rearward towards the trio.

As one fell to the ground, another grabbed at his arm as he spun around a hundred and eighty degrees then bent over at the waist. One dead, one wounded, and the remaining Monk seemingly unscathed went to aid his comrades.

"What are you firing at", demanded the pilot to the back seat crew.

The gunner also had no idea why Jean had fired his weapon and only shrugged his shoulder at the pilot who had turned in his seat trying and get a glimpse of what was going on. Finally after Jean hesitated a moment he responded,

"My finger slipped on the trigger, SIR", he reported sarcastically.

"Jean, make sure that doesn't happen again", the pilot snapped angrily.

They continued flying along, the pilot not really wanting to know what Jean was up to. Jean just smiled, knowing that was all the further the incident was going to go. He sat with his back against the bulkhead propped his feet up on the doorpost and wedged himself in between. His machinegun placed on his lap, as he kept up his lofty vigil.

That night back in the barracks Jean was relating the story of his Monk KIA in a jovial spirit. Mitch just happened to overhear the conversation and listening to the tale was getting his short hairs ruffled. First he thought of the professionalism of the platoon being degraded by Jeans moronic actions. Then he went to pure anger, ok, so he had to admit it, he did not like Jean anyway. But up until now he never really paid much attention to Jean. Since they did not hang out together and as long as they had to fly in the same platoon there was no reason not to at least try and get along. But today was different, Jean crossed a line and Mitch had enough seniority to at least say something.

"So now you're a murderer Jean", Mitchell spoke bitterly.

"A big man killing unarmed priests", said loudly enough for the whole barracks to hear. For a second Mitchell felt better having said his piece.

"That's right, big enough to pound your fucking ass into the ground too", Jean yelled back even louder.

Mitch was not too pleased that he reminded him that Jean was indeed much bigger than he was. Even less happy to see the big guy charging towards his bunk where he was seating. Jean stood in front of him, hands on his hips and spoke aggressively.

"Got something you want to tell me motherfuck", that gross mustache vibrating with each spoken syllable.

Their eyes locked in visual combat, a long stare down was taking place as Mitch carefully weighed his options.

If I tried to stand up just now he could smack me down before we ever got started, Mitch thought. He stayed seated.

Could tell him again how I feel, but that would certainly be another taunt!

Could I win here going fist to fist, no way!

Back off now and kill him later, yea better choice, Mitch now had a plan!

"No Jean, got nothing more to say to you".

"That's right fucker, see that you don't or maybe I'll just have to blow you away like those fucking dink motherfuckers, got it".

Man, he wished he hadn't said that, now Mitch *will* have to kill him. He has made it this far by not allowing those who threaten his life live long enough to make good on their threat. Jean was now his enemy! I'll have to get him before he gets me, Mitch thought seriously.

The Army didn't get the word that Jean and Mitchell are locked into a death match so they still had to go to work every day. He spent the next few weeks planning Jean's death, and just how to make it look accidental. Maybe it was lucky for Jean that Mitchell was not the cold-hearted murderer that he was. Over a period of time and having no further clashes with that big ugly son of a bitch, Mitchell had finally lost interest.

Besides who had time for that? It had disturbed Mitch to know that he could have killed him so easily, a simple reflex of the finger on the trigger at just the right time. No thought or emotion, just like firing at the eligible males, mechanized movement that's all it is. It was not the act of taking his life that held him back. Instead it was the fact of getting caught and spending time in LBJ (Long Bien Jail). It is the same jail that Lieutenant William Calley of the infamous Mi Lai Massacre incident was recently housed in. No, that certainly was not a good option. Maybe that was what kept Jean from fulfilling his threat also. Mitch finally realized that his desire to make it home was far stronger than sacrificing all for that asshole. Maybe Jean was so upset about the dead Americans that he felt taking out his revenge on the monks was justified. Whatever his problem was, Mitch knew it's not for him to become a part of it.

Firebase Schroeder was southeast of My Phuoc Tay, and just north of the Mekong River. The base had been recently turned over to an ARVN artillery unit but there remained a couple of American advisors. When the Americans manned the base, there was not a lot of Viet Cong activity in the area. Peasant farmers occupy the surrounding hamlets and try to avoid Saigon's war and politics. Farmers just farm, that's it, they care little about anything else. It's only when Saigon interferes with their lives that things got fucked up. Now Saigon wants these villagers isolated from VC influence. They have been placed under government protection, whether they like it or not. First they relocated the farmers in the outlying hamlets into the protected villages. Displaced families now crowded together waiting for the war to come to them, as they know it will.

The small artillery firebase was triangular in shape, and had three 105-Howitzer cannon's, one in each of the corners of the triangle. A sandbag perimeter with machinegun bunkers incorporated into the sandbagged wall and half a dozen or so mortar pits inside the perimeter also encircled by sandbags. Several rows of concertina wire surrounded the outside perimeter and since the area was heavily wooded the immediate area around the base had been bulldozed clean. From the air, Schroeder looked like a bald spot on the back of the head of the forest. Strategically speaking the firebase was central to several hamlets and the big guns could reach the Mekong River.

A little further north of Schroeder a hamlet had been visited by a Viet Cong patrol the night before and killed an old man believed to be the head of the village. As a leader he stayed behind to protect his people's possessions. His death was probably just to be made an example of if the villagers did not cooperate with the Cong. When the people complained that the protection they were promised failed to protect, the higher-up's thought it best to aggressively search and destroy the enemy strongholds in the area. The insertions of ARVN's into the outlying countryside produced the desired effect. Battles between NVA and the ARVN's are frequent and fierce. The Taipan's have been kept quite busy providing air support. For several days they have been under fire, some of the ships take hits from small arms. Luckily no one has been hit yet.

Near the end of one long day supporting the ground troops the Taipan's had spent the day laying down protective fire. On the last sortie they expended all of their on-board munitions. It was late in the afternoon and the gunships had to rearm before returning home to Bearcat. It wouldn't do for an armed helicopter to fly home in a combat zone totally unarmed.

Vinh Long is a large American Base southwest of Firebase Schroeder, and also situated one of the branches of the Mekong River. They were all tired and looked forward to getting back to eat, shower, and sleep. On approach to Vinh Long airfield Taipan lead radioed the tower for clearance for the three gunships to land.

"Taipan Heavy, hold one mile east until contact over", the tower radioed back.

"Vinh Long tower, Taipan lead, be advised we need refuel and rearm, over", lead responded with urgency in his voice.

"Taipan's, Vinh Long, roger that but we have a situation here and cannot allow you to land, we hope to have everything under control ASAP, how copy"?

"Roger, good copy Vinh Long".

Flying in circles at high altitude for ten to fifteen minutes, Mitch could tell his pilot was getting aggravated for the hold. Not only did they need to get back but also flying around without armament is a bit unnerving.

"Vinh Long Tower, Taipan lead, can you give us an ETA"?

"Taipan, Vinh Long, some of our soldiers have ahh…started shooting at each other across the runway, we have the MP's trying to suppress the disturbance at this time, can you hold five", the air traffic controllers voice sounded frustrated also.

The pilot keyed his microphone to intercom to tell the peter pilot, "If I had some fucking ammo I'd go in there a strafe that fucking runway", he said agitated, "why the fuck would our guys shoot at each other"?

After another ten-minute delay they finally landed and hovered to the POL point for fuel. After refueling they hovered to rearm, there they talked to some soldiers who knew of the situation that prevented them from landing earlier. Apparently there had been a racial disturbance between White and Black soldiers. Not combat soldiers, rear echelon personnel, people stuck in a war zone, with no war to fight. Away from home, confined and frustrated with their situation, taking it out on each other. No one had been shot, it seemed to be an isolated incident but someone was going to be in big trouble for starting the race riot. Naturally from the aviator's point of view, the whole thing seemed terribly idiotic, not to mention hazardous to the combat crews who had a real war to fight.

The Stars and Stripes newspaper related many stories of racial tensions and other conflicts among American troops. Those guys in the rear needed to get out in the field for a while to relieve some of that pent-up frustration. Perhaps this is a true example of human nature. Could be we are all dooming ourselves to extinction anyway. Mitch was saddened in his thoughts.

Mitch knew that getting up every morning to climb into a gunship to fly around looking for people to kill has in some strange way quelled the aggressiveness in him. He didn't like conflict, never had, now it's his living, not much he can do about that, but he had to try to not let it become him.

His feet had been itching like crazy for days, he found himself untying his boots while they were in the air so that he could scratch his feet. When he pulled off his socks he could see layers of skin peel away and stuck to the inside of the socks. At first he thought it was just athlete's foot. But the skin loss has become so severe that now his feet bled through the thin skin that's left. When Mitch finally decided to see a medic about it, he was told he had a severe case of jungle rot. Although they had some fancy medical term for it, it was still the "rot". Smelled like it too! For the cure, he was grounded from flying for one week. He couldn't put his boots on because his feet needed to stay dry and he needed to apply heavy doses of topical cream. The medic ordered him to change his socks three times a day when he returns to flying. Mitch had the impression that the medic thought that he contracted the rot deliberately just to avoid combat. The Doc couldn't have known Mitchell's distaste for being in the rear.

So now the platoon Sergeant knows Mitch has been grounded and makes his plans to keep Mitch busy while he heals.

"Since you ain't flying tomorrow, you've got guard duty tonight". The word gets around fast in the rear when someone is available for the shit duties.

That night there were two of them in the bunker on the perimeter. As night fell the area was black as hell. Lights were forbidden on the perimeter after dark for obvious reasons, even the faint glow from a cigarette was enough for some sniper in the tree line to get a bead on you. They had taken turns on watch while the other caught up on some shuteye. Then the two were visited by one of the guards from the bunker to the right. He introduced himself as "Stone, least ways that what most people called me". He came by to hang out with them because,

"That guy over there is an asshole, if I stay in there with him I'll end up killing him".

It seemed to Mitch that this kind of hardship was common everywhere in the rear. Why couldn't they be more nonchalant like him? They made some small talk and Stoner asked Mitch why he was wearing flip-flops on guard duty. He explained his medical disability, and Stoner just thought it was funny that a crew-chief who flew all the time could have jungle rot when the infliction mostly affected the grunts that marched through the soggy jungles. Mitch was in no mood to explain that they often landed in the rice paddies in the wet season. And that when they got out stretching their legs or to piss, their feet were wet all day too!

His new friend pulled a joint from his top pocket, lit the tightly twisted end, sucked in a long deep toke and offered it to the other guard who had only slept with one eye shut. The pungent odor caused him to sit up in anticipation. He too inhaled the "doobie" in quick short tokes, with the last one he held his breath with his cheeks bulging as he passed Mitch the small white paper roll. He looked around for a reason to pass but what the hell he thought he's got a week to wear off the effects. They passed the joint around until the roach disappeared in a final wisp of smoke.

They were pretty stoned when their new friend came up with "a fucking great idea", he announced.

"Let's toss a grenade out that I saved, a "Willie Pete" just in case we got over run by gooks", he spoke excitedly. "It's too fucking quiet out here, we need some action", he said nodding his head.

"Maybe we can get the whole fucking perimeter firing at nothing, wouldn't that be the shit eh guys, wad-ya-think".

"Yea cool man, lets fuck-n do it man", now Mitch had two wide-eyed crazies going to get him in some deep shit. As he went to the next bunker to grab his grenade, Mitch began to get a little paranoid. WP's were fun to drop from a chopper but could anyone actually throw one far enough to escape the burning plumes as they blossomed outward.

Stoner returned with the powder blue colored device, he went out alongside of the bunker and he pulled the pin on the detonator.

"Wait man, you gotta get that thing far out there or, we'll all fry", Mitch said.

"Yea your right, I'll climb over the Berm toss it, and then run back".

He began his climb over the other side of hilltop, but as he did his foot slipped and he had to catch himself with the hand that carried the grenade without the pin.

"Whoa shit, I fucking almost lost it", he whispered to them.

But the two of them could see what happened and had already turned to run.

"Maybe we ought to-wait in the bunker", Mitch said to the other guard.

They peered out over the sandbags cautiously to see Stoner slide down the muddied embankment. On the wrong side of the perimeter now, he leaned way back and arched his arm behind him. Then snapping it forward in perfect form he let the grenade fly. It was obvious from the second it left his hand that the trajectory was too high, which meant that it wasn't going to go far enough out to avoid the hot phosphorus plumes. Mitchell's heart went into his throat as the grenade exploded a mere fifty feet out. Then Stoner scrambled to get back over the Berm, but the muddied embankment was too slippery for a rapid retreat as he slid back down on his stomach. He sensed his failing and turned to witness the explosion sending bright white burning phosphorus plumes into the night sky. He quickly rolled over on his back. They all watched in horror as the plumes began to fall all around him. While still on his back he squirmed and twisted, dodged and ducked as the pieces came trailing down so close to him. In what lasted a fraction of time seemed almost hours as the scorching bits narrowly made contact with his flesh.

"What a fucking trip man, did ya see me dodge that shit" Stoner said brushing the mud off his uniform. He was hopped up now big time. It was indeed a miracle that he did not even get even a single bit on him for which we had no way to treat his injuries and that shit would have burned through any part of his body that it made contact with. Stoner had indeed managed to avoid being burned by his intense concentration that could come only from having been stoned. But then again, maybe he would have had a better idea if he had not been so high.

Mitch had become scared straight at the sight of it all and now felt exhausted. Stoner went back to his bunker a little wiser for the experience and Mitch was glad it ended without further hardships for any of them. Especially, if anyone had reported the explosion to the sergeant of the guard, which only meant all the guards were either stoned or asleep. Sure, hope the enemies don't try to make it in tonight. Mitch sat on the sandbags staring out into the dark mass of trees three hundred meters away remembering how much he hated being in the rear.

Having pulled guard duty all night, he slept in late. At nine in the morning it was too late for chow in the mess hall so Mitch took a walk to the base Post Exchange (PX), to buy some real canned food. The PX is a military convenience store and K-mart in one. While there he ran into one of their EMU crew-chief's who had just returned from R&R in Hawaii. Nicknamed "Blondie", he went there, not to see his wife or girlfriend, but to surf. He too was from California and a big Kahuna with the local surf set.

"What-cha looking for", Mitch asked noticing his frustration in not finding it.

"I need some wax for my board", Blondie said excitedly.

"I'm going to Vung Tau with my new board today".

Whoa, Mitch can't believe what he was hearing,

"You got a surf board here", he asked, now all excited too.

"Actually some guy in Hawaii gave it to me when he wiped out in a big surf and got himself all fucked up on a coral reef", he said grinning.

"When the ambulance came to take him away he told me he will never surf again and gave me the board".

"Cool man", He was envious as hell, should of went to Hawaii for R&R.

"So I got it here and one of the pilots who surf's wants to fly over to Vung Tau and try it out, we got the day off and maintenance wants to test flight one of the ships".

Mitch was grounded from flying missions but no one ever said he couldn't go for a ride. Besides, the salt water would probably be good for his jungle rot. Then it came, the highly anticipated question, "Ya wanna come"?

While flying towards the coastal town of Vung Tau with the surfboard on the cargo floor, the three of them rubbed the wax candles vigorously to the surface of the streamlined beauty. For a moment in time the Styrofoam and Fiberglass board will be the time machine that takes them home, to the beach and the surf. He would have paid a great price just to have the privilege of waxing it up. Thinking of actually riding the surf is bringing tears to his eyes.

They arrive at the coastline twenty minutes later just northeast of the city and turn southwesterly to fly along the beach. Unfortunately they see there is little wave action, the whole South China Sea was as flat as a tabletop. Still they wanted their turn if only to sit, or to paddle around on the board for a few moments just to recall what their life used to be.

The helicopter hovered over the water about twenty feet, no more than a hundred feet from the shoreline. First the board went out, then Blondie from his stance on the landing skids as he broke off into a swan dive. Not being able to see the water depth we followed in a classic feet first jump.

The pilot tossed out a helmet bag of boots and dry clothes and of course my flip-flops. It was caught and remained dry on the board to shore.

Without waves the board went little used, so it was decided to walk into the town for a cold brew. An enlisted man's club provided the necessary liquid refreshment and a live band played the same rock-n-roll music heard every day on the AFVN radio station. Soon they decided what they needed was some good ole-pussy.

Surfing the streets in search of short time girls it was soon apparent they were as scarce as the China Sea waves. Along the way they stopped a multitude of service personnel to ask for the best place to find pussy. Finally one Air Force guy whose rank is unfamiliar says, "Go to the end of the street and turn left look for the barbershop, when you go in they will ask if you want a haircut, just tell them NO" the stranger volunteered and briskly marched on.

A short distance later the hunt was over as they stood in front of the only barbershop. Above the door is the number "37",

"Barbershop thirty-seven, this must be the place" Mitchell says.

"I think that guy was bullshitting us, this *is* a barbershop", his surfer buddy is dismayed.

"Well it won't hurt to ask", Blondie replied, opening the front door.

A small metallic bell rang as the door was pushed open. Blondie held the door open with one hand as he peered inside. The room was empty except for the little old papa-san standing behind the only barber chair with one mirror, and one small counter for hair cutting accessories. Beyond the little man is a plywood wall with doorway cutout closed by a red curtain. He looked at Blondie expressionless and asked,

"You wanna haircut", his voice is barely perceivable.

"No thanks papa-san", Blondie said as he turned to walk back out.

Then out of nowhere a head appeared through the center of the curtain, she held the curtain around her neck shielding her body as she spoke,

"GI, GI, come, come".

Her hand appeared below her head as she motioned with her hand for all of them to come to her. Blondie in turned motioned the other two to join him. As he approached the curtain she stood back to open wide the curtain so that we could see beyond her. Cautiously he poked inside only to see a narrow hall and what looked like the cubicles at the steam-bath.

"Hey guys this is the place".

Mama-san explained that the barbershop provided exclusive services to her country's fighting heroes.

"Many GI come here, we do number one job" she spoke proudly.

"Only place to come round the world", she said.

They had no idea what she was talking about, but as long as they were there to get some pussy, who cared?

"How fucking much mama-san", Blondie asked

"Twenty one dowra"

They paid the outrageous fee and each was lead into a cubicle. The tiny room had only a bed with tubular brass head and footboards. The walls were also of plywood and surrounded the bed on three sides. On the left is just enough room to barely stand. Mitch sat on the bed waiting. A woman approached and entered, she pulled close the curtain to the cubicle, and then began removing her clothes. She then motioned for him to do the same.

She wasn't good looking, but she wasn't ugly either and she did have a fair figure, what the hell, who could be picky at this point. She called for the mama-san to bring her something and she tried to make some small talk while waiting. Mitch began to wonder what she and he were going to do. It didn't appear she was ready to lie down so that he could mount her. Now he had his clothes off and she patted the mattress for him to lie down. Mama-san stuck a hand through the curtain, without looking in to pass a wet towel to his prostitute. They briefly spoke to each other in native tongue, then she began to cleanse his groin area with the moist towel. She gestured for him to raise his legs and wiped areas that were normally reserved for small babies.

Foreplay, he thought she was trying to excite him, couldn't she see that this is it baby, I am fucking ready now. Let's get it on! She moved on all fours between his thighs and began kissing, licking and sucking. Then with her arms, lifted his legs to put her mouth and lips where no one has before. Her buttocks raised high as her head disappeared below his chest. Mitch felt strange sensations as her tongue explored uncharted regions. His head was swimming in confused hypnotic colors as she grabbed the manly staff and introduced it to the moist orifice of her face. He exploded in convulsive glory while she held him in her mouth. She used her hands to pump, squeeze, and vacuum every miniscule drop of his virile juice.

The moment he stopped, she stopped. Mitch looked down to see her smiling face as she began to swish and agitate behind her sealed lips and puffed cheeks. Mitch watched in shock as she reached under the bed to pull out an old fashioned brass spittoon. Then with another final swirl around the cheeks and she spat carefully into the brass pot.

"Jeeezus, why the fuck did you do that", he asked in disgust.

"Look you see, I make beau coup pee", she said laughing, meaning she made a lot of Piaster, Vietnamese currency.

She raised the brass pot for Mitch to look inside. He peaked over the large rim and saw the pot half full of milky liquid.

"Why", He had to ask.

She spoke as best she could to explain that she was paid by the weight of the spittoon at the end of the day. Mitchell figured she swirled the material in her mouth to add to the volume with her saliva. Thus with greater weight she also cheated the establishment and she would be over paid.

His stomach ached as Mitch dressed, he was both satisfied and sickened, but really no worse off for the experience. Waiting for the others only a short time they left to find a bar. It seemed strange to Mitch that none of them spoke of their adventure at the barbershop. Did they have the same treatment, he wondered?

Listening to the live music they sat together at a small round table at the bar located on the beach. Beer flowed from the pitcher into plastic cups at a high rate. Time passed and a few more pitchers of beers were downed before their rendezvous with another chopper for the flight home. It was an hour before sunset and the flight was short.

Mitch sat on the floor of the big Huey staring out over the passing sand dunes as they slowly reverted back into jungle. He contemplated his past experiences with prostitutes, Bangkok, Saigon, the steam bath at Bearcat, and began to feel sorrow for their hardships that drove them to their whoring profession.

Diesel fuel was added to the cans of human waste every day, then set ablaze. Indigenous personnel would then stir the putrid concoction with metal rods until completely dissipated.

Chapter Sixteen

Cool Waters

Christmas is now just around the corner, although Mitchell wouldn't have known it unless he had heard it said on the radio. It's hard to predict a season when there are only two, rainy, and dry. Every now and then an announcement is made by the radio DJ on the Armed Force's Vietnam Network (AFVN), about the comedian/actor Bob Hope, coming to Bien Hoa for one of his famous U.S.O. road shows. The show is a Christmas time special to get the guys cheered up who, like Mitchell are thinking about being home with the folks, and savoring a medley of holiday foods.

Last year, Mitchell saw the Christmas special aired from Vietnam at home, in the comfort of his living room. He could remember clearly the folks saying, "what a great American Bob Hope is to travel to a country like that to entertain our soldier boy's". True, the actor/comedian did so a great risk to himself, as well as all those who volunteered to join the road show. There is no real security here and a rocket or mortar attack could come at any time. Mitchell looked around cautiously and thought, how great it would be to get home and say, "hey, I saw Bob Hope in Vietnam, Live man"! Mitchell's reality was very different from his mind's picture. At that moment he couldn't even think of being able to go see a show for entertainment purposes!

Mitchell had put his combat duties as his own top priority. He felt he needed to, if he wanted to survive. He has already seen too many fellow soldiers go by not paying full attention to one's job. So he refrained from thinking about any such kind of indulgence. His luxury was being in the chopper whenever his ship was up and in the air. But just maybe, he wished, he could at least see it on the television. He could just imagine some of the fine looking women that would be with Mr. Hope, there always is. Mitchell began to feel a little sorry for himself.

The band, Credence Clearwater Revival, is singing through Mitchell's headset, ***"better run through the jungle, you better run through the jungle",*** a damn fine song for Charlie ears when we come flying into his territory. He looked below, there is no jungle, just tall grass for as far as the eyes can see.

The new AO has shifted westward deep into a mostly uninhabited area. The EMU's are now inserting the ARVN's of the ninth division into a sector known as The Plain of Reeds. They will operate out of a base at Moc Hoa and fly due west some sixty miles to the intended Landing Zone.

Because of the long range of the sortie, only one insertion will go in today. The sun was high in the sky and the blur of rotating blades over Mitchell's head cast a rapid flickering shadow over the fuselage and crew. The Taipan's are escorting the flight of ten slicks by positioning themselves behind and slightly below the trailing EMU. The clear skies and bright sun blend to create the high heat of the day. Too long flying at low altitude, they've got to get up high where it's much cooler he thought. Flying every day, in a helicopter with no doors on it tends to make you much more aware of the ambient air temperature.

A few puffy clouds could be seen above as Mitch starred out onto the empty palate where he painted his own picture of home and of being at the beach, but not before checking that his seat belt was tight.

The back seat crews have been informed by the front seats, and learned that Charlie is suspected of infiltrating the Delta region by way of crossing the Cambodian border. Enemy patrols have been tracked by "Leerp's" (L.R.P.'s, long range patrols), crossing the vast swamp at night with sampans loaded with materials. Thin trails of matted grass turned brown from the constant migration of the nocturnal people. The many trails curve, and intertwine on the well-traversed paths that disappeared westward over the horizon towards the Cambodian border. Then back over to the east, northeast, beyond the horizon towards Saigon. These trails evidence of movement but no one had been seen in the area in the light of day.

This would not be a good place to get shot down in Mitchell thought. They flew for long periods without seeing anything but tall grass. If shot down, they would be in Charlie's turf. Below, there was nowhere to run or take cover. Mitchell felt a bit uneasy and his sense of survival was now on high alert.

Presumably, NVA supplies for the Viet Cong's participation in their effort to take over control the Delta was being transported by sampan. The water level was insufficient to properly float the wooden craft, especially one loaded with weapons and ammunition. They had to be dragged through the tall grass that easily consumed the identity of a living person down there. When the ARVN's get there, it will be their job to search for any signs of "Charlie" building base camps or stock piling weapons.

After crossing mile, after mile of the grassy wetlands, the flight descended from cruising altitude, for an approach into the LZ. The radio squelched and a voice announced,

"EMU flight, lead, break into trail formation", came the command from the EMU flight leader.

Carefully the flight shifted from the typical four-vee formations into a trail formation, one behind the other, slightly staggering their altitude, trail high, lead low. They closed in their ranks so tight behind the lead ship they flew, seemingly, with the main rotors overlapping the tail rotor of the bird ahead of them. The Taipan's have already hit the deck and have taken up orbiting the LZ. The flight neared the landing area, which geographically looked like everything else in the area except that it was an "X" on the pilot's map. None of the helicopters would actually touchdown, just hover inches above the tall blades of grass while the ARVN's unloaded into the mostly wet LZ.

At three hundred feet C&C gave the order, "EMU flight begin final".

The flight began to reduce their airspeed while descending. The first insertion in a new LZ is always a bit more tense. You just keep your eyes peeled out for anything that might cause the helicopter to strike an unwanted object or booby traps. All eyes were searching downward when out of nowhere, a single engine mono-wing airplane appeared. Diving down from the left side of the formation, it dove under the entire flight just as they were about to begin their final descent.

The radios went crazy,

"What the Fu….."

"Hey, what's going on"

"Pull up, Pull up"

"Breakout, breakout"

"Breaking left"

"Keep it together guy's", C&C finally broke through, "Stay calm, till we figure out who that asshole is".

It was the very first time C&C actually cursed over the radio. Meanwhile the flight had scattered about the sky. From the ground it might have looked like a flock of pigeons being attacked by a Pigeon Hawk. Everyone had been so busy looking out for the other helicopters so as not to pile up on each other, everyone forgot to notice where the bandit had disappeared to. Soon the EMU's were grouped together but still not in tight formation as they circled left while climbing for altitude to protect their precious cargo of dink soldiers from ground fire.

C&C made several attempts to contact intelligence regarding air operations in the vicinity but did not receive a satisfactory reply. Then he commanded EMU lead to reorganize the flight and make the drop in the LZ. The flight started again from East of the LZ heading West for the final approach. Crewmembers had been told to be on the lookout for approaching aircraft and call out any sightings.

The flight was ready to try again and organized back into trail formation. Descending down from five hundred when a slick gunner called out,

"Aircraft approaching, eight o'clock high".

That call was passed on to C&C who was busily trying to read any markings on the airplane through his binoculars.

"Continue your approach EMU's", he announced.

The old, single engine combat airplane was Russian built, but oddly, it had no markings. It continued to close in on the flight.

When C&C saw that it had no markings, he waved off the flight,

"EMU's Abort landing, go around, go around"

The flight held a tight formation while banking out left.

The little plane passed by the flight from below and climbed nearly straight up for the big blue altitude. It disappeared quickly even though many crewmen still thought they could still see just a speck in the heavens. In truth it was very difficult to maintain visual contact on the fast moving airplane when sitting in a helicopter that is cranking and banking out turns to avoid a collision. Disorientation happens rapidly when there are so few references in vast skies to relate to.

C&C was really pissed off now, this was going to be the third and final attempt into the LZ. The Colonel was not going to let some little enemy airplane prevent this combat assault from being carried out. Completing the mission is always the primary objective.

"EMU's, you have clearance to fire on any unidentified aircraft", the Colonel order's were clearly heard.

"Taipan gunships are clear to engage in air to air combat on any aircraft approaching the flight". He spoke slowly and distinctly as if he was reading the words from the Army manual.

Holy shit, Mitchell wondered if air to air combat had ever been done before in a helicopter. Certainly, he had never heard of such a thing.

"OK boy's you heard C&C, keep your eyes open and call out the target", the pilot thought a bit longer, then commented further, "Tell me what direction he's coming from and I'll try to bank over to keep y'all from having to shoot through the rotor blades". This was beginning to sound serious to Mitchell and he prepared himself mentally, keep cool, lead the target, and don't shoot through the rotor blades. He readied the heavy gun in his arms.

Mitchell gave thought to the movies he had seen on TV of world war two B-52 bomber crews firing 50 caliber machineguns at Nazi planes attacking the bomber group. Did he ever see them actually shoot one down, he couldn't remember. Shit what if that little plane has bigger guns, longer range? The powerful bullets could reach them long before his M-60. Mitchell wished he still had that 50 cal. No matter, Mitchell could just imagine shooting down that little bandit and receive a Distinguished Flying Cross. And who knows what other medals would be bestowed upon him for his bravery and accuracy of aim. He looked up, squinting into the sunlight that flickered past the spinning blades above him.

The radios continued to chatter about the unidentified plane with warnings to shoot first and ask questions later. But the tan colored plane never appeared again and the flight was able to complete the mission. C&C was being clever in announcing the flights intention to fire on the airplane over the radio. Apparently he assumed the enemy pilot was monitoring the mission radio frequency and would get the message that his antics were no longer going to be tolerated. Besides he was outnumbered fifteen to one. Still everyone had wondered why the bad guy didn't want the flight to land. He deliberately and successfully diverted the flight twice, but why? Maybe intelligence was right about enemy movement, although it seemed so unlikely in such a remote area.

The mission was successful today, all survived to fight another day, although for a while there it looked as though it could get hairy. Air to air combat, Mitchell looked out to the horizon to find the airborne adversary. From high and behind, the fast approaching airborne killer opens-up on the flight with four heavy guns. A huge fireball filled with the sky with debris of aircraft aluminum and human body parts as several choppers are hit. The suicidal pilot bore down on Mitchell, fifty caliber machineguns spitting hell. Raising his M-60, he visually cleared the blades, and took aim. Hundreds of armor-piercing, anti-aircraft ammunition is in high-speed flight towards Mitchell's soft flesh. He waited for just the right moment and then with one quick burst, the enemy spiraled down, nose first, headed for the solid earth below and trailing a column of thick black smoke. Mitchell's imagination was sure working overtime!

Soon he began to think about something else, Mitchell sat wondering of his high school buddies, where they were, and what they might be doing right now. A little bit of sadness slipped in when Mitchell looked out again to see the sun was setting low in the west. Out to the east as far as he could see, rising smoke poured in to the sky. At first he thought it more of the usual slash and burn agriculture being practiced by the rice farmers. From his perspective it looked like the smoke was spreading faster than they could fly. A wall of dense smoke stretched along for miles, rising ever higher, nearly straight up. Mitchell looked on in awe. The smoke was so dense that it could not be seen through, so it was impossible to know how thick the dark gray wall was. When he noticed that the smoke bellowed up fast then dissipated rapidly he was sure a fire did not create the smoke.

Reaching for the intercom switch to ask the pilot if he knew what was happening, he heard the pilots conversing about a B-52 air strike. He listened in on the conversation. The bombing had commenced, and all air operations had been diverted far from the impact area. The pilot's complained how it was going to extend our flight time home. B-52's flew at extreme altitudes, and when crossing a triangulated radio signal from ground positions, the heavy bombers dropped the "five hundred pounders" on Charlie's party. What Mitchell had thought was smoke was in fact the Earth rising from the tremendous explosions. The devastation created in seconds by the exploding bombs is unimaginable and awesome. A bomb crater will instantly be created and large enough for a water buffalo to swim comfortably in. Problem is, we have more bombs than they have buffs. So the country is dotted by the hundreds of millions of tons of high explosives that rained down on the Mekong Delta.

The flight continued flying parallel to the line of smoke, five miles away, soon after the low rumble of the five hundred-pound bombs falling out of the sky by the hundreds began to shake the aircraft. Mitchell began to imagine what effect the bombs had on any people on the ground. Surely anyone in the immediate vicinity would be vaporized. The helicopters headed home but it was getting late and the pilot's continued to gripe that the EMU's wouldn't return to the "nest" before dark.

Twilight on the airfield and the EMU's have all returned to their "nest", while the Taipan's shutdown in the "snake pit". Maintenance inspections on the aircraft are quickly performed while the weapons are cleaned and rearmed. It is quiet and the only vehicular traffic came from a three-quarter ton truck that came to pick-up crewmembers. A few rode back, but most walked on to the mess hall that stayed open to feed the returning airmen. The cooks hated the disruption of their regular schedule. Since the whole flight had returned late, the mess hall personnel were ordered to serve until every man had his meal.

After finishing his supper of meatloaf, or "buff-a-loaf" as they sometimes referred to it, Mitchell made way for the barracks. Just outside the second floor entrance he thought he heard the sound of water splashing coming from the water tower that was about ten yards away. He stopped, listened but ignored the idea that "Charlie" had infiltrated the compound and was hiding up in the tower.

At his wall locker Mitch stripped naked and wrapped an olive drab colored towel around his waist and went back down the stairs. In the shower building he took up under one of the many showerheads and grabbed the chain pull to release the cool fresh water. It was rare to have the shower all to himself and he enjoyed the solitude. After washing he was at the sink when he heard the sound of someone scurrying about outside the showers. Mitch decided to take a quick look. Nothing, whoever it was had disappeared, strange he thought. There was just enough time to dress and get in a couple of cocktails before the EM Club closed at ten p.m.

Upstairs the platoon Sergeant approached and informed Mitch that he was not scheduled to fly tomorrow. Great, he thought, they would sure as hell find something for him to do. It was already too late to find another ship to fly. Tomorrow he would have to plan his E&E, escape and evade.

Mitch woke with the others for morning roll call even though his head felt heavy from the few extra drinks he quickly gulped down while planning his E&E for today. The duty roster was posted just outside the Commanders office, Mitchell's name did not appear on it. Good, now he would just have to avoid being seen by any Officers. He decided the motor pool would be a good place to E&E. Only enlisted men there, the Officers never got their hands dirty. Besides Mitch had some of his Aussie acquaintances that worked there and he had not seen them for days.

"G'Day mate", Ethan had said from behind his new and scruffy beard.

"Waddya up to",

"E&E"

"Oh, off flight status eh"

"Uh huh, but I'd rather be flying"

"No you wouldn't mate"

"NO, why"

"Cause I need a driver for this ere vehicle to the Bob Hope Show"

Mitch decided that Ethan was just about the best friend a fellow could have.

It was a short 30-minute ride to Bien Hoa, and they had made it just in time to see the beginning of the show. Mitch was impressed with the number of soldiers in attendance. They had seats far back and to the right of the stage but it did not matter, they were there.

Blonde and beautiful actress/singer, Connie Stevens asked for volunteers named "Bill" and chose five from the hundred "Bill's" that had raised their hands in the front rows. She approached the first uniformed soldier and asked his name,

"Bill", as he gave his name.

Then the second, "Bill so and so", he proudly proclaimed.

And the third "Richhh…ah Bill", he said stumbling over the answer. Connie jumped right down his throat, "You're not a Bill", he pleaded with her to stay and she allowed the liar his luxury and the crowd Booed.

She sang lovingly to each a song called "Bill", and Mitch wished his name had been William. Indeed, he just wished he could just get close enough to actually touch a round eyed woman. The sound system didn't quite reach the distance where Mitch and his group sat, so many of the jokes and innuendoes made by Mr. Hope went unheard and they repeatedly asked others what had been said. Then they had to strain to catch a glimpse of the leggy dancer's, but in all a good show. It really made Mitch feel homesick. He hoped he would have the chance to tell folks back home of his experience.

The following day, Enemy troop movement increased over the past month in the Mekong Delta. Remote fire support bases came under frequent mortar attacks and the Viet Cong were perpetrating atrocities on civilians on a scale not before seen. Articles that Mitch read in the "Star's & Stripe's" continue to mention the possibility of a build-up of NVA and supplies on the border in Cambodia.

Another TET offensive is expected in a couple of months that will in all likelihood be far worse than in 1968. That little airplane suddenly had a bit more relevance for Mitchell. He thought of the possible connection and the fact the plane would not have the range to fly back as far as Hanoi to re-fuel, so where did it go? That question must have bothered someone at Military Intelligence also because the EMU's were returning to the west of that area to try to locate a possible enemy airstrip they felt was near the Cambodian border.

After refueling from the long trip from Bearcat the flight moved to a remote PZ to load up the ARVN soldiers.

The usually compliant ARVN's were fired up and ready to go. Quickly, they load into the choppers almost before they touched down. A sense of urgency is felt throughout the flight. Radios are abuzz of rapidly talking commanders directing the imminent battle. Arty has begun to prep the LZ in advance of the EMU arrival. Something big has happened and everyone in the platoon was anxious to find out what was going on. The door gunners were all hoping to add to their KIA scorecard. There was no need for the Taipan's to do anything out of the ordinary, they were professional's and are always prepared for anything.

It was full suppression going into the LZ, despite the fact there are no visible targets, just grass and a few palms. The flight is in, and on the way out of the LZ they received heavy fire. No one saw anything of the enemy and the slicks departed with a few new holes in the ships and one wounded co-pilot.

Taipan's fired a few rockets just to make some noise but the sounds of the ARVN's engaging the enemy indicated the VC were oblivious to the Taipan's presence. The ground commander has not asked for gunship support although it appeared the enemy had pinned down the ARVN's.

C&C had received a radio transmission requesting medivac of the dead and wounded. Taipans were ordered to stay in the LZ to cover the evac. On the first approach the enemy fire was so intense that the medivac had to back off and orbit until ground forces could subdue the shooting. On the next pass it was decided that the Taipan's would escort the medivac ship in. Firing on both sides of the Angel flight they were successful in evacuating the needy. The dead would have to wait until it was less risky to get in.

The ground force began to spread out and secured a perimeter for the next lift in. C&C gave the order again for full suppression but this time the door gunners would cease fire at the last one hundred feet to avoid friendly fire. Again the Taipan's would have to cover both sides of the flight. The second lift went as planned and the slicks were lucky to get out without any crew injured.

Taipan lead informed the ground commander that their fuel situation had gone critical. He released the gunship's to refuel, but wanted his air support back as soon as it was possible.

C&C had already arrived at the back at the airbase to refuel. He would return to the LZ before the Taipan's arrived. While the "guns" were refueling the pilot's continued to monitor the mission and upon C&C's arrival they found the ARVN's under attack. The situation had progressed badly for the ground troops and C&C radioed the Taipan's to expedite their return to the LZ.

It was an hour and forty-five minutes round trip, and when the Taipan's dove in the LZ they could see the battle in progress. The ARVN's have not been able to advance their position and they were taken causalities at an alarming rate. The ground commander gave the Taipan's an approximate location of the enemy but Taipan lead felt it was too close to use rockets for fear of hitting friendlies. Lead decided that the mini-guns could be used in conjunction with the door-gunners but they would have to be extremely careful to avoid hitting the good guys.

After a few strafing runs the Viet Cong had had enough and began to retreat while firing and running away. That turned out to be a deadly decision for the bad guy's. As they distanced themselves from the ARVN's this allowed the Taipan's to use their rockets. Since there really was no place to hide it was a matter of hunting them down in the tall grass and dispatching them. Soon the body count was adding up rapidly. Torn and bloody corpse's laid everywhere. The shooting slowly subsided.

All that was left was a mop up operation and the day finished with only one American wounded, twenty-three ARVN's wounded, seventeen killed, and forty-two less bad guys. All EMU's would return to the nest, and the Taipan's to the snake pit.

Yep, it had been a good day.

A "Victory Fly-over", at Bearcat was initiated as the entire flight participated in the celebration of the day. All the ships had trailed smoke and the rear echelon personnel below could only wonder what had happened.

The pilots were informed by C&C that he had been told by the Vietnamese ground commander that the Taipan's had been credited with saving a whole company of ARVN's. The commander was going to submit to the Taipan's a medal, the "Vietnamese Cross of Gallantry". Of course no one really thought they had done anything out of the ordinary, but it was nice to know they had done some good work today.

The Aussie's mechanics had iced down two cases, wrapped it all in a poncho liner and loaded up the works in the company's three-quarter ton truck. On the flight line they surprised the flight crews with the Victoria Bitter beer in the truck bed. They stood around bullshitting about the events of the day and chugging down the best of Australia's brew.

Mitchell took his time getting ready for the showers, the others had hurried to get clean to resume their drinking at the EM Club. He had wanted to get in another quiet, long refreshing shower. The barracks was quiet when Mitch went down to shower. As he came around the corner of the building he caught two fellow Taipan's climbing the water tower, naked.

"Hey guy's, I am getting ready to shower, how about you wait till I finish", Mitch was a bit irritated that they were about to use his shower water for their private pool. Say, that didn't sound like such a bad idea. Mitch dropped his towel, "Hang on, I am coming up".

The guy's had been sneaking up to the water tower for some time, and Mitch was the only one to catch them. He climbed to the platform and swung a leg over the black rubberized bladder edge and slid down into the dark pool. The water was only waist high but it felt cool and refreshing. Mitch held his breath and slid below the surface. Under the water, in the weightless liquid, he remembered his home and day's spent at the beach. At that moment he was in the best place in the world.

A Huey "Hog" gunship, named "American Woman".

Chapter Seventeen

Boulder Mountain

Somewhere at, or near the Cambodian border, a team of ARVN scouts joined by U.S. Special Forces had made contact with the enemy on the previous day and still had them trapped on a huge rock pile.

A rival helicopter company had accomplished several insertions of infantry troops to support the small scout force that had originally discovered the enemy in hiding. They had met with so much resistance while attempting to flush the enemy out that they called in for the extra ground support prior to an all-out assault. However during the insertions, the bad guy's hiding in the rocks had fired upon the helicopters. Somehow they were able to expose themselves to shoot, and then completely disappear within the rocks.

American Special Forces acting as advisors assisted the ARVN scout's. They suspected the Viet Cong, or NVA had tunneled out a complete housing complex within the mountain of boulders.

The plan was to insert the reinforcements as near to the base of the rocks as possible. There would be enough troops to completely encircle the base of the small mountain. Then the ground forces would assault the slopes and drive the bad guys upwards until they had nowhere to run.

Yesterday when the support troops had arrived, it was late in the afternoon and all hell broke loose. The helicopters of the 211th had been decimated from so much enemy fire. Most of their ships had been shot down, or otherwise rendered incapable of further missions. By the time the troops were in the LZ and the downed choppers had been extracted it was too late for the assault. The ARVN's were ill equipped, and had not trained for a night assault. So the advisors had argued with their superiors to halt the mission until the following day.

The ARVN ground forces had bivouacked at the base of the mountain last night to prevent an escape by the occupants within. Camped out in small groups they surrounded the mountain. Their food and additional supplies needed for nighttime reconnaissance were brought in by helicopter. They had been outfitted with extra PRC25 radios and Starlight scopes to see into the darkness. Parachute flares fired from mortars, and plenty of Claymore mines to secure the encampments were also provided.

"Charlie" harassed the ground troops with sniper fire, and exchanges of machinegun fire were heard around the mountain all night. Fortunately there were no reports of casualties.

A bright orange blazing ball slowly rose out of the distant horizon. The light of a new day began to spread across the South China Sea and onwards to the muddy banks of the eastern Delta, across vast areas of rice paddies, then westward towards the plain of reeds and Cambodia.

In the tiny Vietnamese villages and hamlets the roosters start to crow, and cooking fires are stoked and prodded until ready. White smoke pours from the chimneys of the remote hooches while farmers strap the water buffalo's to the plows and the children play. Out in the plains the bird's stir, feeding on insects that can only now be seen, and the contingency of U.S. advisors, Vietnamese Scout's and ARVN ground troops enjoy a morning meal in the field.

A heavy fire team of three Taipan gunships, and three EMU support slicks for the anticipated sorties such as medivac, and re-supply, make up today's flight. The flight had departed Bearcat an hour earlier than usual. It had remained dark until they completed refueling before heading out to the AO. The three slicks remained behind until called for. The lead ship, Taipan One Six, departs and is in route with his fire team. It was a long flight west to the Boulder Mountain. The co-pilot was constantly reviewing his maps and seemed frustrated that he could not accurately predict their position as he cross referenced with the navigational instruments.

"I think we have crossed the border", he stated.

"Not possible, were not allowed to", the pilot reiterated.

"But I've checked and double checked and I think…"

"Forget about it will ya, they wouldn't send us out where we're not supposed to be, right", the pilot had been sarcastic.

When they first spotted it in the distance it was the only object visible above the reeds. From ten miles out it was unimpressive, at five miles it's an oddity, but now at two miles, it was a wonder! Mitchell could see the culmination of boulders rise magically upwards from the reeds. For seven hundred feet it rose up in the middle of nowhere, surrounded by nothing. An oddity of thirty to forty foot high boulders piled on top of each other to create this unnatural protuberance. A steep and solid fortress with unlimited places for hiding, this mission was beginning to get interesting.

The massive boulders at ground level had a large amount of shrubbery and grass entwined between the solid rock, the rest of the mountain, really just a large hill, was mostly bare. The way up to the top was in-between the large rocks, in the cracks, where falling pebbles had created narrow pathways. Initially it is slow going to get the troops to assault the hill. The dense shrubbery at the base was difficult to penetrate and some are using machetes to cut out a footpath. Gradually they climb, encircling the hill. All the troops were climbing at the same pace. When one group attained a slightly higher point than the rest, they stopped while the others caught up.

"Tiger tooth, Tiger tooth, Taipan One Niner", the pilot called for the U.S. advisor to get a sitrep. "Tiger tooth", was the call sign for the Special Forces lieutenant who planned the assault and was the man in-charge of the ground forces.

"Taipan One Niner, this is Tiger tooth"

"Roger Tiger tooth, we have been briefed on the mission, what is the situation at this time over"

"One Niner, we have friendly forces on the hill at the one hundred foot mark, be advise we have taken fire all night and advise you to stand off the hillside to keep a safe distance"

"Roger Tiger tooth, will comply, we can fly above your troops to recon their advance"

"Excellent One Niner, will advise when we make contact, Tiger tooth out", Mitchell understood that the Lieutenant meant, "contact", was with the enemy.

Mitchell sat looking straight out at the hillside. He was amazed at the size of the boulders and wondered how they came to rise in this particular spot. The ground was so flat in every direction and mostly marsh. So how did this mountain of stone rise, and when? Clear blue skies prevailed above, and a sea of green reeds swayed in the breeze below. Gray boulders were the only odd color for as far as the eye could see. The troops continued to slowly climb, searching as they went for any sign of the occupants of Boulder Mountain.

"One Niner, Tiger tooth", "Go Tiger tooth"

"My troops have discovered a possible entrance into the interior of the mountain, I'll be halting the troops to send in a team to check it out"

"Roger Tiger tooth, we'll swing around to your position"

The Taipan gunships remained at the five hundred-foot level while coming around to the southeast to get a visual on the cave entrance. Barely a hole large enough for a man had been bored into the solid rock and obscured by debris of straw and grass. One man at a time had to crawl into the hole with just a flashlight and a pistol. The possibility of booby-traps made the search that much slower going as every inch of the dark orifice was carefully scrutinized.

After realizing the search would take a long time the Taipan's continued to circle the mountain at the five hundred-foot mark. Flying at a slow sixty knots they observed the troops down below at a standstill.

Mitchell had been day dreaming again and sat looking out but not really seeing anything other than what was in his mind. He was bored, he really thought something good was going to happen but now an hour into the mission and nothing but rocks.

The Helicopter got in closer to the slope and continued a clockwise rotation around the hill just above the halfway mark. Mitchell noticed a huge boulder that had cracked in two. On the face, it was thirty feet high, straight up, and the crack divided it into two equal parts. It had to weight hundreds of tons. The gap was maybe two and a half feet across and went from top to bottom. An ARVN soldier stood at the bottom of the crack, watching.

His head followed the chopper as they flew by. A few minutes later when they came around again, he was still there. Mitchell observed him lift his weapon as if to aim at the passing helicopter. Initially this pissed Mitchell off as he really did not like anyone aiming guns at him, but then he noticed that the ARVN soldier, recognizable by his uniform, had held an AK-47. That stupid fucking gook is going to get himself killed if he keeps pointing that weapon at me, Mitchell thought. Then Mitch looked down the slope about two hundred feet and saw the troops sitting, waiting.

"Ahh Mr. Davies, did you see that gook back there with the AK-47" Mitch reported to his pilot.

"No, where"

The helicopter banked left, away from the hill to rotate around and pass the cracked boulder again.

"See him, just standing there, before he raised his AK to aim at us", Mitch hoped that would get that soldier reprimanded. Then the pilot remarked,

"Why is he the only one with an AK, all the others have M-16's"

This surprised Mitchell that he hadn't noticed that!

"I've seen it before when the ARVN's used captured weapons", Mitch replied as an excuse for not being more attentive.

"Well let's check this guy out"

They continued to fly at a leisurely pace as not to alert the soldier to anything unusual, although the pilot requested Mitchell to keep his eye's on him and to return fire if he used his weapon against them.

"Tiger tooth, Taipan One-Niner"

"This is Tiger tooth, Go"

"Roger, we have a soldier at the five hundred foot mark, he has an AK that he aimed at us but my backseat say's he did not fire, copy"

"Roger, copy, stand-by one, let me see if we have anyone up there"

In a minute's time, the advisor returned to the radio.

"Taipan, did you say the soldier had an AK"

"Roger Tiger tooth"

"And he is at the five hundred foot mark"

"Roger"

"Ahh Taipan, be advised we have no troops reporting at that elevation, are you certain"

"Roger that Tiger tooth, we got a good visual on him, he is wearing what appears to be an ARVN uniform and he is there at this time"

"One Niner, Well sir, you know that anyone can get access to the uniforms but we have no troops reported with an AK, or at that elevation, I expect your visual is Victor Charlie, can you engage"

"Roger, Taipan's engaging, keep your troops down"

Realizing that he just looked eyeball to eyeball with the enemy while pointing a weapon at him, Mitchell began to reposition himself, ready to repay the favor.

Davies rolled the aircraft left again to do a 360-degree turn.

"I am going to try rockets first guy's, hold your fire till the rockets are away, I am going to get in close so keep a sharp lookout, I'll break out left"

Then the lead pilot informed his two wing ships of his intentions and suggested they climb to a higher altitude to set up a possible air strike to provide cover.

Davies unlocked the HUD and swung the "head's up display" into position.

In the back seat Mitch and the gunner looked straight ahead over the pilot's shoulders and past the windshield. The chopper was now perpendicular with the crack and the soldier who continued to watch the helicopter flying directly at him.

The chopper yawed slightly back and forth until Davies had the soldier in his sights. The soldier must have thought the chopper would soon turn away, and waited until he was absolutely sure that the charging helicopter was making an aggressive move on his position. Only when the chopper was too close for comfort did the soldier turn to run into the crack in the boulder.

Mitchell thought for sure that he was going to get away, when just then he heard the single rocket whoosh as it left the pod and he glimpsed the rocket flame that headed towards Boulder Mountain and the crack.

In what could only be described as a "one in a million shot", the rocket disappeared into the narrow vertical space. There was no flash of explosion, or shattered debris, only a small amount of white wispy smoke that appeared after a few seconds from the top of the crack. It was hard to imagine not eliminating the threatening soldier as he had just turned and disappeared a scant second before the arrival of Mr. Davies rocket that followed him in.

"Un-fucking believable shot", the copilot exclaimed.

"It had to hit him in the middle of his back just as he turned", he added.

"Tiger tooth, this is Taipan One-Niner, we have ceased fire, and have one unconfirmed KIA, copy that"

"Outstanding One-Niner, will confirm when we get to that mark"

Although Mitchell hadn't been able to fire a shot, still he would not have missed that rocket shot for all the rice in country.

It was time to refuel and Mr. Davies informed Tiger tooth that they were breaking off. Now lunchtime the Taipan's would join the EMU's sitting back at the base waiting for their first mission.

Tiger tooth and his troops had made contact soon after, but it was much lighter than they had expected. They engaged the enemy inside the mountain and chased some upwards on the surface. Several NVA had been killed and they had captured a dozen prisoners. The EMU's were sent in along with the Taipan's as escorts to retrieve the captured and the dead.

It had been reported that the troops on Stone Mountain had discovered a complete hospital dug out inside the mountain. There were dozens of rooms and weapons of every make and description had been found. Judging from documents discovered, the mountain was some kind of headquarters for the North Vietnamese Army that was crossing the border deep into the South. This worried some high level Commanders back in Saigon.

The partial remains of a NVA Soldier were discovered at the five hundred-foot mark in a crack in a boulder that led into a large room. In that room scattered sacks of rice displaced by the rocket indicated that food had been accumulated to feed hundreds of personnel.

Mr. Davies received his first confirmed KIA. Fellow pilots had congratulated him, although he took it all in stride.

By late that afternoon all the troops had been extracted with the exception of a small force that held the captured pile of stone. The ARVN troops along with the Scouts had gone unscathed and the Taipan's did not fire another shot. The Scouts found evidence that an unknown number of the enemy had slipped out during the night through secret tunnels that led them past the sleeping troops in the middle of the night.

Several days later, in an area known as the "Wagon Wheel", named for the way multiple roads came together like the spokes of a wheel towards a hub. The area is the easternmost section of the plain of reeds. Mitchell's helicopter is at this time the oldest aircraft in the Taipan arsenal. The ship had only recently began to get "buggy", bugs appeared in the form of intermittent warning lights, Batteries draining from poor wiring, and hydraulic leaks popping up for no reason.

The troops that had been lifted into the LZ earlier that morning had been roaming through swamp all day in search of stockpiles of weapons and were anxious to get back to their base camp. Like the past days, no enemy had brazenly challenged the ARVN's so there was little combat activity.

When C&C called for the Slicks to retrieve the soggy troops, it was decided the Taipan's would escort them as opposed to arriving ahead of the Slicks for recon. It is a relative short hop so the Taipan's climbed to cruising altitude with the Slicks, they are now at approximately two thousand feet.

In the center of the instrument panel a yellow light flickered on, then off. The co-pilot is flying the aircraft and was watching the EMU's in formation. The pilot noticed the light appear briefly but it happened so fast he could not tell which light had momentarily illuminated. The warning lights are mounted in a sub-panel called the, "master caution panel", each light is mounted one above the other, in two columns.

Reaching to lightly tap on the warning panel, the pilot tried to induce a lighted response.

The co-pilot noticed the tapping maneuver and made an inquiry.

"What-cha doing"

"Thought I saw a light come on"

After reviewing the instruments, the co-pilot responded,

"Everything's in the green"

"I don't know for sure it lit, maybe it's a short or something".

"Yea, the moisture this morning was bad", the co-pilot offered.

Mitchell overheard the two talking on the intercom, and unbuckled his seat belt to check it out. He reached over the center console and depressed the "Test" button to illuminate all the lights, they had all lit up.

"Probably the fucking bugs again", he noted.

A few minutes later the light reappeared, and the pilot noticed that it was the "transmission chip detector" light. Normally this would mean that pieces of metal had been attracted to the magnetic sensor inside the transmission to indicate enough metal chips had bridged a gap of the screened end of the sensor. Then the light blinked off.

"Well that's weird", said the pilot.

"Whad-da-ya think, contact C&C", the co-pilot asked.

"Naw, let's see what happens"

They flew on for several more minutes before the light blinked on again.

"This is really not right", the pilot was sounding concerned.

The light burned on steadily now.

"Well I think we got a problem here"

The pilot keyed the mic and announced,

"C&C, Taipan One Niner, over"

"Go Taipan"

"Ahhh roger, we have a chip detector lit, request permission to land to check it out"

C&C knew that a pilot reporting a chip detector light was a serious event, and granted the permission. There are four chip detectors, engine, transmission, and two for the tail rotor gearboxes. If the components have been timed in, as in "not new", then to have a chip detector illuminate usually means that component has failing gears or bearings and the aircraft is grounded immediately.

"Roger One Niner, do you require assistance", C&C asked knowing that he had a flight of Slicks to protect but if One Niner had to land into an unknown area, having an armed escort might be of some help.

"Roger, we will require one wing ship"

Ok, good luck Taipan"

"Roger"

Nearly at that same moment the co-pilot exclaimed,

"Have you done anything to the throttle".

The Pilot responded, "No why"

"I've just lost a hundred RPM down to sixty-five-hundred"

The pilot took control of the aircraft and asked the co-pilot to get a fix on their position and "eyeball a good LZ".

As the pilot lowered the collective, to descend altitude, he too, noticed a further reduction in the engine RPM.

"We better get this ship on the ground quick, we're losing RPM fast"

With that they headed for the ground. The pilot was unsure to dive to initiate the landing in the shortest possible time, and cause additional stress on the aircraft, or descend at a lessor rate and not further aggravate the problem. A transmission failure at this altitude would mean falling out of the sky like a rock.

"We're down to fifty-nine hundred", the pilot stated.

"I hope we get this machine down before the rotor stops in mid-flight".

"Fifty-six hundred", the co-pilot called out.

"I can't go any quicker down", the pilot exclaimed.

"Well it's a race to the ground then", replied the co-pilot.

"Yea, well we better win then or…".

Mitchell listened for any unusual noises coming from behind the rear bulkhead, but did not hear anything. He informed the gunner to buckle up tight, while he cinched up his own belt. Then he watched the rotor speed gage and tried to calculate their time to the ground. Of all the way's to die here, Mitchell never thought that he could just fall out of the sky.

"Passing through eleven hundred", the co-pilot inform them of their current altitude.

"Crank up the throttle a bit, see if that will extend our flight", then the pilot added, "slowly".

"That's it, we don't want to put any more load on the tranny".

The front seats were doing what they could, but the RPM's were declining faster than they were descending.

"Maybe we should auto-rotate", asked the co-pilot

"I'd be afraid to cut the power, we may not get enough rotor speed".

Mitchell looked at the gunner who was looking around nervously. He knew he too was concerned that their situation was declining.

"Six hundred feet", the co-pilot warned.

The gunner reached over to intercom Mitchell,

"I think I'll jump when we start to fall".

"Why would you do that", Mitch replied.

"I don't want to burn when we crash".

"Stupid fucker, either way you're going to be dead, what's the fucking difference".

Mitch looked at him disgustingly and added,

"Just keep your ass in that seat, and tighten your fucking seat belt".

"Four hundred feet"

A noise began to emanate from the behind the bulkhead, a high pitched grinding noise.

"Mr. Davies, I hear grinding now", Mitch reported.

There was no reply as the ship was beginning to slow its forward speed.

"One hundred feet, sixty knots"

"Awe shit, I don't know if…"

The pilot nosed the ship downward, the view of a rice paddy filled both windshields. The ground rushed up towards the anxious faces of the crew.

Just as it looked the impact was going to be really rough, the ship flared back hard for only a few seconds and leveled off a few feet above the earth and fell the remaining distance. With the remaining thirty knots of forward airspeed the ship slid and bounced forward on the muddy surface.

"Roll off throttle"

"Pulling fuel pump circuit breakers", added in rapid succession.

The aircraft stopped sliding at nearly the same instant that the rotors grounded down to a dead halt.

"Well were down".

Mitchell jumped out with the gunner who began to set up a perimeter just in case Charlie sighted their forced landing. Mitch helped the pilot out of the aircraft then opened the engine cowling to inspect the transmission. Looking over the aircraft he found both chin bubbles had been broken and the ship is covered in chunks of smelly wet earth. A couple of long deep trenches created by the landing skids in the mud extended behind the ship for sixty feet or more. They had landed in an open paddy far from any hooch's or tree lines. The wing ship that had witnessed the incident had already radioed for a rescue mission of the crew and ship.

Within minutes a slick had landed and picked up three crewmembers. Mitch was left with his ship to "Hook up" with the CH-47 Chinook helicopter that would be there in a few minutes more. A mechanic that had flown out with the slick gave Mitchell a large nylon looped belt and instructed him how to secure it around the rotor hub and then hook it under the Chinook. He also warned him not to grab the hook until the crew-chief had grounded the two ships or he would get the jolt of his life. Just what I need is another jolt, he thought.

The large Chinook with its two main rotors appeared and descended to a hover directly over the top of the downed gunship. Mitch climbed atop the chopper and strapped the hub with the nylon belt. A hook on a cable hung below the bottom surface of the large helicopter. Mitch could see the crew-chief peeping down from the hole where the cable went up into. With hand signals to indicate that it was safe to make the final hook up, he then had to shimmy up the cable into that hole in the bottom of the Chinook.

Safe inside, the two helicopters, one on top and one slung below, lifted off and headed for home.

The crew-chief lay on the floor on his stomach with his head looking down at his load swaying. He had a hardwired control in his hand to release the load if it looked it would swing up into the mother ship.

"That ship nearly killed us today", Mitch had told the crew-chief.

"Couldn't you just say it began to swing up, and let her go".

He really hoped now he would get a new ship to crew.

SHORT! Having made it near the end of an individual's "tour of duty", jittery solders joke to see who is shortest.

Chapter Eighteen

Hunter / Killer

"Yea though I fly through the valley of the shadow of death, I will fear no evil, because I am the badest son-of-a-bitch in the valley", stepping back he looked at his handy work admiringly. Then he again dipped the brush into the pint size can of red enamel paint as Mitch put the finishing touches on his new helicopter.

His new ship had been transferred from another Assault Helicopter Company that was being sent home as part of the troop reduction plan. The war was over for the men but the helicopters would have to stay. It had come from Texas only four months prior where the ship was reconditioned to almost "like new", and was "oh-so-much better" than his last ship. Mitchell had become one of the most senior members of the gun platoon. This new ship was a sign of that seniority. The FNG's would envy his aircraft, and pilots would clamber over each other to have the first opportunity to fly it. But there was still much to do to have it ready for the next mission.

This was his first ship with any doors at all, although they had removed the large cargo doors before it arrived, it did not matter to Mitch. Again he dipped the small paintbrush, then touched the paint to the pilot's door just below the window. With a steady hand the name "HELL FIRE" was completed now on both sides of the aircraft.

Pellitier, the gunner was busily re-arming the rocket pods, carrying two at a time, and then he shoved the 2.75in diameter rocket with seventeen pound warheads into the pod until he felt the telltale "click" that let him know that they were locked in position. Then he pulled and twisted the contactors that delivered the low voltage to the center of the firing cap. The cap also held the guidance fins in place, and when the rocket was fired it melted into a sharp metal fragments. Those molted bits often stung the back seat crew in the legs projected rearward from the rockets thrust as they left the tubes at more than five hundred miles per hour. After loading thirty-eight rockets he brought in two empty 50cal. ammo cans, and began to weave in the belts of 7.62mm, two thousand rounds in each for their M-60's. Five smoke grenades hung on the wire and the stainless steel water cooler was set in place. The gunner sat twisting his black handlebar moustache into tightly woven and opposing spears as he waited for Mitch to conclude his chores.

After polishing the windshield and the chin bubbles, Mitch went over the aircraft to check all the fluid levels again, gearboxes, transmission, and hydraulics. He drained some fuel into a C-ration can to inspect for the presence of water or other contaminates in the fuel. Crawling under the aircraft to the center, he inspected the "hell hole", a void under the transmission where the mounts and hydraulic tubing could be seen. He climbed atop the cabin to ensure that the rotor head components were all within tolerance. From the tail rotor to the battery connectors he was now satisfied that "Hell Fire", was ready for combat duty the next day. It was just after sunset when the two of them walked off the flight line.

Mitchell stared at the pictures hanging in his wall locker. No, not the ones he clipped from Playboy magazines, the ones of his family and girlfriend. It seemed an eternity since he was last home. He wondered if everyone else has changed as much as he felt that he had. When he closed his eyes to try and find some comfort in conjuring up an image of his family, he could no longer get a clear picture. Sometimes he really had to struggle to get any kind of image of his past home life. Mitch worried that they might forget him, as he seemed to be losing them. Maybe it was for the best, he reasoned, if he died here, then perhaps it would be easier on his love ones to forget him. It was a difficult period of his tour. He has lived longer than his life expectancy as a helicopter crewmember. Was it possible to go the full term without something tearing at parts of his body? He thought not, but still he had been hopeful that whatever came it would be only enough to get him sent home as a whole person.

His solemn mood had been interrupted by the platoon sergeant shouting into the barracks to make his announcement,

"Adler, Collins, Jenkins, Oxford, Pellitier, and Picot, you guys get to sleep in late tomorrow", the Sergeant had no longer finished calling out names of the Taipan Chief's and Gunners when someone remarked,

"Well there's a first, who the fu…"

The Sarge interrupted,

"You six are crewing for a new mission beginning tomorrow, your scheduled takeoff is twelve thirty hours".

Then Adler spoke up,

"What's the new mission sarge".

"Ask your pilot, I don't have any details of the mission"

How odd, Mitch thought, a new ship and now a new mission! Then he realized the names were all of the most senior crewmen, oh this can't be good!

That following morning they had awakened at the normal hour and tried to fall back asleep. The noise level made by those whose schedule was unaffected by the new mission was tweaked up from the norm just to irritate the late sleepers. But the laid out crew remained still, knowing that the others would be soon out the door. An extra couple of hours sleep would do well with battle weary troops, although they worried about the price that would have to be paid for the extended rest.

It was impossible to sleep after the morning flight had taken off. The flight of choppers half circled the base to a heading that took them south. The agitation in the air rumbling under the twelve EMU ship's rotors while they departed was a familiar sound. But the now alert crew felt they had been left behind as the noise gradually dissipated. Outside the barracks the rear echelon personnel have begun to assemble for morning roll call. It had been some time since Mitchell has heard Reveille played over the loud speaker system. By dawn they've usually completed the morning rituals and were airborne, and half way to the AO.

In the mess hall Mitchell observed many unrecognizable faces as the soldiers sat in friendly groups, each engrossed in conversation. He has spent so little time in the rear and soldiers rotated in and out of the unit so that it seemed to Mitch that everyone he saw was a new guy. As he wiped the food tray with the remaining piece of toast to soak up the last of the egg yolk, Mitchell wondered what he would do with the remaining time. He still had hours before takeoff, enough time to get in a steam bath? Probably not open at this hour, he reasoned. Couldn't have a drink at the club, it too was closed. Can't go to the tower for another swim, couldn't risk getting caught, then having it off limits for good. He hadn't written a letter home in months because he still had nothing he wanted to tell anyone. Mitch was just bored, bored with everything except flying. It was all there was to do that separated him from the drudgery of life in the rear. In fact he was beginning to enjoy the combat action in some perverted way, he had become good at it, and felt at ease even when things got hot. Sometimes he wished for a little action when things were slow. Mitchell became numb to the fact his life was in danger every second, and death was always was a heartbeat from reality. At anytime, anywhere he was, a rocket, mortar round, sniper, booby-trap, or failing aircraft component could end his tour of duty. He gulped the last of his coffee and decided to try to sleep some more.

By ten a.m. the heat was unbearable in the barracks, the tin roof absorbed the sun's heat and transferred it inwards. The little electric fan that Mitch had nailed to the wall at the head of his bed did little more than stir blistering molecules at high speed. Often a "Viet-Cong fly" would buzz the ears to annoy him, shoo-ing did little to discourage the filthy buggers. In fact, they could become incensed by the attempt to keep the combative insect from landing in their "zone", and go on the offensive and attack an eye or nose orifice. More terrible is when there is more than one. The hooch maids had arrived, and are busily sweeping, and collecting dirty clothes to be hand washed in the shower building. Another maid stacked the boots for the daily polishing. The VC flies did not harass the natives.

High pitched voices of the women blubbering loudly in Vietnamese now further aggravated Mitch as he squirmed in the heat. The women not used to having any soldiers in the barracks while they went about their chores continued to chatter amongst themselves. They began to laugh loudly and Mitch could not take it any longer.

"Shut the fuck up", he screamed out, but not at anyone in particular.

"Numba ten G.I., you talk bad to mama-san", the younger Vietnamese girl sassed back.

"Why you talk like dis", she questioned.

He ignored her to keep his temper from committing a crime of heat.

Sweat poured off Mitch and soaked his sheets, when it became impossible to stay in the barracks any longer he decided to dress and head out to the flight line.

Scrutinizing his freshly reconstructed aircraft brought a kind of relief of knowing that his survivability probably increased by tenfold with the new ship. The anxiety of having to fly in a ship that he did not trust to keep them alive would be gone now. All he needed was a crew and a mission to fly. Mitch opened the pilot's door and sat in the seat. He scanned the instruments, the artificial horizon looked new, he observed the condition of the N1 tach, and EGT gage. The altimeter and the airspeed indicators were obviously original but they had most likely been rebuilt. Mitch reached down to wind up the eight-day clock being careful not to wind it too tight. He mentally reviewed the start-up procedure.

Mitchell had learned to fly in school while training as a crew-chief but only flew a simulator. He had taken off ok but lost control in flight and crashed and burned. It was a relief to know it was a simulation and he hoped to never having to find out for sure if he could save himself. But now with his experience in actual flight he was much more comfortable at the controls. He could only fly the Huey when the co-pilot wanted to sit in the rear seat and fire the M-60, or when his ship was just out of maintenance and he would go along on test flights. But he loved flying the helicopter and flew whenever the opportunity arose. He had become proficient in keeping the altitude and airspeed within tolerance, but he was never able to bring the ship to a hover and land. The controls were super-sensitive and a sneeze while holding the cyclic control would rattle the aircraft. Still, in an emergency, he knew he could perform a running landing and most likely save himself and the ship if he had to.

Soon the pilots appeared with their gear, helmet bag, maps, pistol and c-rations.

"Afternoon Chief, are you ready", Mr. Flemming asked?

"Yea, but ready for what", Mitch responded

"We going to be flying Hunter/Killer missions this evening"

"Really, that sounds like it could be fun", although Mitch didn't really understand what Hunter/Killer missions actually were.

"We'll see about that", the pilot climbed into the cockpit while the co-pilot, Mr. Preston did the pre-flight.

All they have known up until now, is what they had done in the escort role providing cover for the flight of EMU's, that, and a few sorties when the EMU's were safe. New missions required new tactics, safety procedures and more training. But this was going to be a trial by fire. There would be no additional training, and the tactics would be learned in the field, as the Taipan's are one of the first Delta units to fly the night missions. Somewhere, someone had a lot of faith in the experienced crews of the platoon. With three months left on his tour of duty, Mitch really did not like taking unnecessary chances, but never the less welcomed the chance to do something different.

Suddenly Mitchell realized that he and his gunner did not have their C-rations. Dashing behind to the next revetment where another Taipan ship was being readied and found that none of the crew had any meals. Usually, in the morning the table was stacked with the brown boxes of sustenance, but it was all gone by the time they had finished their late breakfast and they hadn't thought of eating C-rats for supper. After convincing the gunner to run as quickly as possible back to the mess hall to beg the head cook for the meals in a box, Mitchell tried to find out more about the mission.

Mr. Flemming was a good pilot and he and Mitch had flown missions before. Some pilots had ego's larger than an over inflated fuel bladder, but Flemming was a good guy and a sensible aviator. He seemed too young to have had much experience as a gunship driver but his skill was already honed to a sharp edge. Mr. Preston also had experience and was already an aircraft commander. Mitch wondered why he was co-piloting today.

Everything seemed to be different, the chopper, the pilots and flying at night. It had been said before, that too many new changes for one mission weren't good and could lead to serious problems. So what set of circumstance prompted the Taipan's most experienced crews to gather for a special op's mission. He could only wonder, Mitch had only to worry about his duties for now, and hope that "HELL FIRE" would live up to its name.

Mitchell prodded Flemming while he prepared for flight,

"So what's all this about Mr. Flemming"

"Gooks, coming over the Cambodian border into the Delta at night", he replied while pushing in the appropriate circuit breakers to begin the start-up procedure.

Not satisfied with that, Mitchell pressed again.

"But what are we going to do about it"

"Find em"

"How, at night, can't see shit out there"

Flemming was busy with his maps now and trying to organize the codes for the mission, and really did not want to explain what he already knew. But he understood that his crew chief did not get briefed on the mission as he had, so he offered a little more.

"We are going to have a Flare-ship with us"

"Oh", Mitchell said, "that's good to have"

"Uh ha", Flemming was now engrossed in his preflight duties and Mitchell had lost his attention.

Taking off on schedule they headed for familiar territory. It felt strange to be flying south at this time of day, but Mitchell anxiously waited to find out what this was all leading up to. As was normal, the middle of the day is quiet, radio communications have dissipated, artillery is quiet, and there is little air traffic in the skies. It seemed that the war shut down for the lunch hour, a mid-day truce as it were. Allied, and enemy alike retreated from conflict to nourish themselves and regain their strength for another round of evening clashes, before it was time to rest the body.

The air is cool and Mitchell's eyes slowly closed as he blocked out the mechanical noises to clearly hear the composition of Diana Ross and the Supremes singing "Reflections". The sweet melody filled his ears, *"oh I am so alone now, no love to shield me, trapped in a world that's a distorted reality,* the music replaced his dreams, *reflections of the way life used to be"*. His heart ached for home but he was trapped in the Nam, and home was a million miles away, and thousands of years to get there.

Following the end of the monsoon season signals the return of the gray dust. Hell Fire hovered over the tarmac creating a dust storm. Finally the chopper sat down on the fuel pad. The pilot radioed C&C to find out where they were to stand-by.

"Taipan's sit tight at Ben Tre, you will be contacted by Firefly Two-Eight to begin sorties, how copy!"

"Good copy, standing by, out"

After fueling they hovered again to a position alongside the active runway and shut down until they were contacted. It was always "hurry up and wait" in the Army. They were used to it now and quickly made the best of down time. Eating and sleeping were always the priority. Sometimes a game of football was in order or a game of spades in the shaded interior of one of the choppers. But this afternoon was different. The pilots spent much of their time going over special aspects of night missions. Honing their tactics provided in the mission briefing, the pilots used their hands to indicate each respective position the fire team, as they would be in the air. Exaggerated body movements, and shuffling of feet into small circles in the dirt, the pilots saw what only they could.

"Altitude should be a priority," said Preston.

"We will not have the usual references, and the horizon will be invisible in the darkness, so keep a sharp eye on the ball", he continued, referring to the ball in the Artificial Horizon, an instrument to indicate the helicopters relationship to the natural horizon.

Then Mr. Flemming spoke to the other five pilots,

"Keep the interior lights dimmed, watch your night vision, and don't look directly at the flares"

And then Flemming added,

"We'll be keeping more distance between aircraft when on mission, so we don't pile up, ok"

The radio squawked at 1630 hrs. and the orders to "crank-em-up", is transmitted. Firefly Two-Eight was on the horn now giving Mr. Flemming the co-ordinances of the AO where the search portion of the Hunter/Killer mission will commence.

Taipan's arrived on station just before sunset and began flying a zigzag pattern around the AO. To Mitchell it seemed all pretty much routine until the unoccupied Sampan was spotted in a shallow watery trail left in the tall grass. A small tree line rose from the grassy depth almost a klick or so to the West. This time of the season the water levels were very shallow and a Sampan would barely float. The trailing gunship was sent to a lower orbit to inspect the craft. Lead and wing stayed at five hundred feet to cover the lower aircraft.

The sun fell below the horizon casting eerie shadows over the landscape. Then from the edge of a darkened tree line to the right of the flight, three green balls erupted from the base of the trees and streaked upwards over the top the lower aircraft and disappeared to the left.

"We're taking double "AA" fire, lead"

"Roger, do you see where it's coming from", Flemming asked.

"Chief reports he thinks it came from the tree line at two-six-zero degree"

From below, the trailing aircraft climbed up to rejoin formation with the fire team. Then another burst of green balls came directly for Mitchell's ship.

"Oh shit, we're taking fire", he anxiously reported.

The "green balls" were the tracers of the Russian manufactured fifty-one caliber anti-aircraft guns. They seemed to pop out of the trees and fly directly towards the nervous eye's that just prayed to see them fly past. They looked to be the size of a basketball when approaching and then would zip by narrowly missing the vulnerable aircraft. All the crew chiefs had opened fire towards the trees in hopes of suppressing the fire. At the same time the three ships banked to aim their rockets towards the base of the trees.

More bright green tracers flew by and Mitchell was getting really nervous now. If they were to get shot down here in the dark a rescue might not be possible until dawn. Although the muzzle velocity of the fifty-one is measured in hundreds of feet per second, from his point of view, it seemed they passed much slower. He knew there are four rounds in between each tracer that could not be seen, so to see six tracers meant that twenty four more anti-aircraft bullets were out there zipping through the dark sky. The enemy was firing short bursts in hope of disguising their location. Mitchell depressed the trigger again but couldn't see where his bullets were going. The muzzle flash was so bright and flames spewed from the end of the barrel that it had blinded him from the target. He quickly learned to hold the weapon lower as to see over the flash and use his red tracers to guide them onto the general location of the anti-aircraft battery in the trees.

At the first firing of a salvo of rockets, they left the tubes with a surprising bright flash and trail of sparks. Night firing of machineguns and rockets were enhanced in the obscurity while never before having been witnessed by crews that had previously only flown missions during daylight hours. Mr. Flemming nosed the aircraft up and simultaneously banked right at the bottom of their run. A loud "ping" was heard just after the cease firing by the gunners.

After the first strike the wing ship reported to Lead that he had seen the green tracers, "got very close to the your ship"

"Roger I think we're hit", Mr. Flemming responded.

"Cross check good", the co-pilot told Flemming. Both had quickly scanned the instrument panel for any sign of component failure.

"Rog, but I feel a vibration".

Mitchell did not feel what the pilot referred to but he assumed the vibration was more in the cyclic control in the hand of Mr. Flemming.

"Chief take a look to the rear"

Mitchell leaned far out to view the tail-boom that was intermittently lit up by the red rotating beacon of the anti-collision light.

Mitchell's heart sank, as he could barely perceived the large gaping hole, the size of a fist in the tail rotor shaft cover. Its sharp torn edges turned outward to indicate this was an exit hole. If the Fifty-one caliber went through the cover, it most assuredly went through the shaft. If the shaft failed in flight they could end up going in like EMU One-Five did so many months earlier.

"There's a big hole in the TR cover", Mitchell reported.

"Be specific chief, did it hit the shaft", the pilot asked.

"Can't tell for sure, the hole is in the center of the forward cover, so it must have hit the shaft", Mitchell knew that this would temporarily halt the mission.

Mitch asked the gunner if he could see the entrance hole on the left side.

"Nope, too dark, can't see anything"

Then he made a mental note that a flashlight might be a good thing to have on future night missions.

So after one air strike, the fire team headed for a friendly base to check out the damage. On solid ground again and on a dimly lighted base Mitch went to work. With a screwdriver he turned a couple Zeus fasteners and lifted the tail-rotor cover over on its hinge. To their great relief the 51-caliber bullet had entered from under the tail boom, left of center, while the aircraft was banking. The single round went through the hallow tail boom at an angle exiting at the top, right, just under the shaft at a slight angle and through the cover without touching the shaft.

All the pilots in the fire team had come to see what the fifty-one had done to the company's new ship, one of them having had the only flashlight in the group passed it to Mitch for the inspection. Having found but a scratch on the shaft, Mitch reported,

"Good to go men"!

The nervous hand of the pilot had caused the vibration. Double "A"fire would make the bravest pilot a bit fidgety, especially at night. Knowing that a fist sized hole existed in the TR cover and that the integrity of the shaft could cause separation any moment didn't help matters either. They had all been a bit nervous but only one hand was on the "stick". Nothing more was said about the vibration to the others. Ironically Mitch was relieved that it was his pilot and not his new ship.

"Let's find those bastards, and give-em a little taste of Hell Fire", Pellitier too, was relieved that his life had not been unduly put in jeopardy.

The crew had felt relief and a bit invincible for not having been shot down by the AA. So they fueled the ships rearmed the pods, and grabbed extra ammo for the M-sixties.

In less than an hour they were back in the AO. The trailing ship went into a low orbit again to try and draw fire from the same tree line. Meanwhile, lead and his wingman stayed high to roll in on the targets when they showed themselves. The Lead and wing ship, turned off their navigational lights, while trail exposed himself to the anti-aircraft gun! The crews had regained their night vision when the first burst of tracers lit up the tree line.

"Trail, get outta there, your taking fire"

"Roger, rolling out left"

"Leads in on the target"

"Got-cha covered lead", announced the wing-ship.

Skies were ablaze with tracers, red from the Taipan's guns firing downwards, and green from the enemy in the trees shooting back up. One at a time, they would dive down from their strike altitude into near blackness with only the accuracy of the instruments to alert the pilot when to pull out of the dive, and clear the target for the next gunship. The exchange of tracers crossing paths in the night sky went on for two air strikes. Long bursts of machinegun fire from each gunner saturated the tree line. When the trailing ship fired his mini-guns, lead was climbing one hundred eighty degrees to his right. They could see what looked like Trail, pissing down a steady stream of red tracers into the trees. Then the rockets exiting the pods would momentarily illuminate the interior like a flash of bright white of a strobe light and quickly fade before exploding into the trees. Another climbing turn to regain lost altitude. Mitchell squeezed the trigger and began firing even before the next dive. Holding the trigger and concentrating on the target he barely noticed the shadow of the bullet traveling down the barrel. The barrel was white hot now and Mitch could see the faint specter of live rounds through the hardened steel as it passed down the guns bore.

Fearing that the barrel might warp and capture a bullet on the way out, then the next bullet would ram the first causing the hot barrel to explode into fragments, it was time to change barrels. Mitch lifted the barrel locking tab to disengage the barrel and gas cylinder assembly. But he needed to twist the assembly approximately thirty degrees to release it. Not able to touch it, even with his gloved hand he kicked it loose and then shook the machinegun to dislodge the barrel assembly. Finally the barrel fell out just as the gunship was setting up for the next run. Quickly Mitch grabbed the one spare barrel and replaced it into the gun's breach. He loaded the belt of ammo then turned and began firing again, down they went, Mitch and the gunner both firing leaning out to the limits of their seat belts to aim forward into the target. Then near the bottom of the run Mitch felt a searing pain in his left foot.

The nerves in his leg all signaled simultaneously that something was terribly wrong. Mitch jerked upwards and his helmet slammed hard against the rear bulkhead. His pain was agonizing and he had lost his breath. Reaching for the microphone switch he tried to report that he had been shot. But the helicopter was still on mission and at least he was alive, he waited. Able now to gulp short breaths, he tried to regain his composure to inspect his injury. He felt sick at the thought of taking off his boot to find a mutilated foot, but his anguish was so great and he thought that by removing the boot it might relieve some of his pain. Trying not to look while he undid the laces of his leather combat boot, it was difficult to see anything in the gloom of the chopper's interior. He could smell something burning, maybe I've got a burning tracer lodged in my foot, he thought. He quickly unlaced his shoe as to save some portion of his foot before burning beyond recognition. The pain was excruciating. Fumbling with his right foot to kick off the left boot, as he really didn't want to touch his wound, it finally came free. As he slid his foot out he strained in the darkness expecting to see his blood, but noticed smoke coming from his discarded boot and the sock still on his foot. Reaching for the black smoldering leather form he held it close to his face. The laces and the top of the boot had been badly burnt. Mitchell pulled his sock off the inflicted limb to find only the top of his foot badly burned. He realized now that the white-hot barrel he had shaken out the gun fell onto his foot and burned through before he felt anything in his intense concentration while firing.

The peter-pilot noticing that the right gun had not fired recently turned into the cargo area and noticed his crew chief fumbling with his boot and keyed his mic,

"Chief, are you hit"

"Burned, just fucking burned, I burned myself", he almost cried happy tears for not having been shot.

"Do you need a medivac", he questioned.

"Naw, I'm ok", Mitch responded in an exasperated voice. Then extracting some ice cold water from the cooler, he poured it over the burn area and went back to work.

He was really pissed off now and was eager to extract his revenge on an enemy that stood invisible in the black foliage. His anger fueled by the intense pain in his foot drove Mitch into a frenzy of shooting. He sprayed his bullets everywhere to prevent any of the bad guy's escape of his wrath. When he finally ran out of ammo he wished they would over fly the tree line so that he could use his grenades. Hell, he would even throw his C-ration cans at them. But discretion was the better part a valor, especially at night so they headed back to Ben Tre for fuel and ammo, and maybe a Medic to look at Mitchell's foot.

On the radio Mitch heard that Firefly Two-Eight had been standing by while the Taipan's went through their exercise. Assuming that Firefly would be at Ben Tre, Mitch looked around during the refueling process and did not see any other ships that appeared to be standing by. In fact the base was quiet and the Taipan fire team were the only operating aircraft. Locking the fuel cap in place, he replaced the fuel hose neatly next to the fuel bladder. Then Mitch inquired,

"Hey, what happened to Firefly"

"He's on station, standing by, waiting on us", Flemming responded.

"What kind of chopper carries that much fuel"

"Firefly is a C-130 aircraft and can stay on station all night", the pilot looked at Mitch and added,

"Ok, here's what we are going to do, Firefly will cruise at ten thousand feet and drop parachute flares, then we will fly around the light from the flares hopefully catch a few bad guy's and dispatch the targets", he looked at Mitch to see if he understood.

"Oh, I got it now, thanks", Mitch replied.

In reality, Mitch could have asked a hundred other questions but was happy to get what he had so he decided to just roll with the program.

Huge bodies of stars filled the dark but otherwise clear skies. Mitch sat looking out over the dim terrain. Nothing could be seen from down below, it was all pitch black with the exception of flickering reflections of small pools of water scattered amongst the reeds. He wondered how they would ever spot anyone with the yellowish glow of a flare. A voice on the radio announced the commencement of the flare drop. A yellowish glowing dot appeared in the sky well above, and ahead of the helicopter. It began small and quickly brightened as it fell. After a few moments a small white parachute could be seen directly above the light. As the parachute flare dropped to about two thousand feet, it began to illuminate the terrain below. Weird shadows danced and flickered over an area the size of four football fields. A circle of light appeared now even brighter under the flare. From a distance the light formed an inverted light cone in the blackness, with the narrowest point emanating at the flare then widening outward until the radius of light formed on the surface of the earth. Slow banking circles are made as the two Taipan gunship's orbit just outside the cone of light. The trailing ship remained at a higher altitude and was a greater distance from the light to provide cover for either of the two ships circling. With their navigational lights switched off, they were invisible to anyone on the ground inside the circle of light. The trailing aircraft would keep his nav lights on to draw fire from the enemy, as he was at a safer altitude. The Nav lights would also serve the lower two ships so they wouldn't collide with trail in the event of an emergency climb out. Meanwhile crews visually searched inside the lighted area for anything to target, pilots remained vigilant keeping the craft airborne and in control.

As the first flare faded out before ever getting close to the ground another was dropped from the high flying fixed wing C-130 aircraft. Shifting to the next cone of light the Taipan's continued circling the cones of light. Then another flare is dropped in what now appears as a straight line towards the Cambodian border.

After the drop of the seventh flare Mitch called out a sampan sighted. The pilot in command cleared Mitch to prep the area using intermittent bursts so that the enemy could not target them by observing the source of his machinegun fire. Every time he let up on the trigger, the aircraft had moved considerably more forward. It would be nearly impossible to lead the moving target without knowing exactly where it was.

He first drilled holes into the wooden boat to render it useless when the waters returned. Then he laid down intermittent fire surrounding the perforated boat. His bullets were penetrating the landmass with a few red glowing tracers ricocheting off in indiscriminate directions. Something in the reeds moved, but it wasn't a man, it was much larger. After a few more bursts a water buffalo came into view as the flare fell closer. The dark gray color naturally concealed it in the dimness of the reeds. Curiously, the beast did not run, instead he trotted in circles as though he couldn't find a particular direction to run in. As the light drew nearer the ground it became apparent that the buff was tied to a stake by the ring in his nose.

"What the hell is he doing way out here"

"Probably used to carry weapons in from the border", the pilot responded to the question proposed by the co-pilot. It was obvious to Mitch that someone brought the animal to this location and secured it for the night.

Charlie was definitely in the immediate area, he knew how to hide but he couldn't make that animal disappear, that is until the flare burned out. The pilot called for the firefly ship to circle and drop another flare.

"Firefly Two-Eight, we have possible contact below, request another drop in preceding zone"

"Taipan Leader, roger, stand by for drop"

It took several long minutes for the flare ship to circle and return to the area and make his drop. Then another couple minutes for the flare to ignite and float under the parachute to an altitude where it actually illuminated the ground. But every area looked the same as another. They strained their eyes to witness any familiar thing below. Without visual ground references it was impossible to know if the drop was in the same place or perhaps drifted off in another direction, whatever the case the great horned beast had disappeared. Shoot first, worry later, would be the future creed of the Taipan hunter/killers.

In fact there was no C&C ship to direct fire on targets, it was now the responsibility of the fire team's lead pilot to clear all gunners on potential targets. The mission was lagging behind and fuel had its limit on the chopper's ability to linger on station. So the heavy fire team moved on to another area marked on the map selected by military intelligence as a probable point of transgression by the enemy. Another hour on station and it was time to refuel for the long ride back to the snake pit.

It was now long after midnight the missions concluded, there would another night, another time. The Taipan's were learning the lessons of the night missions, soon enough they would conquer the Delta nights too! Looking around the interior, Mitch thought of how surreal the night flying was. Dimly lit red lights on the instruments provided the only cabin illumination. Although in blind light they could perform their function without fail by reason of the experience of each. Training and familiarization was the key to survival now.

Mitchell's foot throbbed as his adrenaline wore off. The medic had wrapped it tight, and he had slid the bandaged appendage back into a loosely tied boot. He thought of the hour, or so it was going to take to perform his daily maintenance before retiring for the night. He would have to hobble around the aircraft checking what he needed to make the ship ready for yet another mission. The maintenance section would be notified to replace the tail rotor cover with the fifty-one cal-sized hole in it. And tomorrow he would scrounge up the flashlights, first aid kit…and what else did he need? His mind was tired he couldn't think anymore tonight.

They had flown more hours tonight than usual during the daylight hours. There had been no down time for lunch or waiting for another combat assault. Instead they had eaten their C-rations while refueling. Now they had a little break for the ride to Bearcat. Mitch had difficulty lighting a cigarette, he pulled off his Nomax glove then he slapped the Zippo against the palm of his hand trying to draw down any remaining fluid to the wick. Their time had passed quickly tonight and Mitch thought that was a good thing. Although he couldn't remember exactly how many days he had left on his "short timer's calendar", but he knew his time could go faster with the new missions. He took a long hard draw on the smoke.

His teeth began to chatter, lip quivering, and a cold chill ran through his body. Damn, it was cold at night. One thing more to be remembered, tomorrow night, bring a flight jacket!

A **"Slick"** takes flight after unloading troops in the LZ (landing zone), in an area known as "the Plain of Reeds"

Chapter Nineteen

Rescue Mission

Waiting for an empty latrine was never an option, one never knew when the opportunity to sit was going to happen again. With his pants down around his ankles, Mitch sat with his derrière covering the hole cut into the wood platform. He always tried to take up on one of the end of the six holes so that anyone else who entered would hopefully sit a few holes away. This would allow some air to vent without being pelted with the odor that emanated from the disturbed fluids in the cut drums below. It was so unpleasant to sit there when most all the holes were occupied. Only inches apart, GI's would be conversing as they intermittently grunted before another bombing run. This would cause the small latrine to become filled with explosive toxic fumes, very dangerous stuff in the heat of the day. At times, the aroma of urine and feces would be so strong that some FNG's would have to swap ends to belch out material not yet processed by the intestines.

Having finished his business at the latrine, it was time to get to the ship ready for yet another night of flying. Mitch had everything he needed now and Hell Fire proved to be a strong and dutiful helicopter. He was totally satisfied with the ship and felt a kind of bond with it, even a bit excited to fly. Trusting machinery to keep you alive might seem frivolous to some, but to Mitch it served to reduce his apprehension of crashing at night.

It was the third week of the night missions and there had been plenty of action. At times it seemed the war had totally shifted from day to night. Charlie was extremely active in the Delta. There had been attacks on nearly every hamlet and village. Villagers were agitated that the Army of the Republic of Vietnam had not halted the aggression that was building all around them. Many of the outlying village leaders were now cooperating with the VC to protect their people. Of course this was not going to save anyone in the South. The VC still murdered the peasant old men, women, and children to ensure they would never serve the Saigon regime ever again.

The hunter/killer missions have been successful in that Charlie was being disrupted with his crossings into the Delta. An unusually high body count accompanied those successes but without the ground troops to confirm the Taipan's enemy kill's it was harder to determine now, and is mostly estimated.

Just a few days ago while flying at low level, the odor of a rotting VC corpse rose from the ground and slammed the crew like a ground to air missile. A male victim clad only in black shorts was laid out in the open at the edge of a tree line, his bloated body filled with gasses in the soft tissues that grossly distorted his appearance. Lying on his back, with arms and legs stretched upward, fattened fingers spread out so that he appeared to be crawling on the sky while holding a basketball between his legs. They circled to try to determine if there were any more bodies and some hint as to just who might have terminated him. The smell drove them off before anything significant could be determined.

They really had no way to know just how many had amassed just beyond the border or how many were escaping detection. Right now there are not enough experienced crews to be out flying around at night. This is some tense stuff requiring max concentration, and completely ignoring the pucker factor. Hunter/killer teams aircraft commanders had to train their own replacements if they wanted a night off. Experienced night pilots would instruct new co-pilots who have been flying as AC's with the EMU's during daytime operations and would now have to fly as co-pilot again until brought up to speed on the special aspects of night missions.

That whole first month the fire team spent concentrating on keeping safe with no loss of aircraft. The difference between VFR (visual flight rules), and IFR (instrument flight rules) is literally day and night. VFR was daytime and good weather flight, while IFR is nighttime and/or foul weather. Hence the night missions were always IFR. That meant safe flight was dependent on the instruments and learning how to avoid hazardous obstacles and keep vigilance on other aircraft while in flight. This might sound common place but in fact it took incredible focus and the ultimate in teamwork. Pilot and co-pilot had to work together as one, when one's concentration was diverted, even for a second, the other had to instinctively take over flight command or cross check instruments. Back seat crews had to be mindful of the pilot's night vision and not blind them with muzzle flash. Maintaining ground reference, keeping your situational awareness and knowing exactly where you are is crucial to surviving. Learning to read the terrain by distinguishing the difference between pitch black, charcoal black, and various shades of dark gray has become a useful talent.

All this would hopefully lead to no loss of airmen either. With the war winding down and whole companies of soldiers going home, the Taipan's made survival the number one objective.

Darkness was a good friend to have when all was going well. Viet Cong never trained to shoot down invisible aircraft. The Taipan's were indeed invisible at night, except on those few nights when the moon aided the enemy. All in all things were good and the professionalism of the Hunter/Killers became apparent to the other members of the unit. Pilots and crewmen began to volunteer to fly the hazardous missions. But the night fliers were still in a "trial by fire" mode and newly inducted pilots had to work in slowly.

Sunset fell on the Snake Pit as the Hunter/Killer team prepared for another night of missions. Once again, the soft ticking sound preempting the rising whine of the turbine that was the call to be in your seat and buckled up. But Mitchell was standing adjacent to his seat although his helmet was on and already plugged into the communication system. He waited to stretch his legs for as long as it was possible.

When it was time he then slid onto the small square canvas patch that was his seat for hundreds of prior missions.

"Coming up", the pilot announced.

"Clear right", Mitchell responded immediately by anticipating the call.

As a seasoned crew-chief Mitch had the routine down pat. He knew his job well and was confident in his performance. Sure there had been the usual mistakes but they had always been minor in nature and straightened out before anything to cause harm to anyone could develop. As a gunner he was one of the best, able to determine legitimate targets and then expeditiously neutralize them. His ability to assess the pilot's skills as good, better, or best determined what he would need to do in advance of any orders from the front seats. Since Taipan gunship drivers were recruited from the slick platoons, all had enough experience to fly the craft. They just needed to hone in on the special aspects of the gunship role. Mitch thought highly of all pilots but newbies, especially those who have little time in country made him feel a little bit uneasy.

From his right rear seat he intently watched the young officer in the front left seat to ascertain his competence. He finally determined that although this was the co-pilots first night mission, he had undergone sufficient prior mission time and would probably hold his own. Then Mitch slid his ammo can across the floor from the left of the seat and placed it in front between his legs.

The tower reported the "winds calm, density altitude two niner-niner two, Snakes cleared for take-off".

Three gunships heading South, Mitchell no longer thought of home, he was short and one way or another he would be home soon. Instead he glanced over the engine instruments, and then repositioned his chicken plate under his seat. They had made this trip so many times he knew instinctively how long it was going to be before they landed to carry out the first refueling. With the remaining time he went over in his mind what procedure he would use if they went down at night. It was good to reenact the scenario in one's mind over and over until you were sure it would be done without so much as a moment's hesitation. He checked the batteries in the flashlight to be sure he had a signaling device. In addition he now paid particular attention to where they went and in what direction the friendlies were.

The night sky was partly cloudy and there was a quarter Moon high above. At times it seemed that the light of the Moon was completely absorbed by the darkness of the ground, at least until reflected by water or some other such shiny object.

Departing Saigon terminal control area far to the East of the Asian megalopolis the sodium street lights amber luminescence reflected off the cloud base that hovered over the capitol city. Soon there would only be the dim glow of smoldering fires in sparse hamlets and an occasional flash of artillery rounds impacting the earth. Those direct fire orders, and co-ordinances that were given to remote fire support bases from the Grunts out on night patrol.

After the first flare extinguished itself about a hundred feet above the terrain, a second flare had already begun its decent from the C-130 aircraft. The Taipan's rolled out of their orbit to establish a second orbit around the ever-brightening flare. For the next hour they chased one flare after the other. No contact had been made but it seemed the number of trails carved into the reeds had increased. Zigzag patterns made from West to East sometimes connecting then breaking off into another direction but still in the general heading of East. No eligible male's had been spotted and that was discouraging to Mitchell because a little gunplay always made the night go by faster.

When Mr. Flemming determined the fuel situation was close to critical he called for the Taipan's to refuel. The firefly ship would go to some base somewhere to land and have their supper, probably in some nice cozy Air Force mess hall with plenty of good eats. On the other hand the Taipan's would shut down alongside some airstrip in the middle of nowhere and eat their cold canned C-rations. Mitchell regretted not enlisting with the Navy or Air Force as they always ate better meals, and slept on thicker mattresses too.

After refueling and eating Mitchell went to chat with the pilots. The new guy, a peter-pilot, was an EMU pilot for only a short time and volunteered because many of the more experienced pilots were getting short and did not want to risk the change of duty. So with fewer pilots to train they began to sort out the less accomplished, although it was still a voluntary mission.

Mr. Stanley was but a couple years older than Mitch was but to him, he looked much younger.

"So what do you think of the Hunter Killer missions", Mitch had asked.

"There seems to be a lot of hunting, but so far no killing", he replied.

"Well when the fucking shit hits the fan, it will be a different story"

"Yea, it's the craziest thing I've ever done", interrupted Flemming.

"We account for the highest ratio of kills versus hours flown", he continued.

For a short while they continued to chat about whom did what to whom, and quickly solved most all the Army's problems. After a time, Flemming opened the right side door, grabbed his helmet and slid it onto his head. Then reached into the cockpit to key the mic-switch on the cyclic control and checked in at the prescribed time to make contact with the firefly ship.

"They have been trying to raise you on the op's freq. Seems you have another mission to fly", responded the firefly Captain.

Quickly Flemming reached in and dialed up another frequency that would connect him with operations back at base.

"Get your team up quickly, will contact you with co-ordinances after your airborne, this is a high priority sortie", the voice commented.

Flemming shouted at the two ships behind them,

"Crank-em up".

Pilots and crews felt the sense of urgency and hustled themselves into their respective positions.

With all the rotor's now turning they pulled in pitch and lifted off into the darkness.

Mitchell switched to the UHF and monitored the communications.

"Fire base Madeline is under a mortar attack, they have requested air support", informed the ground based voice.

"Take extreme caution, we have been advised that Madeline is engaging an estimated battalion of NVA"

A battalion of NVA, how many is that Mitchell wondered? He didn't really know how many that meant, but it sure sounded like a lot of the hardcore enemy. He now wished he hadn't wished for the gunplay to make the time go faster. Then he heard Flemming say that it would take twenty minutes to get to the co-ordinances given them. Mitch sat patiently waiting for whatever came.

Firebase Madeline was situated on a small peninsula where two rivers forked off in different directions. As the Taipan's approached from the Southwest of the co-ordinances given to them, all the lights at the base had been extinguished. The waters surrounding the Firebase reflected what little moonlight peered through the scattered clouds. The landmass was black and other than the perimeter, no details inside of the base could be recognized. On the approach and still a couple of miles out, several flashes of explosions that momentarily lit up the base had occurred. Machine gun fire and the red burning tracers followed the impact of explosions and it could be seen that whoever was in that firebase was shooting back towards the Northeast.

Approaching the target area at ninety knots airspeed, and at two hundred feet, the helicopter bucked slightly and the wind rush increased as they dove in lower. Now just one hundred feet, they buzzed the firebase. Flemming was lead ship and mission commander,

"Wing, Trail, follow me into the target area, lights out, watch your separation, let's see what we have here, then we can establish attack pattern".

Flemming then added another command,

"Gunners hold your fire until we identify the friendly positions".

Flying directly over the firebase Mitchell looked down and saw several barely distinguishable human forms running from a bunker to the perimeter of the base. Apparently the base ceased their fire upon the arrival of the gunships and took advantage of the time to resupply the reinforced protective barrier that at times like this was never high enough. Passing over the river that forked to the Northeast the Taipan's entered an area that was littered with large trees. At an altitude of sixty feet the Taipan's roared overhead and the enemy on the ground decided it was time to reveal themselves to the choppers. Almost in unison, mortar fire erupted on the ground all around the gunships, at least twenty positions were identified on that first low level pass. Quick radiant flashes illuminated the ground positions nestled in among thick standing timbers.

Mitchell observed one mortar position that seemed to fire at an automatic rate. Each flash of the mortar leaving the tube would reveal the enemy position, but the flashes were in rapid succession, almost impossible for mortar fire. Normally it took time to reload after each firing, drop one round down the tube, then wait till it fired, pick up another projectile and drop again. But the rate these were firing at was never seen before.

Mitchell's ship flew directly over one position between a clearing in the trees and he saw five enemy soldiers on their knee's surrounding the mortar tube. Each of the NVA had a mortar in each hand. All held their projectiles out at the ready. The first would drop one, it fired, and then that same individual would drop the one in the other hand. A pile of projectiles was positioned behind each soldier so that all he had to do while the others fired their two rounds was to reach around and grab two more. By the time he did that the other four loaders had completed their drops. Continuous rapid firing towards the poor guy's in the FSB continued. They needed help, and fast.

As the Taipan's banked right to set up an air strike, Mitchell witnessed a large explosion on the ground ahead of the aircraft. Passing over where there had been a mortar position, the fire's glow revealed five enemy bodies laid out from the epicenter of a horrific explosion. Burning fires replaced the mortar tube that had blown up. Either the tubes couldn't take the stress of that much firing or someone had managed to put two rounds in the tube at one time causing the tube to literally explode apart killing all at that position. Taipan's score five, enemies, zero.

There were so many positions that losing one did not matter much to the Taipan's and it certainly didn't make the mission any less hazardous. Sporadic machinegun fire from below could be heard but the dark aerial combatants at high speed in the night sky were impossible to find. Adrenaline was flowing like the Niagara Falls, Flemming commanded his fire team.

"Taipan's strike from the West to the East, avoid any fire past the river on the right, strike altitude one five hundred". After an acknowledgement from his wingman and trail, he announced,

"Climbing to strike altitude now"

After completing a climbing three-quarter turn around the target area, they were now directly West and continued the ascent.

"Call out five hundred, and I'll bank out right", Flemming instructed the peter-pilot through the intercom. "Call out five hundred", is the command to monitor the altimeter and disengage the air strike at safe altitude. Mitch heard the order and knew that it was time to start firing. When the gunship leveled off, Flemming cross checked his instruments and almost immediately began to dive in on the target area. Mitchell and his gunner opened up first, the bright muzzle flashes illuminating the cockpit. Streams of red tracers poured down into the target area some ricocheting off in indiscriminate directions. Flemming fired a salvo of rockets leaving a stream of sparks on their way to deadly destruction. Another salvo left the rocket tubes this time Flemming punched off six rockets. Mitchell was out to the limit of his seat belt, he leaned out to fire straight ahead. His aim changed with every flash of a mortar fire on the ground. His night vision all but gone from all the bright flashes, still he continued to fire blindly into enemy positions.

Without warning, a stupendous loud BANG and the sound of aluminum ringing like a church bell. Simultaneously Mitchell felt a hard impact on his body and his M-60 is being pulled from the grip of his right hand. His eyes closed as he felt the scrapping of raw earthy material pinning him to the exterior of the aircraft. Suddenly he found himself completely disoriented, then he felt more impacts and thought he was no longer inside an aircraft. With a death grip on his machinegun he struggled to right himself before the aircraft rolled over on top of him. With his left hand he reached for anything that he could grab onto. He was sure they had crashed, but the fear of being on the ground with a Battalion of NVA was still more frightening because it meant certain death and Mitchell was not ready to die, not just yet damn it!

Quickly he struggled to upright himself, he had taken a hard knock that sent him backward and nearly upside down while still with his seat belt loosely around his waist. When at first his feet touched the floor he became aware of his awkward position and then he could pull himself back in. The pressure of the seat belt was rested and he could feel relief on his lower extremities. Back in his seat it took a couple of seconds for him to realize they were still in flight, but just barely. The ambient sounds were unrecognizable, never had he heard such noises, and Mitch was sure they were going to fall out of the sky at any moment. All of the interior lighting had been extinguished.

Quickly he looked around to assess the damage, although it took a moment to identify the debris inside the aircraft. He soon realized they had hit a tree. A large tree limb had penetrated up through the cargo floor exactly in the middle between Mitch and the gunner. The immense limb shoved up and through the aluminum plates and crushed against the rear bulkhead. Bits of plexi-glass, small branches, and leaves, cover the floor. Hurricane winds swirled around pelting the crew with bits of rubbish further aggravating the ability to make notice of the extent of the wreckage. Mitch looked up to see how much damage to the windshield there was, but it was all gone. Both windshields and the "green house" windows above the pilot's heads had been destroyed.

Bouncing up and down and heavily yawing, strange and very loud whooshing sounds came from above. The rotor blades had been compromised and would surely disintegrate at any moment. Then he tried determining the condition of the pilots, unfastening his seat belt he reached for the back of Flemming's seat. In the low light condition seeing anything was difficult but their night vision had returned in the darkened cabin. Peering over the pilots left shoulder he noticed the chin bubbles were gone. He saw the right tail rotor pedal was gone and he could see that Flemming had already one foot behind the left pedal and the other in front, thus enabling him to use the pedal. Something hit Mitch in the face and he grabbed onto Mr. Flemming's com-cord that was swinging in the flurry of air. Plugging his helmet back into the system, he reached around and plugged himself in also, to his astonishment it still worked.

"What happened", Mitch yelled.

"We hit the tree's", Flemming shouting back.

It wasn't the answer Mitch wanted but it would have to do for now. The helicopters severe vibrations cause their voices to vibrate further making communication difficult. Mitch looked out and saw a flash of moonlight illuminate an open area on the ground.

"We can put it down right there", he said tapping Flemming on the shoulder to get his attention.

"We're still flying, I think I can fly it", Flemming spoke with uncertainty.

Mitch did not want to crash again should the blades fall off or something else fail. He really just wanted to get out and on the ground again. Fear gripped him, as he thought of the possibility of another incident.

"No, put it down", Mitch tried to assert his authority.

"I'm telling ya, I can fly it"

"See, I got pitch control, the cyclic is a bit tricky, but I can operate the pedals"

"Besides there's a lot of enemy down there", Flemming's apprehension was beginning to show.

"OK, where are you going to go", Mitch asked.

"We're close to Vinh Long, I am going to try to make it there", then he added, "Check on the crew".

Flemming's voice was stronger now and Mitchell felt more confident in his pilot than he did in Hell Fire.

Checking over the gunner, Jimmy's head was down, and he moaned loudly when Mitch tried to lift his head. He seemed delirious and Mitch was afraid to do anything more for the time being. Trying not to get hung up on the branches piercing the floor he threw out some loose limbs that were scattered about. Then he checked the co-pilot, leaning over the center console the co-pilot was bleeding profusely from facial and neck wounds. His blood had completely saturated the front of his flight suit, and he seemed to be barely conscious. Mitch tasted something salty in his mouth and wiped his lips, blood, his, or Stanley's he couldn't tell.

"How much time before we can land", Mitch yelled into the mic.

The wind rush was so loud, and the whistling sound coming from the blades was scary as hell. All the bouncing and shaking didn't help either.

"Couple of minutes more, but I got a problem", Flemming shouted again.

Mitchell's heart sank, he knew they were going to fall out of the sky at any moment.

"I've got no aft cyclic"

Looking at the huge tree parts sticking through the flooring,

"Yea, one of these tree limbs probably jammed the push-pull tubes", Mitch bellowed out remembering all the hardware that was buried under the deck plates.

Mitchell knew right off that aft cyclic was needed to flare the craft and slow it down.

"How fast we going", he asked.

"I can't slow under ninety knots", Flemming responded.

"Can you radio ahead and let Vinh Long know we're crash landing", Mitchell asked hoping maybe they had a better answer.

"We've lost all the radios, they won't know we're coming".

Flemming continued to fight the controls, and the helicopter responded with a heavy yaw and a bounce. Flemming then added another bit of news,

"I am hoping they don't shoot at us coming over the perimeter, with any luck One Eight saw what happened and will let them know we're coming".

A sudden bright idea, Mitch looked out aft to see if anyone was following them.

"Hey, both our guys are behind us" he reported to Flemming

That comment gave hope to them both that they just might survive.

"Great, they must have seen what happened, get in your seat and buckle up".

Taking another moment to look after the co-pilot, Mitchell felt the full rush of the wind pelt him. Small bits of debris still swirled about the cabin. So with their courage slightly elevated, they limped on through the sky.

Vinh Long was one of the largest bases in the Delta, and the streetlights could be seen from miles out. As they approached, Mitch sat pondering what he would do on touchdown, jump or hang tight. Would the aircraft hold together for a crash landing, hell they still might not even make it to the base, he thought. He reached over at the gunner's seat belt and made sure it was tight. With all interior lights out it was eerily dark and Mitch couldn't see Jimmy's face to know how he was doing.

With Vinh Long in sight they were on a perfect approach except the airspeed was too high. With the collective control Flemming lowered the chopper. Still over dark jungle they headed straight and level towards the Song Co Chien River then over highway 4 that paralleled the river at this point. The South Westernmost edge of the base was in sight now. Beyond that the active runway was now visible. Again the disabled machine bucked and yawed hard left then right. Mitch placed a foot against the door post and pushed hard to wedge himself against the bulkhead. Passing over the highway Mitch leaned outward saw the raised perimeter of the base. And just past that he could see a fire truck alongside the runway.

As altitude decreased, their sense of the speed over ground was more apparent. Over the highway it was void of any traffic at 3:00 am. Then the perimeter passed by a mere ten feet under the crippled craft. The fire trucks had switched on their red rotating beacons and were already in high-speed pursuit of Hell Fire.

Flemming shouted, "Looks like seventy knots at touchdown, brace yourself"

Mitch raised both hands straight up to secure himself in case of a rollover.

The metal landing skids were inches from the PSP steel landing strip. Another fire truck appeared at the left door just as the two metal parts touched. Flemming rolled off the throttle immediately and the sparks shot out from under the skids. Hell Fire slid at high speed down the runway. At times it tried to yaw one side or the other, but Flemming was still fighting it utilizing the tail rotor with his one pedal. Mitchell could feel the heat from the friction of the two metals spraying white-hot bits of molten steel. They rapidly passed the fuel depot that was midway down the runway.

Slowing to a point where the tail rotor no longer had any effect on the machine, it began to slide sideways. Mitch's heart jumped into his throat as he visualized the ship rolling over into a fireball. Decelerating rapidly the ship stopped before turning ninety degrees to the runway.

Mitch jumped out and nearly fell to the PSP, without knowing it he had been injured on the inside right knee that was hit by tree limbs. He hobbled to Flemming's door to get him out before any fire's started. Sliding his side armor plate back and assisting him with the seat belt, he then went to the co-pilot. As he came around the front of the aircraft the spotlights on the fire trucks lit up Hell Fire's damage. He stood momentarily frozen at the incredulous sight. All the plexi-glass gone, the nose of the aircraft ripped away exposing what was left of the Avionics compartment and the still secured battery.

Before he would get to the peter-pilot the rescue people were cutting his seat belt away and three rescuers are gently lifting him down. Two medics with a stretcher stand nearby waiting for the patients.

The main blades finally came to a halt. Mitchell looked up to see the source of all the loud whooshing, the rotor blades had been severed at the tips. With nearly a foot or two gone and exposing the shredded honeycomb aluminum, pieces hung and flapped in the light breeze. Besides throwing the critical balance out of whack causing the severity of the vibrations, the stresses on the mast and transmission should have caused the whole thing to come apart. He wondered how they ever flew so far in this condition.

More medical personnel appeared and examined Mitchell and Flemming, they were asked if they needed to be more thoroughly examined at the base hospital, but they declined. The bruise's cuts and scrapes could wait till they were back at Bearcat. More and more servicemen appeared, soon there was quite a gathering of onlookers commenting on the condition of the aircraft. Standing in the dark with the assembly of soldiers, Mitch overheard one ask his buddy,

"I wonder how many were killed".

A full bird Colonel appeared and informed the two crewmen, that a Slick would be leaving to ferry them back to Bearcat as soon as the fate of the others were known.

A slick landed and parked alongside the active runway a short distance from the wreckage of Hell Fire, it had arrived earlier and they supposed it was the ship to take the crew home to Bearcat. Flemming and Mitch quietly went to sit while they waited. They sat on the floor of the Slick with their legs dangling over the left skid, and quietly conversed.

Not able to hold it back any longer, Mitch asked,

"What the fuck happened anyhow".

"I never heard Stanley call out five hundred, we flew directly into a tree"

Had Mitch heard any call for five hundred, he thought not.

Mitch then recalled the feeling of rolling over on the ground while nearly upside down and barely holding onto his weapon, and conveyed that to Flemming.

"We hit more trees on the way out, clipping the tops of the trees behind the one we smack directly into", then added, "you were probably disorientated".

"Damn near knocked me unconscious is more like it, but why did it happen at all".

"This was his first night out, he evidently was paying more attention to the fireworks than the altimeter", Flemming spoke quietly trying to make sense of it all for himself.

After close scrutiny of the doomed Hell Fire, the two of them agreed that it was remarkable they had survived. The first impact caused the helicopter to ricochet of the tree trunk upward. That upward deflection caused Hell Fire to become airborne again. But the ship had clipped several more treetops before gaining enough airspeed for flight. Flemming then rapidly cross-checked the flight controls and quickly determined what worked and what did not. Truly his expertise and undaunted nerve allowed them to survive this night. But Hell Fire would never fly again, her structurally damaged airframe surely exceeding the cost of repair verses replacement.

Mitch asked, "What do you supposed happened to those guy's at Madeline"

"I asked the Colonel about that and he said they called in air support from a spooky gunship, which should hold them till morning"

"But there was a lot on enemy out there"

"In a couple of hours there will be enough aircraft on scene to wipe the area off the map"

"Some rescue mission, eh"?

"I think this is the first time I didn't complete a mission".

"That fucking peter-pilot nearly got us killed"

"Can't blame him, I was the AC, should have crossed-checked better"

"You saved our asses man, he should have called out five hundred, any fucking idiot could do that"

"Well maybe we both screwed up".

"No sir, this was his…", Mitch was interrupted by the Colonel who appeared to inform them that they would be lifting off soon.

"What about our gunner, sir", Mitch inquired.

"May have broken his collar bone, we're going to keep him for observation, he'll be ok son".

Then Flemming asked of Mr. Stanley, what was his status.

"He's right there", the Colonel said pointing behind the two of them.

"He's got a few stitches but he's fine now".

Suddenly Mitch felt very bad about the comments he just made about Stanley. The two of them sitting talking, thinking no one heard their private talk. Mr. Stanley had lay there on the floor on the right side of the aircraft, in the dark and never uttered a sound to defend himself.

He had felt guilty about the incident and probably agreed with the remarks said about him.

It was a very long and silent ride back to Bearcat, Mitch searched his conscience and forgave Stanley of the incident, although he never told him that. Mitchell realized that all who climb aboard a gunship to fly over hostile territory in the obscurity of the night assume the risk that anything can happen. No one person is a crew and all share the jeopardy equally. It would serve no purpose to condemn the co-pilot for his error in judgment. They had all made mistakes in their experiences in combat, some lesser and some greater. No one can ever be completely prepared for warfare.

The Taipan Patch, reptile wrapped around a 2.75 in. Rocket and Mini-gun. This was exclusive to the third platoon of the 135th Assault Helicopter Company gunships.

Chapter Twenty

Deros

The odor that filled his nose shot up into the most sensitive area of his sinuses. His eyes flashed open...what the fuck is that fucking smell?

Trying to cover his face to avoid the awful pungency, the pillow only suffocated him. It was difficult to breathe and he was becoming irritated that someone would burn something outside his barracks to impart that God-awful smell. He had enough, throwing the sheet over violently he charged out of his bunk and stomped across the floor. The screen door slammed back nearly coming off the hinge. Someone is going to get such a fucking ass kicking, his thoughts mustering his temper into a frenzy. Skipping several steps at a time towards the landing he flew around the corner of the building. In his aggravated state he found two hooch maids sitting on the ground with dead fish fillets opened on fly ridden newspaper. Disbelieving the raw nerve of someone to dry out rotting fish under his window to make Nuoc mam sauce for their fucking rice made him nuts. Angrily he grabbed the newspaper and folded the contents within. The young hooch maid bitch screamed in Vietnamese and tugged at his arm to stop him from spoiling their next meal. Mitch aggressively pushed her hand away and marched a few yards to the rear of the latrine and deposited the fermented fish wrap into one of the full steel drums.

His valuable sleep time interrupted by the hooch maids just added to the way things were going. Everything seemed to be working against him. Now how could he possibly get back to sleep? His whole body vibrated with the tension of that little skirmish with those two. Oh how easy it would have been to just slit their throats. Storming back upstairs he tried desperately to go to sleep again. Sweat poured off him while his mind raced at the speed of light.

With so little time left in country he had to fly the aircraft of the other crew-chief's, sometimes even a fucking newbie's ship. Mitch picked at the last of his scabs from the scrapes and cuts received from crashing into the trees. He hated not having his own chopper. Not knowing the intricate details of his own machine could get him into real trouble, he simply did not trust anyone else's ability to do a better job than he at keeping the aircraft flyable. There was only three weeks left on his tour of duty. He was far too short to be flying combat missions, let alone flying them in an unfamiliar aircraft. He would have to be extremely diligent when performing the pre-flight inspections. It wouldn't due to get killed after all he has been through from a damn mechanical failure.

Sleep evaded him until it was time to prepare for another night of missions.

Going downstairs again for a shower before heading out to the flight line, he entered the shower building. Twenty or so hooch maids were washing their GI's clothes under every available showerhead. Since most of the aircrews were already out flying, and the rest were working at their job functions around the base, the showers were the place where the maids laundered the uniforms. Mitch was still too pissed off to care, he dropped his towel and quietly commanded, "Di Di Mau". The three girls utilizing his overhead spigot gathered their wash without looking at him and moved out of the way. The women giggled and spoke softly in their slang French influenced Asian language, but dared not to look directly upon Mitchell's nakedness. Even the hooch maids respected those who had been hardened by combat. They treated the veterans much differently than the newbie's. Nobody dared to antagonize the short-timers. His own mama-san, a middle aged woman, who looked better than most because she did not indulge in Betel nut chewing, would tread lightly whenever he was around! She knew his disposition and cautioned others not to aggravate him. Although Mitch had never been unusually abusive to her, he had a reputation for being short tempered with the indigenous people. In truth his frustration was due to his being annoyed by the way things were going. It seemed that having new ships, gunners, and pilots seriously reduced his chances of survival. With these odds, he was just waiting to get himself killed. Really not sure what it was, but the tension some days was intense and caused his nerves to vibrate like a tuning fork.

While dressing into his Nomax fire retardant flight suit an unfamiliar face entered the barracks. Walking past Mitch and down a few feet on the opposite side of the barracks he laid an overstuffed duffel bag on the bunk that had been stripped of its bedding. Clandestinely watching as he began to unpack he thought to himself that the soldier looked too young to be in the Army. His look was a bit too clean, fresh haircut and clean pressed uniform. A gunner who apparently rotated back home formally occupied that area of the Taipan's hooch. Since the former gunner flew days Mitch did not know of his departure date and had just assumed that everyone was out on daytime missions. The replacement seemed nervous about moving in.

"Name's Mitch", he offered to break the ice.

"Jack, Jack Wilkins, friends just call me JW"

"Where you from man"?

"Mississippi", he replied in a heavy southern drawl.

"Just got transferred to the platoon eh", Mitch inquired.

"Shit man, just got to Vee et naam"

Mitch quickly remembered being pretty much in the same boat so long ago. He pained at the thought of this poor guy having to start a tour of duty in the Taipan platoon.

"You mean you just got in country and they put you in the gun platoon"

"I vol-un-teered"

"You fucking volunteered, are you fucking nuts or something", Mitch wanted to tell him to get out before it was too late.

Mitch knew Vietnamization was causing a deficit in personnel, more were being sent home than were arriving, but bringing in kids to do a man's job was just plain suicide.

"How old are you anyhow", he had to know.

"Twenny"

"Kind-a young for this shit aren't you"

"Why, how old are you", he responded.

Mitch would have to lie if he was ever going to convince the kid that he should rethink his career.

"Twenty-one"

They exchanged more personal information and the newbie let it known that he was married and that his wife recently gave birth to a baby boy.

Mitch sat down on the bunk next to the young father and asked if he knew what the Taipan's did, recounting his own conversation with J.J. when he first arrived in the platoon. The newbie listened intently as he spoke for a little less than hour before Mitch had to fly.

Nine days later in the snake pit…

The crews gathered around their respective ships performing the pre-flight preparations. Minutes later they were airborne passing over familiar territory, even in the darkness they could always recognize the first leg of the mission to the first refueling base by the twisted shapes and shadows of the land masses and tributaries.

Thinking that maybe it was just in his mind, but life's innocence seemed to have deserted him. Laughter was a rare occurrence these days and when he did laugh it was usually over a morbid thought or deed.

They had joked about the killing and how the bodies looked when mutilated by bullets or explosives. They laughed to tears when an RPG had hit an ARVN soldier in his crotch, nearly splitting him in two. Corpses with missing limbs or heads were no longer an oddity. He ached in ambiguity about his feelings of returning home before it was too late to be human again. His desires to mentor the newbie's and protect his platoon mates in stark contrast to home and family, but to stay was risking never going back, physically or mentally!

In his upside down world of night to day, flying, fighting when all were asleep, except the enemy, Mitchell's sense of time had been diluted.

The night's seemed to drag on, although he made every effort not to think of going home, still it had crept into his mind. So soon and yet so much time, anything could happen at any time while he continued to fly the missions. Had he come this far only to be eliminated at the very end?

Ever diligent to catch the enemy before they could get off a single shot, all eyes searched the black terrain for anything suspicious. They called it "the lucky BB", the solo bullet that would bring down the heavily armed flying tank. One hit in a vital spot and down they would go. Even surviving the crash still meant having to deal with Charlie in his backyard. Apprehension, not fear fueled these thoughts with no distractions available to transform them.

Fiercely swirling cool air within the cabin is the primary indicator that they were in flight. Missing was the sensation of the ground passing below and the blur of the rotating disk above his head no longer flickered in the suns light. He sat crouched in the seat at the edge of the door opening, his right sleeve flapping hard in the breeze. Mitch pulled on the tab to zip up his flight suit to the top stop then retied his black scarf around his neck. Preservation of the pilot's night vision was always enforced while in the air, so the dim red blush of the instrument panel lighting was the only source that revealed the other three crewmembers, weapons and ammo boxes. They flew in a heading known only to the pilots who navigated the dark skies with maps, compass, and radio beacons. Mitch pulled a wrinkled pack of cigarettes from his sleeve pocket. Drawing out a crooked stick he held the Zippo tightly cupped in his hands to the end. Drawing in the smoke deeply, he slowly exhaled and felt a warm calmness blanket him.

Flying through the night they searched for the elusive enemy. Taking a break only when it was time to refuel and have dinner out of a can. Hours of hunting, scanning vast areas for the proverbial needle, then at zero one hundred hours, the conclusion of another night of missions came without incident and it was time to return to base. Climbing to cruise altitude for the hour-long flight the temperature dropped one degree for every hundred feet. With the mission over the back seat crew switched the radio chatter off to listen to AFVN. Mitch closed his eyes to concentrate on the music. Then after a few moments visions of life back in the "World" as he remembered it played on the brain screen.

It was nearly 2:00 am by the time he got to the showers. On the final climb up the flight of stairs a flash of light and muffled explosion occurred in the near distance. It seemed to come from somewhere near the flight line. Mitch realized immediately it was not a mortar or rocket attack. He hesitated on the stair to determine the cause.

Armed soldiers in helmets and flack vests ran towards the flight line, followed by trucks speeding in pursuit. In short order parachute flares popped high above the flight line. Mitch felt it prudent to get to his locker and put some clothes on.

"What's going on", asked the aviator in the top bunk.

"Don't know, I think something blew up on the flight line", replied Mitch.

"I going to see if my bird is ok, wanna come", he asked?

"No, and don't fucking wake me up when you come back either"!

Following others towards the revetments, a shirtless soldier who rushed past Mitch shouted back that three VC sappers had gotten through the wire and tried to blow up some choppers on the flight line. Mitch slowed, then stopped and turned back towards the barracks. Being unarmed, there were others better suited for a search and destroy mission, he was far too short to take any unnecessary chances. Besides those rear echelon boy's needed some excitement and there were many more of them.

Inside it was "lights out" in the barracks, it seemed as though half his life was spent in the dark. Mitch was sure he knew what it was like to be a vampire. He even felt an uncomfortable ache in the light of day and the glare of the sun would pierce his eyes like small daggers.

In his GI issued olive drab skivvies, he pulled down on the camouflaged poncho liner that was his blanket. Then he folded once the silky smooth material that had been cooled down from the small electric fan that was never switched off. Even in the darkness every detail of the barrack's interior was distinct to his keen night vision. Mitchell wondered if he would miss these accommodations, long passed was the memory of what his bed at home felt like.

Looking down over the rows of neatly aligned bunks and visualizing the faces of sleeping crewmembers there were many newbie's coming into the platoon. Realizing he hardly knew anyone, and that many of his good acquaintance's had already rotated back to the World without a proper sendoff.

Flying night missions prevented Mitch from joining the usual celebratory caucus for having survived combat. Although he had seen his share, they were never really cheerful occasions. Leaving your platoon mates in a precarious environment while you, yourself head for the safety of home always ended in hostility. Upon consumption of great volumes of alcohol either the transient, by refusing to leave and having to be "forced" home, or by jealous comrades who almost always made a drunken comment regarding cowardice for leaving them behind, would start the ruckus. Sometimes only a yelling match, but other times the fists flew.

When his time came Mitch would leave quietly, it was enough to just get out alive and in whole. Soon, his time would come. He pulled the sheet tight around his neck to keep the vermin out and slept.

Four days later in the Taipan hooch;

Third bunk right, all night long his flatulence had been stored in the ever-expanding chamber until this moment of release.

"Man, I'll bet you left a stain in your fart catcher with that one", an autonomous voice blurted out from the other end of the barracks.

Holding the back side of his waist band away, the Aussie twisted at the waist as if to look into the rear of his non-regulation underwear,

"Yea, best I go wipe me arse and change me skivvies mate"

Mitch awoke to the boisterous report of the escaping gas. Slowly he placed his feet on the small woven carpet to keep the splinters of the bare plywood flooring from piercing his tender pups that were still recovering from his case of Jungle Rot. He opened his wall locker and noted he had eight days left in country. Eight days, way too short to be flying! He hesitantly got dressed into his Nomax flight suit.

On the flight line he mutely pleaded not to see any action again this night while prepping the aircraft for mission time. Getting the hell out of this country was his only priority now. Fighting hard to keep out the demons of despair, the voices warned that doom was imminent. Every negative scenario became the sole thought that consumed him. Anxiety ran amuck within the reluctant soldier. As darkness surrounded the airborne vehicle every flash of light, no matter how faint, whether a reflection upon diminutive bodies of water or a distant star on the horizon, each became a potential enemy muzzle flash.

When the chopper banked to alter course Mitch reached to switch to UHF to hear what was going on. What he heard was his fire team being redirected from their Hunter/Killer mission. A potentially risky situation was forming, especially for someone who has only a week to go.

"Firebase Freedom reports heavy enemy activity", the faint voice crackled through his helmet.

"They believe attack is imminent and request a preemptive strike, can you oblige, over"

"Affirmative, good copy", the pilot responded.

"Will need to refuel, then will arrive on station in two zero minutes, copy?"

"Ah roger that Taipan leader, contact Freedom on one-two-one-decimal-six"

Watching the fading lights of the air base where the heavy fire team had refueled, Mitch hoped to be back there again soon.

Mitchell's pilot dialed in the frequency and hailed the threatened firebase.

"Taipan gunships this is Firebase Freedom, over"!

"Ah Freedom, Taipan lead, go"

"Roger lead, we have beau-coup Charlie laying in a tree line just south of the base, request airstrike to commence with parachute flare over the target"

"Roger Freedom, negative artie until we have cleared the target area, how copy"?

"Ok, roger ahh, will hold all fire until you have completed your strike"!

The lead pilot then prepares his heavy fire team,

"Taipan's, strike to commence on flare over target from Southeast to Northwest, strike altitude one-two-zero-zero, break left, away from Freedom", the radio clicked then he continued,

"All guns call out return fire"

Mitch knew this order was for the newbie's benefit, no one had to tell him when to call out when they were being fired on. He kept an eye out for the trees too!

The flare ignited, illuminating the thick mass of foliage below. Ominous shadows danced over the dark terrain as the bellowed parachute of the flare floated slowly downward. Taipan's are now at strike altitude and could see the base out to the North. Circling approximately 120 degrees apart, down they went one following the other, firing rockets and machineguns when suddenly Mitchell's gun jammed. In a panic he felt for the spent round that would be found at the ejection port, nothing! He lifted the breech, tore off the first few rounds thinking that maybe that he had a dud bullet, then reloaded and squeezed the trigger again, nothing! A sick feeling came over him as he felt sure that Charlie down under him would know his weapon was jammed and would take advantage of his predicament. Quickly he tried again to no avail, then reached for the M-16 and began firing with that.

"Fucking piece of shit", he yelled at the gunner while shaking the gun at him.

"If you want to die here, just keep fucking up these guns, and you will", he continued in frustration.

"Gimme your gun, you take this fucker and fix it", Mitch exerted his authority on the new gunner whose name he didn't even care to know.

Within a minute the gunner had the gun working after discovering the gas piston had cracked in pieces and replaced it with the spare barrel. Mitch realized he could have done the very same thing and in fact should've. Feeling like maybe he should apologize, but then again it was just the way things were with him these days.

Climbing again for altitude, they circled the target area, dove in and fired again until expending all their ammunition. Telltale red trails through the night's sky created by the tracers disappeared into the ebony jungle. The destruction caused by the lethal projectiles known only to those unfortunate persons at the receiving end. With the work finished, it was time again to rearm and refuel. The firebase would now use their howitzer cannons to complete the assault, and that should suppress any thought of an attack by a hopefully now demoralized enemy.

On landing at the remote base, Mitch grabbed his flashlight to do his post mission inspection of the aircraft. Starting with the blades, as they usually received the most undetected holes, he worked his way towards the hubs and found an indentation under one hub. Climbing atop the helicopter to closer inspect the damage he discovered they had indeed been shot at, and hit!

Charlie had learned that a single shot, well placed, had almost the same effect as a barrage of machinegun fire without giving away their position on the ground. This gave some credence to the idea that the highly trained NVA was either in the area, or was instructing the VC in night operations. Damage was minimal largely due to the hub being one of the hardest metals on the aircraft. But Mitch was perplexed at what angle the round had impacted the hub? From below the aircraft, the round would've most certainly have had to go through the airframe, but there were no other impacts. Finally he crawled under the ship, still not observing any bullet entry's he scrambled into the hellhole, known for its difficulty of entry. Only a contortionist or a crew-chief could negotiate the hole. Inside the round open port under the aircraft and below the transmission, Mitchell found the armor-piercing bullet stripped of its copper jacket laying only inches from where he sat on the other side of the bulkhead. Fortunately the bullets destructive capabilities were diminished over the distance to reach the helicopter, as firing upwards is always a disadvantage to firing down. He gathered the small steel core of the bullet and some pieces of the copper and shoved them into his pocket.

Returning to the sanctity of the snake pit, the helicopter hovered sideways into the L-shaped revetment. The landing light illuminating the dirt and debris kicked up in the rotor wash. Mitch closed his eyes and waited for the chopper to settle in on the pad.

Even before the blades came to a standstill Mitch made his entries into the logbook to report to the TI, the slight damage to the hub.

"Mutha-fuckers, almost got me", Mitch exclaimed to the gunner as he grabbed all the weapons and headed off with them. Opening the engine cowlings, Mitch began his periodic inspections with a flushing of the engine. Recounting the night's events he grinned at the thought of having been right in his thinking that they were doomed if the guns didn't fire. He knew his adversary well by now, and learned to respect Charlie for his abilities. Mitch added some hydraulic fluid to the reservoir, and removed some minute metal particles from the engine chip detector.

Soon after landing the pilots were gone, they had little else to do and would usually be the first off the flight line. He felt strangely good for having survived another night of missions and looked forward to a shower and finally to sleep. He finished safety wiring the chip detector and wiped up around the engine deck then closed the cowlings. The gunner returned from cleaning and repairing the guns and then replaced the spare barrel. Together they readied the ship for tomorrow's flight.

In the mess hall they chow'd down on thin dried out pork chops that were mostly bone and fat, powered mashed potatoes and canned green peas, then apple cobbler with ice cream for dessert. Mitch wished they kept the recreation room open so that he could get a beer. It had been more than a week since he had an alcoholic drink of any kind. They walked from the mess hall towards the Taipan hooch together, six rear seat gunners and chiefs, tired and in bad need of a shower. Begrudgingly they dragged themselves up the flight of stairs. Shoulders slumped and dragging-ass they entered the dark barracks trying not to disturb the sleeping day shift, but they did so without taking any overt action.

Mitch opened his wall locker, the steel door slamming back against the steel frame of his bunk. He threw his flight helmet, ammo bandoleer and M-16 rifle inside thus creating just a bit of noise. Then sat on the bunk to unlace his boots and felt a soft crunch. He leaned to the side to pull out an envelope from under his rump. He recognized the manila folder as the same size he had seen before placed on his platoon mate's bunks just prior to returning home. His first thought was he wasn't ready yet to leave, but then it was probably his DEROS orders for next week. He opened the folder with the stamped official seal of the United States Army and pulled out its contents. In his hands he held the official order to return to the States. Letting out the air from his lungs he noted his DEROS date. This can't be, he strained again in the dim light that filtered through the screen door that illuminated the landing outside. It was true, he would go home the day after tomorrow! This night's mission would be his last he would ever fly again in Vietnam. His excitement brought his heart rate up and his breathing was rapid. A kaleidoscope of visions swirled within the cranium that in turn induced a robust quantity of emotion. But the one he felt most strongly was sadness.

A crewmember walked past towards the door with his towel wrapped around his waist and flip-flops noisily slapping at the bottom of his feet. Mitch began to wonder if he should go home. If he stayed he could help these new guys who really needed to be mentored. If anything happened to them he would feel responsible for abandoning them in their moment of need. And what of the pilots, sure only the seasoned pilot flew the Taipan gunships, but wouldn't they likewise need the best crews? What did his seniority mean if he had to go home? Then what if he got home and couldn't cope with the humdrum existence back in the real world. Mitch knew that he had become too accustomed to the daily adrenaline rushes. At this point he was addicted to the stimulant that sharpened the senses and made him feel powerful. Even now he was too pumped up to sleep and he did not want to even try! But there was no one to share his excitement, the Hunter/Killers were clean again and tranquil in their repose. They had no idea that Mitch's next flight would be the freedom bird that would carry him in earnest to his salvation.

Mitchell was the last into the shower hooch. How different everything looked knowing that it was the last time to view his surroundings, he never paid any attention to the carvings into the wood shelves that jutted out below the mirrors. The names of those now long gone, remained in posterity as testimonials to having existed, and showered in this same place. Fumbling through his shaving kit Mitch pulled out his Swiss manufactured nail cutter and rotated the small nail file out and began to carve.

Sleeping in late the following morning Mitchell finally withdrew the papers from the envelope and found a lengthy list of requirements for separation from duty in Vietnam. Quickly he found that more than one day was needed to comply with all the incidentals and paperwork. He truly wished there were time for a beer at the club.

It was late in the day when his chores had been concluded with a lot of help from the guy's in the rear that prioritized his departure. His platoon mates had already lifted off for another night of sorties deep into the Delta. Crews on the day shift were still on the flight line cleaning up after a long day. Mitch decided to get that ice-cold beer he had tasted on the back of his throat for the past week. There would be time later to pack!

It seemed that the noise level in the recreational room had been elevated, but it was difficult to see why. A blurry figure stood next to Mitch,

"Eh, there you are mate", the Aussie slapped Mitch on the back nearly causing him to fall over as he stood leaning on the bar.

"Bean-ny, ole pal, good to almost see you", Mitch responded although not sure if the words were intelligible.

"Been ere long?"

"Bout a year, but I got an early out"

"Right then, I hear your going home?"

"Ah ha, that I am, I think", Mitch wiped the dribble of beer off his chin with his shirtsleeve, and tried to focus in on his friend.

"Benny, I think I want to stay but I need to go home"

"Sure mate, I'll see to it you get that freedom bird, what time is your departure".

"Oh seven forty five in the am", Mitch wasn't sure if the answer was correct but he did remember the time.

"No worries then, we'll get ya off", Benny promised, and then offered,

"A've another drink mate, this one's on me!"

Fellow aviators continued to arrive for Mitchell's celebration and bought more and more drinks until he could not drink anymore. Eventually he was carried out, dragged to the barracks, then up the stairs and dumped fully clothed on his bunk.

At zero five thirty, the platoon Sergeant took several minutes to awaken Mitch from his alcohol-induced stupor.

"Get a move on Collins, I've got a three-quarter ton waiting to get you to Tan Son Nhut, ya wanna go home don't cha?"

The words were ineffective to motivate him, but the constant shaking of the bunk finally caused a stir. Mitch suddenly realized he had not yet packed.

"Oh shit Sarge, I feel like shit"

"Not to worry kid, you'll feel better when you're on that plane, you'll have plenty of time to sleep, now get your ass in gear"

Sweat ran off Mitch's face like a monsoon downpour even soaking his undershirt as he finally boarded the MAC-V Freedom bird. All the returning servicemen were seated as the stewardess announced solemnly,

"Gentlemen, please fasten your seat belts", and that was her only statement. Not another word had been spoken, all were eerily quiet in their seats.

The plane rolled out onto the taxiway and extended flaps. Holding short of the active runway for a brief period before lining up on the centerline, the aircraft shook slightly as the pilot performed an engine run up before releasing the brakes and throttling up. Picking up airspeed the plane vibrated at various degrees before the nose lifted followed by the main gear. A loud shout of joy erupted mixed with whistles and claps from the uniformed passengers.

"Were coming home baby"

"You can have your fucking real-estate Charlie, I'm outta here"

"Take me home freedom bird, take me home"

"Fuck the Army" said one,

"Fuck Vietnam", said another,

"Fuck the gooks", shouted still another.

The comments released from a year of pent-up emotions reverberated throughout the cabin.

In just moments the cabin was quiet again as the aircraft climbed to cruise altitude and the country that time had ignored disappeared rapidly below an overcast sky.

Mitchell tried to recall the previous evening festivities to no avail. He sorely wished he had not drank so much and tried to remember if he had said a proper good-bye to his mates. Well I suppose it really doesn't matter, he thought, I'll never see any of them again. In his mind he could conceive no circumstance that would bring any of them together again. Once more the feeling of sadness overwhelmed him but he fought it off with thoughts of finally being on his way home.

Osaka, Japan was the return fuel stop. Everyone deplaned and shopped for gifts to bring to love ones, it was late evening and the city was well-lit and bustling with people. There was little about Osaka that anyone wanted to remember because the next stop would be in the real world, Oakland, California.

Just before noon on a bright sunny day the squeal of the tires making contact with the runway ignited elated shouts of joy of their arrival on U.S. soil. The doors to the plane opened filling the cabin with a surge of the sweetest smell on earth. A tingling of every nerve ending swelled under his skin, Mitch breathed in deeply and exhaled. On the stairs he looked down to see some of the first passengers out, on their hands and knees kissing the asphalt. With dampness in his eyes and lump in his throat he walked towards the terminal building ignoring the sneers and taunts of the anti-war protesters who came to greet them.

For Mitch the war was over, outward conflict replaced by an inner friction of having no awareness of his fellow soldiers at Bearcat, and the inability to shake off his sense of duty to them. While he painfully reentered a new existence, those he served with carried on.

In the following few days in a remote village deep into the jungle Delta the EMU's mission was to insert a small band of troops. At the behest of a village elder, reporting that a large cache of weapons in his immediate area had been located, wanted them removed. He feared the VC would use them against his people at some point, but had no knowledge of any enemy movement in recent weeks.

A flight of four slicks with a few volunteer GI's on each to load up the weapons cache was sent into the area. Escorting them is a light fire team to provide air support, just in case. On arrival into the LZ, the village where the elder reported the cache could be seen off towards the two o'clock position and appears to have been vacated. A suitable LZ has been spotted but is surrounded by tree lines. The four ships form into a diamond formation and half circle the LZ at high altitude while the Taipan gunship's recon at low level below.

"EMU Two-Eight, negative contact, looks like your best approach will be from the southeast, Aaah at one five zero, straight out departure looks ok, copy"?

"Roger Taipan lead, enter one five zero".

Holding the diamond formation the EMU's descend towards the LZ. The Taipan's have repositioned to cover the inbound slicks. Taipan Three-Six, Mitchell's former ship, was on the right, Three-Three on the left, both holding high and slightly to the rear of the formation.

Although trained as a crew-chief, J.W. is flying today with Three-Six as a gunner until he gains some mission experience. Today is his third mission. His pilot is a seasoned gunship driver and a short timer. He never dwelled much on going home, and was considering reenlisting for another tour of duty.

All four ships touchdown and the volunteer troops dismount the aircraft. They will locate the weapons, and then call back the choppers for lifting out the captured load. The ground troops spread out to form a defensive perimeter.

EMU Two-Eight pulled back into a hover to begin transitioning back into the air. Behind him the three ships are still sitting on the ground, when at the edge of each corner of the LZ, four camouflaged screens made from bamboo wood and fresh woven palms falls forward to expose the manned anti-aircraft batteries...

Troop Dismissed

(The end)

Epilogue

Near the end of this book, in one brief sentence, it is stated, "While he [Mitchell] painfully re-entered a new existence, those he served with carried on." The phrase "painfully re-entered" has connotations of a physical abnormality; however, this was not the case.

April of 1969 was considered the height of America's involvement in Vietnam, so the war did not end with my rotation out of Vietnam. I chose not to end the book with my separation and leave the reader with the feeling that was "the end." For the war went on for many more years, and thousands of combat assaults later, many more would die on both sides.

Know this: All combat soldiers suffer some degree of pain. Non-combatants can also suffer due to enemy actions or from witnessing trauma. In a combat zone, there is no "safe" place; therefore, the constant threat of harm and the stress it produces is ever present. Civilians, too, are subject to these stresses, which may account for the radical attitudes found in many war zones.

Some figures put the number of vets who served in Vietnam at 3,145,000; of those, 776,000 were combatants. Could they all show some sign of post-traumatic stress syndrome [PTSS]? The answer is yes! Certainly, 776,000 would have developed a disorder or PTSD [post-traumatic stress disorder]. Others developed "chronic" PTSD in variable degrees. Without some sort of therapy or treatment, the effects of PTSD can and will last a lifetime!

The degree of PTSD is attributed to many factors, some of which are the intensity of the combat involved, the amount of trauma witnessed, the term of the events, and the degree of morality and character makeup.

This is not to say that all Vietnam vets have a disability that is uncontrolled. Certainly most vets have indeed progressed well and repatriated back into civilian life as normally as the next guy or gal. But somewhere deep down, there is a repressed vault of recollections of a period of time that generated the stress disorder. Most will learn to livewith that as a means of survival, and well they should. Since recognizing the symptoms is a large part of the problem, most are at least aware of the fact that there is a good chance that they may have suffered PTSD, and are either consciously or unconsciously keeping it suppressed! If there are no outward or ill effects, let sleeping dogs lie!

When I returned home, there was no PTSD as a recognized disorder, and therefore no treatment. If I was doing something that seemed peculiar to others, and they were aware that I was a Vietnam veteran, then I was merely deemed to be "another crazy vet."

Personally, I did feel different from the rest of the civilians I had contact with, including my family. But it was more like isolation in terms of being able to connect or relate to anyone other than another veteran. I never felt more comfortable than I did when speaking with another Vietnam vet, regardless of his branch of service or MOS [military occupation specialty].

Now I am going to tell you something you may have not heard before. Posttraumatic stress syndrome is not the only serious affliction of veterans. The Vietnam War produced thousands of adrenaline junkies, and this is potentially more dangerous and devastating than the emotional aspects of PTSD.

Adrenaline is a powerful drug; it is the substance that prepares your body for defense or survival. Some have likened it to cocaine or heroin in its addictive ability and the potential effects on the brain. An adrenaline rush is usually accompanied by an increase in endorphins, and keys in the fight-or-flight response. Adrenaline is a hormone produced by the adrenal glands in the body. When it is produced in the body, it stimulates the heart rate, dilates blood vessels and air passages, and has a number of other minor effects. Adrenaline is naturally produced in high-stress or physically exhilarating situations.

Once I met a gentleman, whom I will call "J.D."; we were in the process of doing business. Afterward, we were having drinks at a bar and he told me he was a veteran and served in the Marine Corps. I found that interesting, since I knew him to be Cuban born, and I assumed that he was a more recent refugee, like many others in Miami at that time. He explained that he immigrated to Miami with his wealthy parents in the early 1950s. Upon reaching his early twenties, he enlisted, because he hated everything about communism and was not content to let Americans stand alone in resisting all that the "Commies" stood for. I do not recall all his accomplishments, but he did some highly risky and exciting stuff. As a paratrooper, he once bailed out of an airplane at 40,000- plus feet with oxygen, setting a world record.

At this time, I too was involved in high-risk [sport-related] activities. I knew I was a junkie, but thought if I made a conscious effort to be safe at my endeavors, I would do little harm to my body. I told my Cuban associate that I too was a veteran, and told him of my activities. I will never forget the little smirk as he called me a "juice junkie."

J.D. said not to be offended, and said he had been bothered for many years by his own addiction, only recently having learned of a means to control it. He had discovered that police officers were involved in a trial program to be trained to control their adrenal gland output simply by doing some basic exercises. These were to control the respiratory and cardiac rates while responding to a potentially high-risk call. It started at the time of the call. If a dispatcher reported "a man with a gun," for example, that usually got the officers to start juicing up. By the time they would reach the scene, they were sufficiently drugged.

Sometimes the drug clouded their ability to react to given circumstances with reasonable restraint.

They began to wear heart monitors on their wrists, and controlled breathing enroute to the scene. It was a simple exercise that is now practiced nationwide. I too practiced these steps, along with a little meditation, and found success in reducing the effect of adrenaline output. That little bit of knowledge may have saved my life, because high risk for long periods will eventually catch up with you as you require more and more "juice" to get the high.

I am not opposed to high-risk activities; I just think that to do them as safely as possible, your mind—which dictates the decision-making process in any activity—should not be subjected to anything other than rational planning and execution.

So if you are a veteran or a sports enthusiast with an overactive adrenal gland, be aware of the symptoms of a juice junkie. If you are involved in high-risk activity, practice the breathing exercises, monitor the heart rate, and add a little meditation. This can lead to a healthier and extended life.

If you would like to learn more, go to your Web browser and type in "PTSD" or "adrenaline junkie."